I0799929

POSTCARD HISTORY SERIES

Lordsburg and La Verne

in Southern California

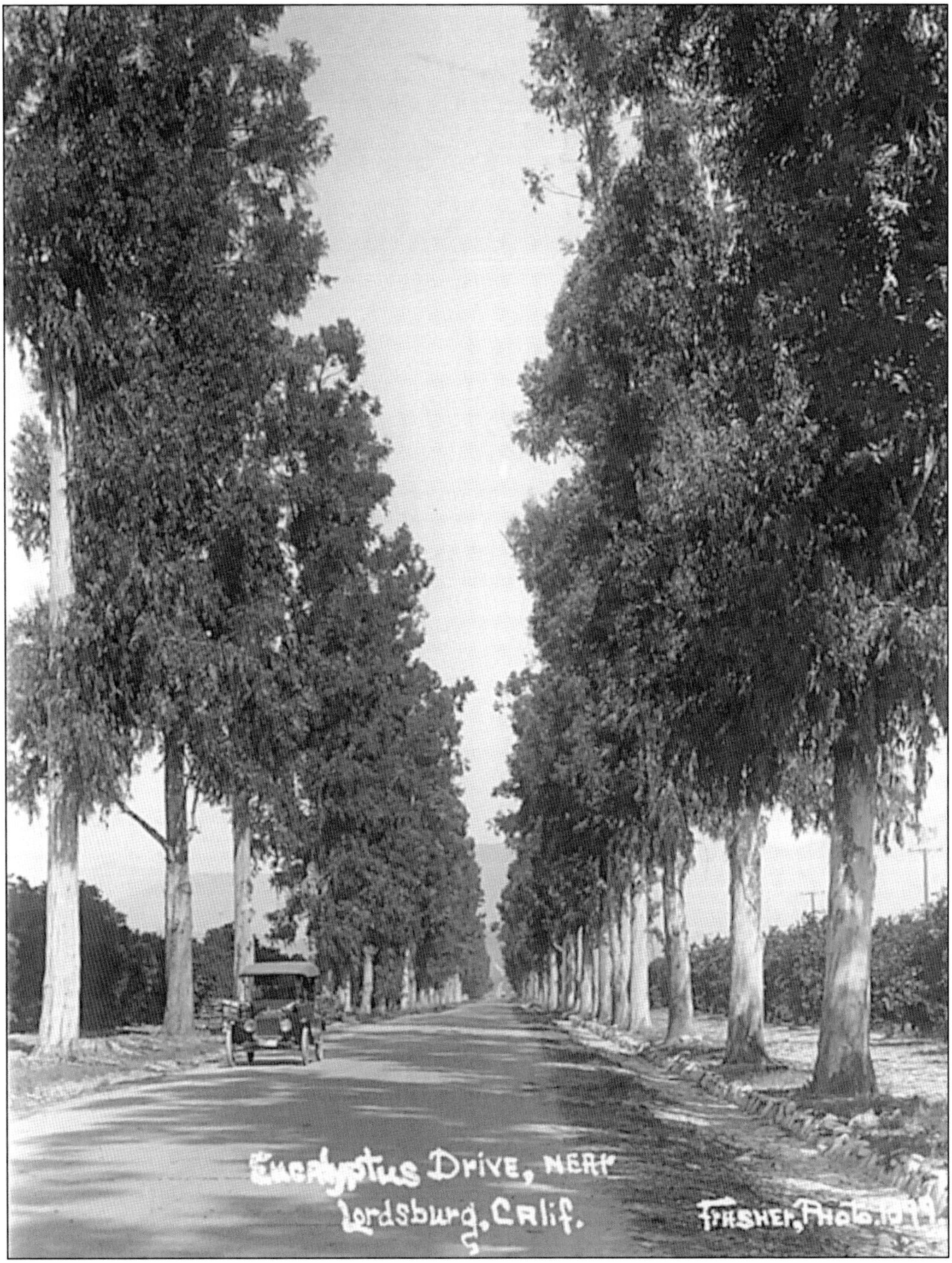

Eucalyptus Drive, near Lordsburg, California. This view was taken on North Garey Avenue between Bonita Avenue and Foothill Boulevard. These Eucalyptus trees were planted with cuttings sent down from San Francisco from original trees from Australia. Seth Richards' 360-acre citrus ranch, which at one time was the largest citrus ranch in the world, surrounded the drive on both sides. (P/P: Frasher Photo No. 1899, Burton Frasher, Wapato, Washington; courtesy University of La Verne, Wilson Library Archives.)

POSTCARD HISTORY SERIES

Lordsburg and La Verne

in Southern California

Marlin L. Heckman

ARCADIA PUBLISHING

Copyright © 2000 by Marlin L. Heckman.
ISBN 978-0-7385-0249-6

Published by Arcadia Publishing
Charleston, South Carolina

Printed in the United States of America

Library of Congress Catalog Card Number: 99-066624

For all general information contact Arcadia Publishing at:
Telephone 843-853-2070
Fax 843-853-0044
E-Mail sales@arcadiapublishing.com
For customer service and orders:
Toll-Free 1-888-313-2556

Visit us on the Internet at www.arcadiapublishing.com

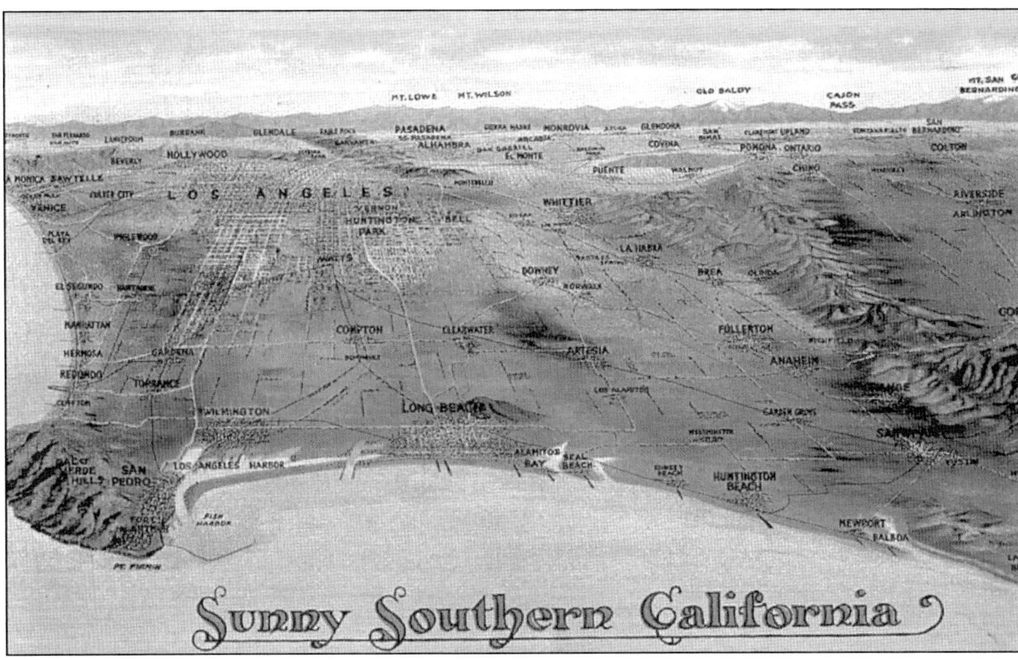

SUNNY SOUTHERN CALIFORNIA. While this early-20th-century map of the region does not show Lordsburg/La Verne (near San Dimas and Pomona, just under Mt. Baldy), it does show the expanse that became the Southern California area seen today as almost one continuous city. (P/P: Western Publishing & Novelty Co., Los Angeles, No. 617.)

Cover Photo: **LA VERNE BOAT IN FRONT OF LORDSBURG CYCLERY (SEE P. 84 FOR DESCRIPTION.)**
Except as noted, all images in this book are from the author's personal collection.

Contents

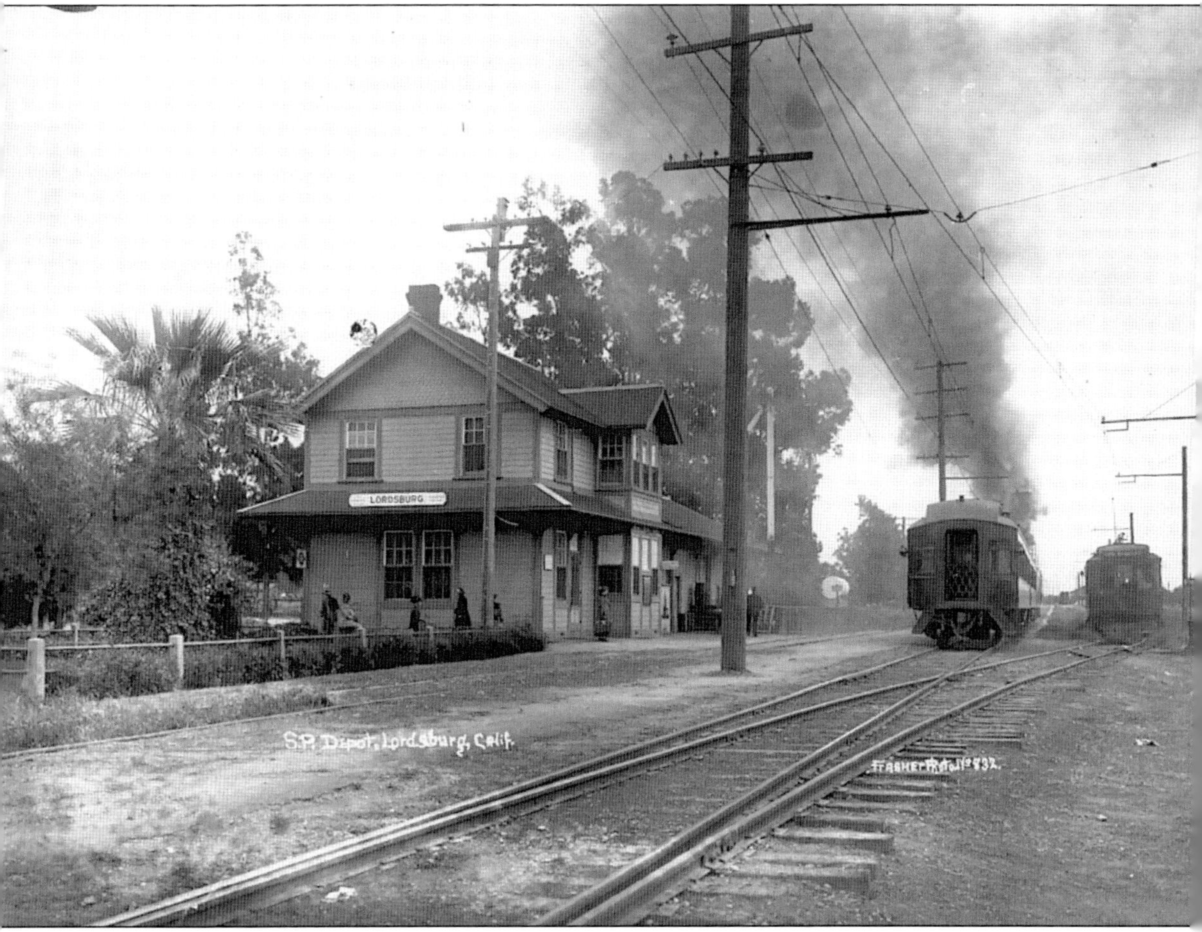

The Lordsburg Southern Pacific Station. This building, located on Orange Street between D and E Streets, was built in 1896 and served as a station for the Southern Pacific Railroad and the Pacific Electric Railroad. (P/P: Frasher Photo; courtesy University of La Verne, Wilson Library Archives.)

INTRODUCTION

With the coming of the Santa Fe Railroad to California in 1887, many "new" towns sprang up along the potential route. Some lasted only a year or so, and some are still alive more than a century later. One of these new towns was Lordsburg. Mr. I.W. Lord and others, wanting to capitalize on the coming of the railroad, built a large hotel and advertised lots for sale only to have the land boom collapse before any paying guests ever materialized. The hotel building sat empty for four years and then was opened, in 1891, by members of the Church of the Brethren, as Lordsburg College and the town of Lordsburg began to grow around the college. The college prospered for ten years and then was closed for the year 1900-1901, reopening in 1902. Today its successor, the University of La Verne, has 40,000 graduates around the world. The town of La Verne, successor to the town of Lordsburg, has a population of approximately 32,000 residents.

An article in the April-May 1907 issue of the *California Student* described Lordsburg as follows: "Beautiful in situation is this upland town with its rose-embowered homes, its orange groves and its smooth streets shaded by pepper trees, and the avenues of Palms and Acacias. . . Twelve transcontinental trains and six local trains stop here and there are six daily mails."

Tiring of the name Lordsburg as early as 1912, both town and college yearned for a new name, but Mr. Lord was still living and took offense at the suggestion. I.W. Lord died in March 1917, and in August of that year both town and college took the name La Verne, from the orange district north of Lordsburg. Because of the acres of citrus groves encircling the town, Lordsburg/La Verne was identified as the "heart of the orange empire." Many railcar loads of citrus fruits were shipped by the La Verne Orange and Lemon Growers Association and other cooperatives in the area during the high years of citrus production. By the 1940s, however, a quick-decline citrus disease killed many of the trees, and by the 1960s, houses had replaced most of the groves.

About five miles south of Lordsburg/La Verne was the city of Pomona, five years older and a faster growing city on the Southern Pacific rail line. In 1909 Pomona was the fourth largest city in Los Angeles County with a population of 8,000. Ganesha Park and the over-400-acre Los Angeles County Fair grounds was located between the two cities of Lordsburg/La Verne and Pomona. Three miles to the east was the city of Claremont with Pomona College, which was started in another land boom hotel building. These three towns share delightful locations with unmatched views of the mountains, including the 10,000-foot San Antonio Peak, known as "Old Baldy," to the north.

During the early years of the 20th century, venues of entertainment in Southern California involved rail and automobile transportation to the mountains, the beach, the desert, and neighboring communities. A Sunday drive might have included a visit to the lion farm, the ostrich farm, or the alligator farm. One could have visited strawberry fields and citrus groves. A trip to the ocean beach might also include a boat ride to Santa Catalina Island, some 26 miles off the Southern California shore. Hiking, horseback riding, and camping were other options available.

Californians have always been proud of their land, climate, and flora, and postcards presented a way to share feelings about these with the rest of the world. The railroads were great supporters of this boosterism even after the land boom and bust of the 1880s. March 11, 1911 was designated by the Southern Pacific Railroad as California Invitation Day and large postcards were printed for people to send to relatives and friends. The message was: "California wants people like you. Now's your chance to come out here. We've got sunshine and green grass and wild flowers right now, and all the comforts of an ideal home to offer you. You'll like it here all right. There are special low rates on the S.P. beginning March 10th and in force until April 10th. Ask your ticket agent. No excuse for not coming to see us and the things we are proud of. Perhaps you don't believe what we say about our climate and State. Come and see for yourself. We'll make good every way. Come on. Yours in hopes."

Lordsburg College was also part of the California boosterism craze, with its advertisement in the May 28, 1891 issue of *The Southern Californian* aimed at recruiting students for the new school to be opened in the fall: "Some things to think about. Students who attend Lordsburg College need not: 1. Wade snow; 2. Fear cyclones; 3. Go wading mud; 4. Tie up their ears; 5. Freeze their feet and fingers; 6. Endure blizzards and hot winds; 7. Long all Winter for springtime to come to see green hills, grass and pretty flowers. But they can all the year see: 1. Ripe fruit; 2. Green grass; 3. Living fences; 4. New vegetables; 5. Beautiful flowers; 6. Snow on the mountains; 7. Magnolias, grevillas, eucalyptus; 8. All kinds of semi-tropical fruit; 9. Mountain, hill and valley scenery; 10. Oranges on trees, lemons on trees."

The postcards in this volume represent the first 30 to 40 years of the 20th century in Lordsburg/La Verne and its Southern California setting. The cards range from the undivided card (address only on the back) to the white border and real photo cards.

As an aid to deltiologists (postcard collectors) the abbreviation P/P identifies known publishers/photographers for each card and there is an index for those entries. Postmarks are also noted for postally used cards.

One

Lordsburg College and La Verne College

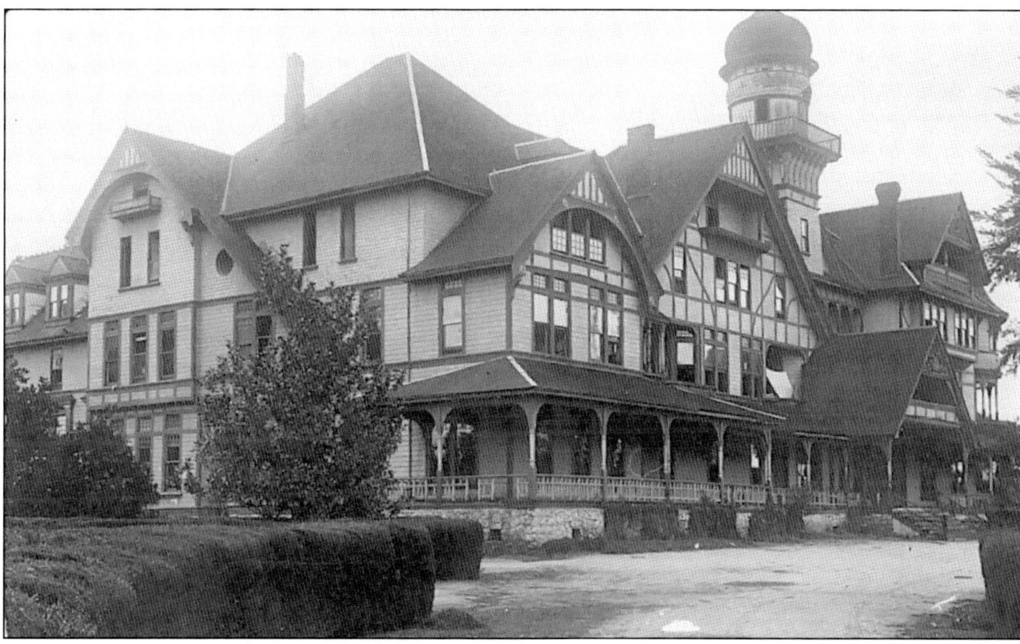

View of Lordsburg College Building from the Southwest Corner. This hotel/college building was built in 1887–88 by land speculators who lost out due to the collapse of the land boom. (P/P: Frasher Photo; courtesy University of La Verne, Wilson Library Archives.)

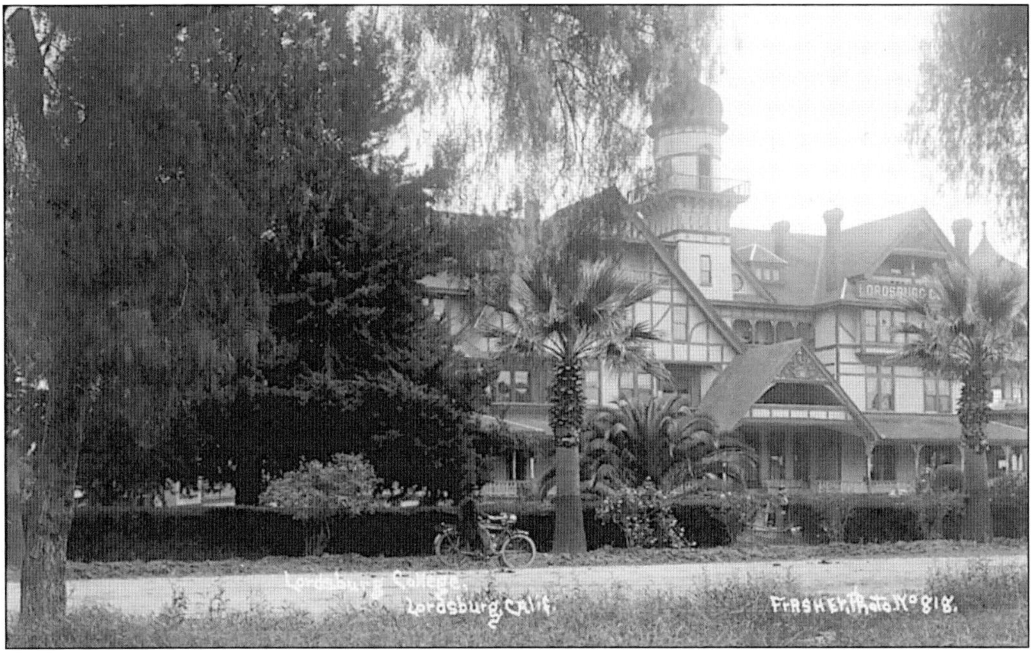

Lordsburg College, South View. The Lordsburg Hotel opened in 1888 but never had a paying guest, so in 1889 a bid to purchase the building for the purpose of opening a school was accepted. Lordsburg College opened it doors in October 1891. (P/P: Frasher Photo, No. 818; courtesy University of La Verne, Wilson Library Archives.)

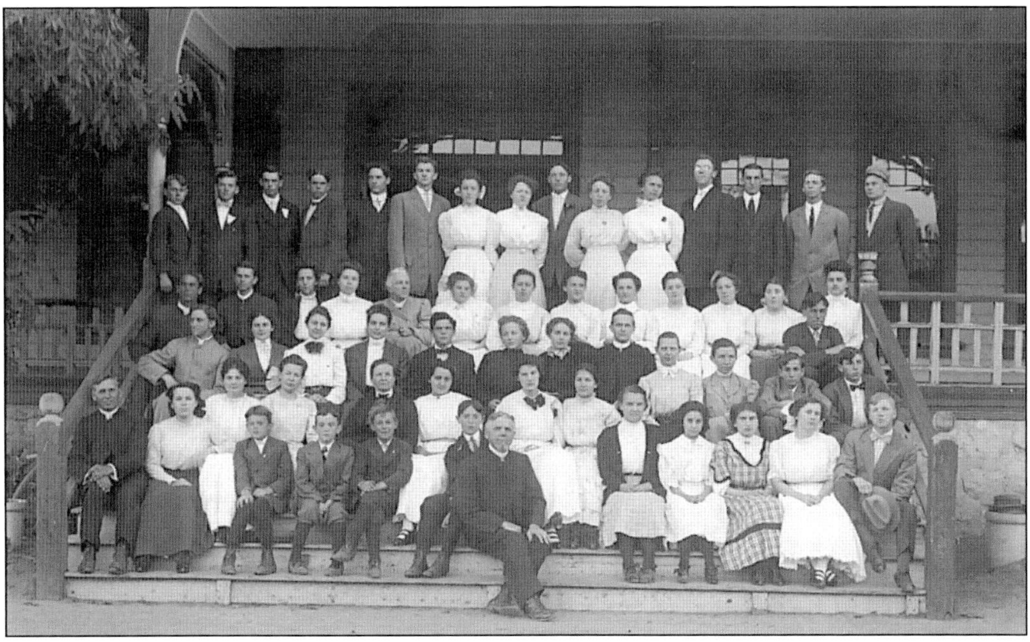

Lordsburg College Students and Faculty, 1909–10. The school began with 65 students in 1891–92. It was closed for one year from 1901 to 1902, but by the 1909–10 school year, the student body had grown in numbers. (P/P: unknown; courtesy University of La Verne, Wilson Library Archives.)

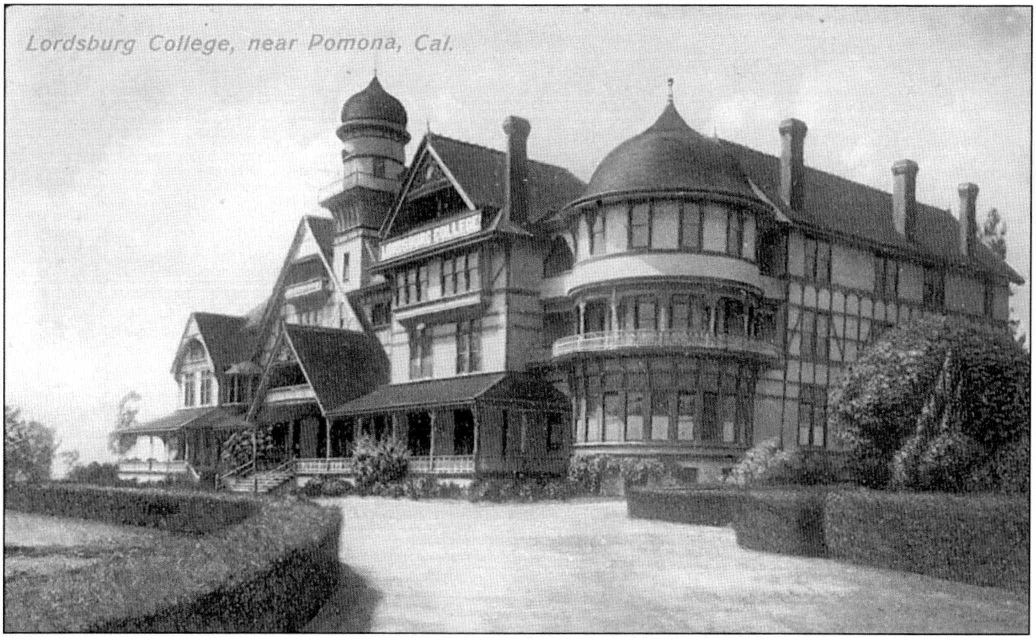

LORDSBURG COLLEGE, NEAR POMONA, CALIFORNIA. The college building was surrounded by manicured gardens. This card identifies its location as "near Pomona," although after 108 years, the University of La Verne, successor to Lordsburg College, still faces the question: where in the world is La Verne? (P/P: M. Rieder, Los Angeles, No. 4250; made in Germany; postmark: February 1908.)

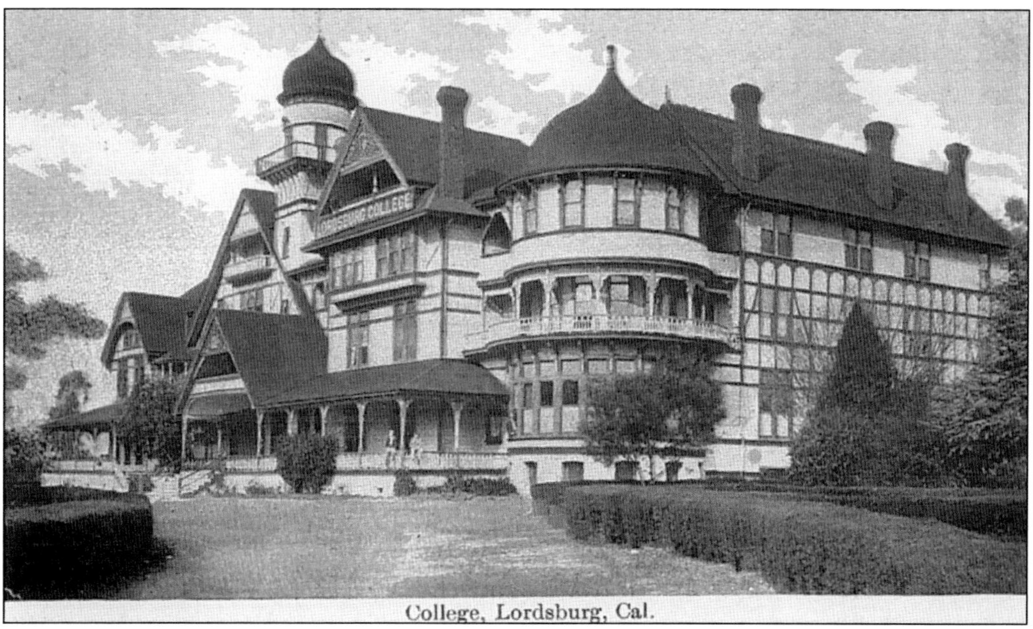

COLLEGE, LORDSBURG. This building provided offices, classrooms, library, chapel, dining hall, and dormitory rooms for students and some faculty. (P/P: unknown; postmark: October 1913; courtesy Jack McCaskill.)

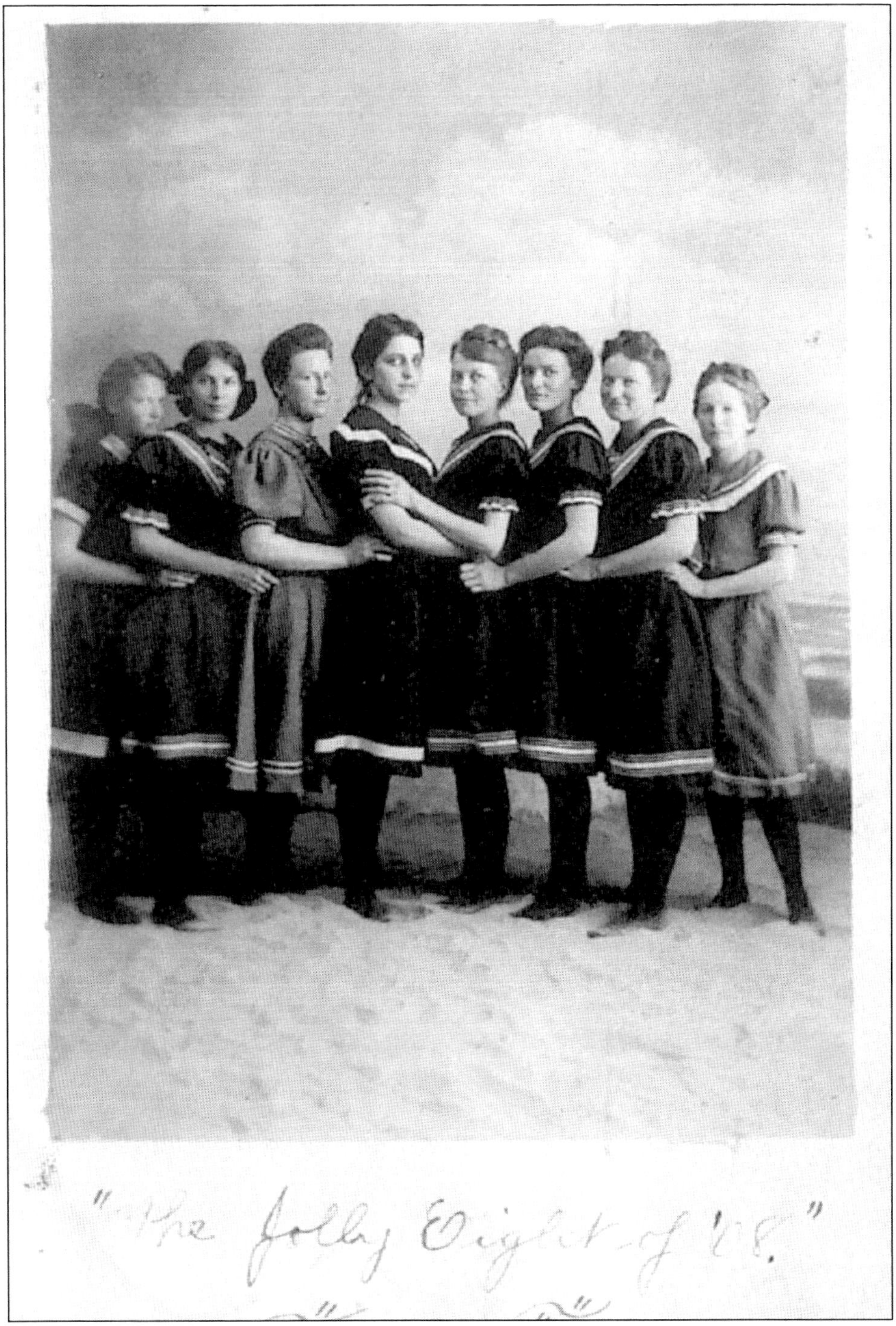

The Jolly Eight of '08. Lordsburg College students in 1908, these women went to Long Beach and lined up for a beach photographer. Note the backdrop of clouds and waves that touches the sand just behind their feet. From left to right are Bertha ?, Edna Neher, Lizzie Neher, unknown, Mary Lichtenwalter, Clara Mabel Brennamen, Susie Neher, and Lottie Neher. (P/P: unknown; courtesy Ernestine Hoff Emerick.)

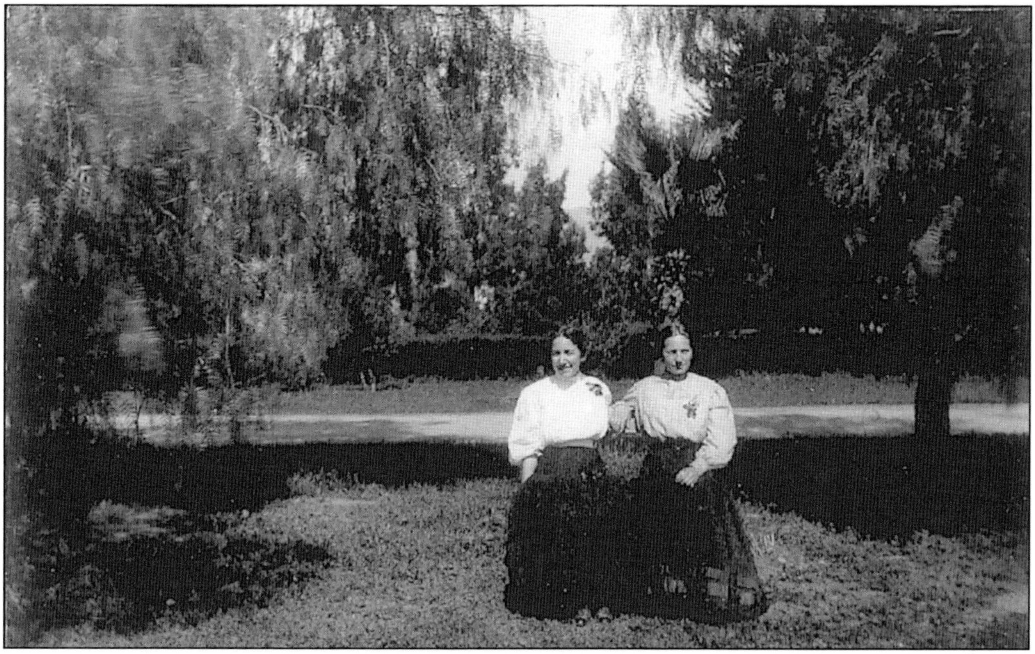

Mary Lichtenwalter and Lottie Neher on the Campus of Lordsburg College. This picture postcard was intended for Lottie's friend Ernest G. Hoff, whom she later married. (P/P: unknown; courtesy Ernestine Hoff Emerick.)

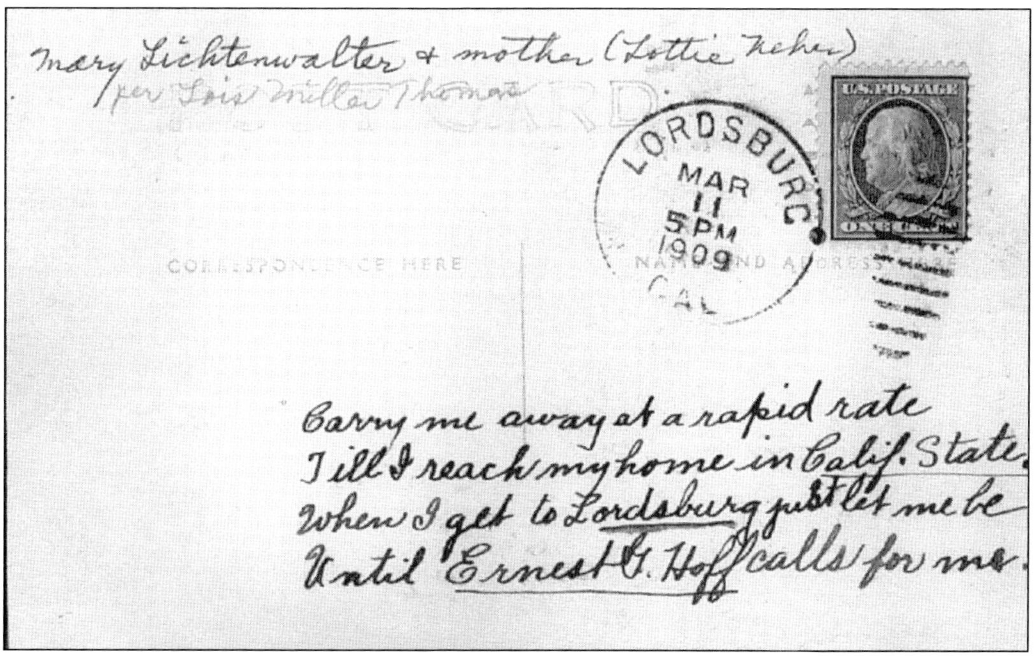

Unusual Address on the Card Above. Even without a zip code, this card was received, as addressed and mailed in Lordsburg, California, on March 11, 1909. (Courtesy Ernestine Hoff Emerick.)

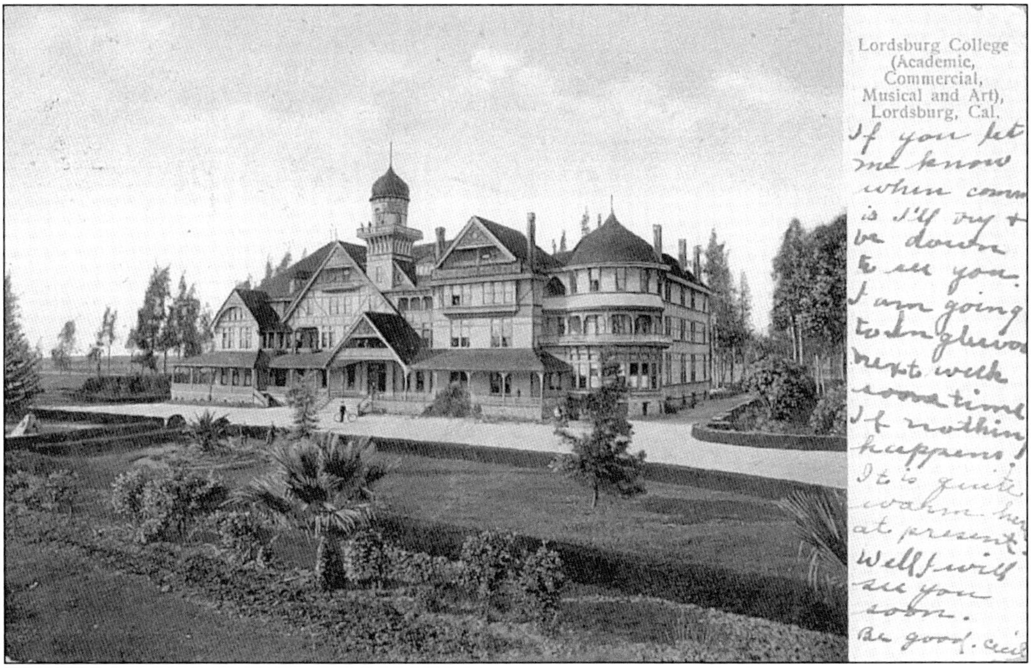

LORDSBURG COLLEGE (ACADEMIC, COMMERCIAL, MUSICAL, AND ART), LORDSBURG. Cecile Whisler wrote, "We had commencement last night and I was one of the graduates." The college catalog shows that Cecile Whisler of Lordsburg graduated in 1910 as a student in Bible and Piano. (P/P: M. Rieder, Los Angeles, No. 3484; made in Germany; postmark: May 1910.)

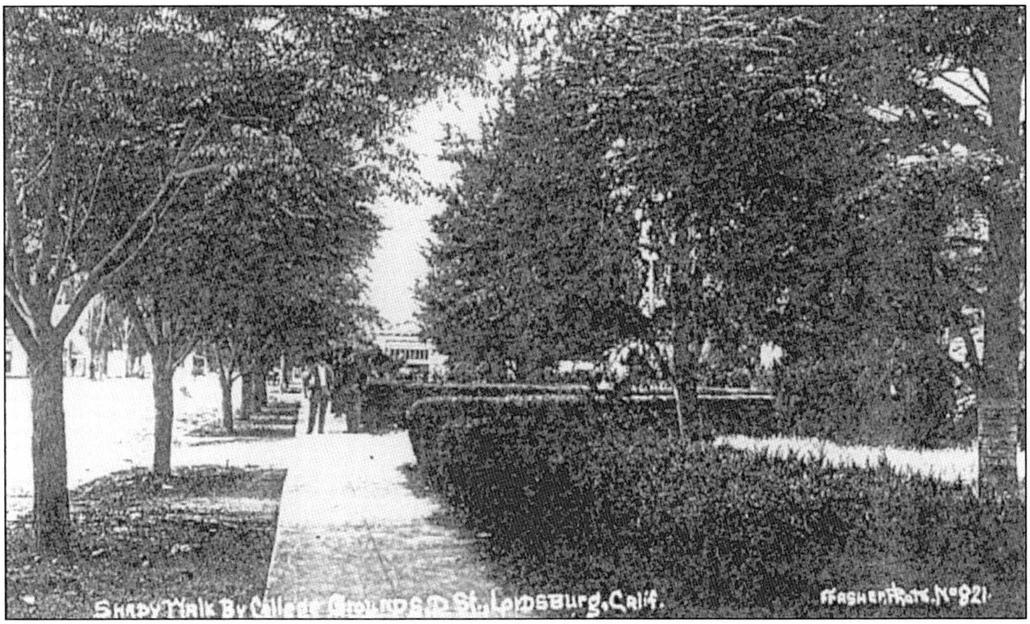

SHADY WALK BY COLLEGE GROUNDS, D STREET, LORDSBURG. This is the east end of the block in which the Lordsburg College building was situated. The building at the end of the walk is the Pomona State Bank, at the corner of Second and D Streets (see p. 35). (P/P: Frasher Photo, Burton Frasher, Wapato, Washington, No. 821.)

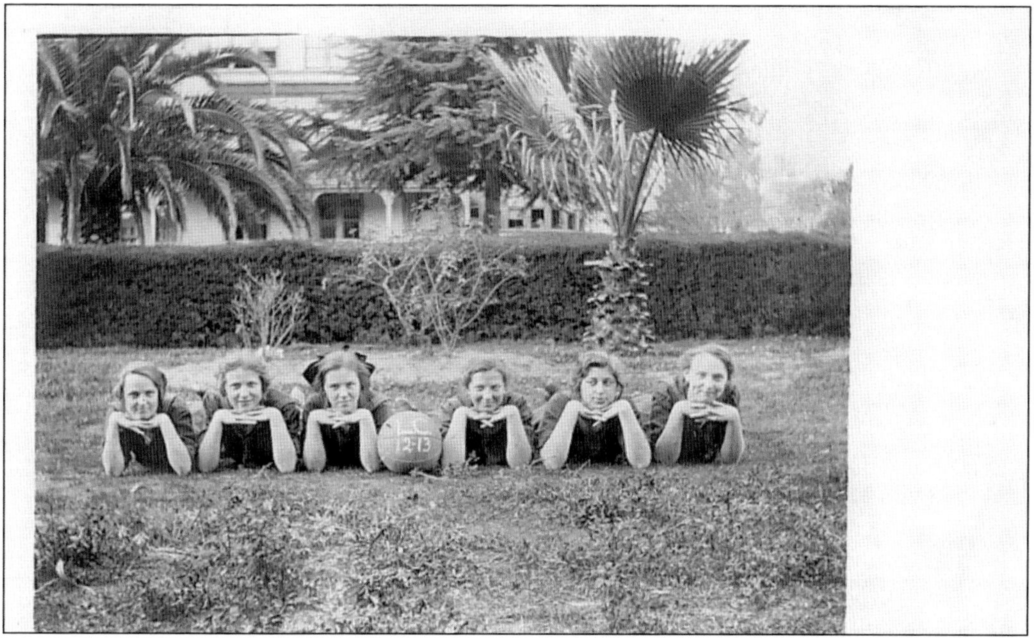

Lordsburg College Women's Basketball Team, 1912–13. No identification of team members was possible, but their coach was Ruth Blickenstaff. In November 1912, they were successful in beating the Bonita team 26 to 9. (P/P: unknown; courtesy University of La Verne, Wilson Library Archives.)

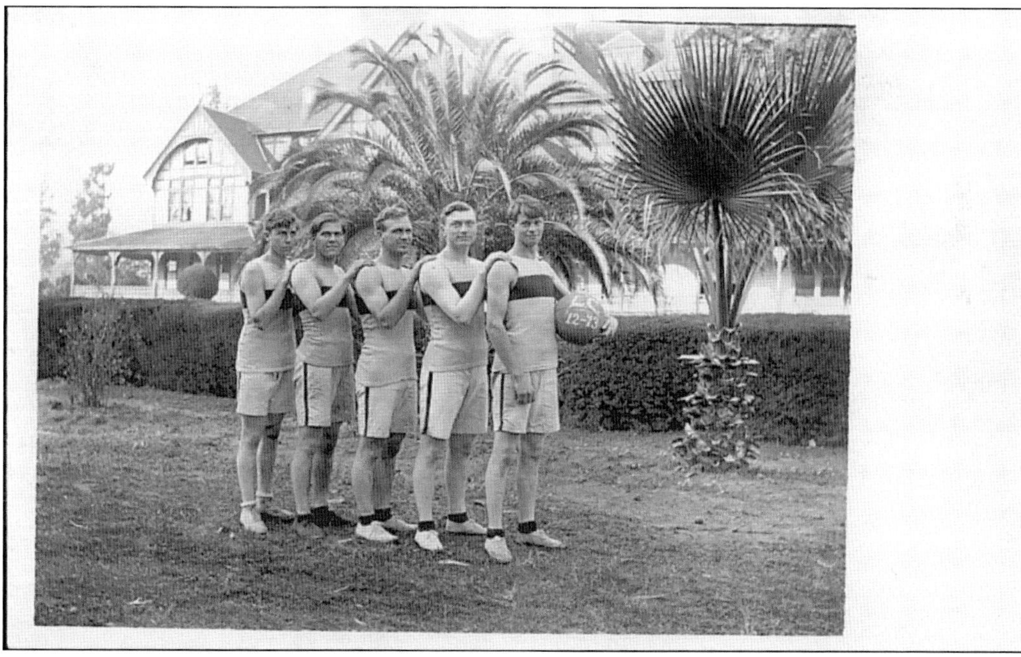

Lordsburg College, Men's Basketball Team, 1912–13. From left to right are Luke Minnich, John Overholtzer, Raymond Evans, Paul Dresher, and Jesse Brandt. (P/P: unknown; courtesy University of La Verne, Wilson Library Archives.)

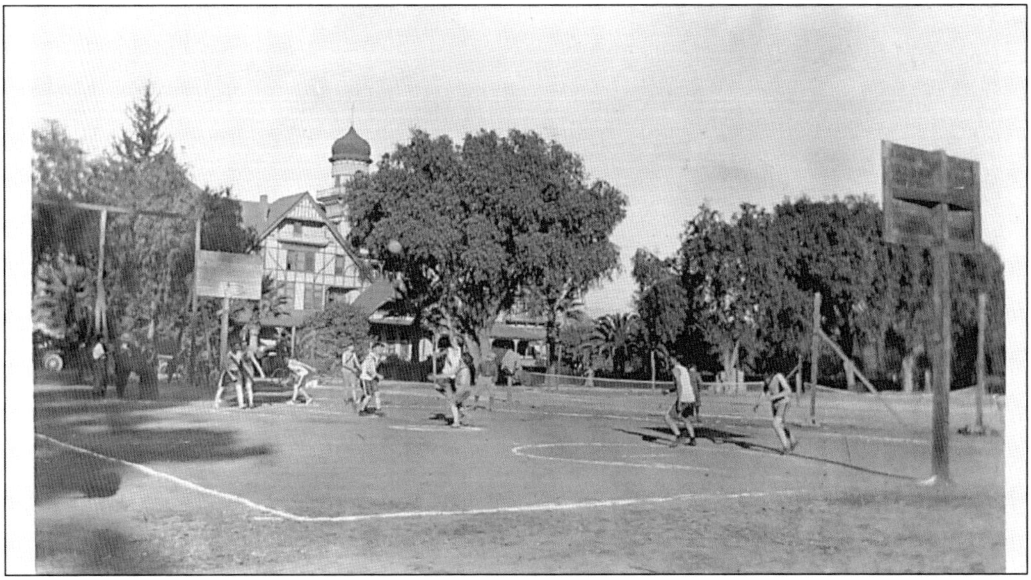

College Basketball Court, across Second Street from College Building. Physical fitness and sports played an important part in college life. On October 12, 1912, the *Lordsburg-La Verne Leader* reported, "The girls who are athletically inclined have decided that the boys are selfish with the basketball court. As a result of this a great army was seen to enter the athletic grounds armed with pickax, shovel, rake and hoe. A wilderness of weeds is being transformed into a new court." (P/P: unknown; courtesy University of La Verne, Wilson Library Archives.)

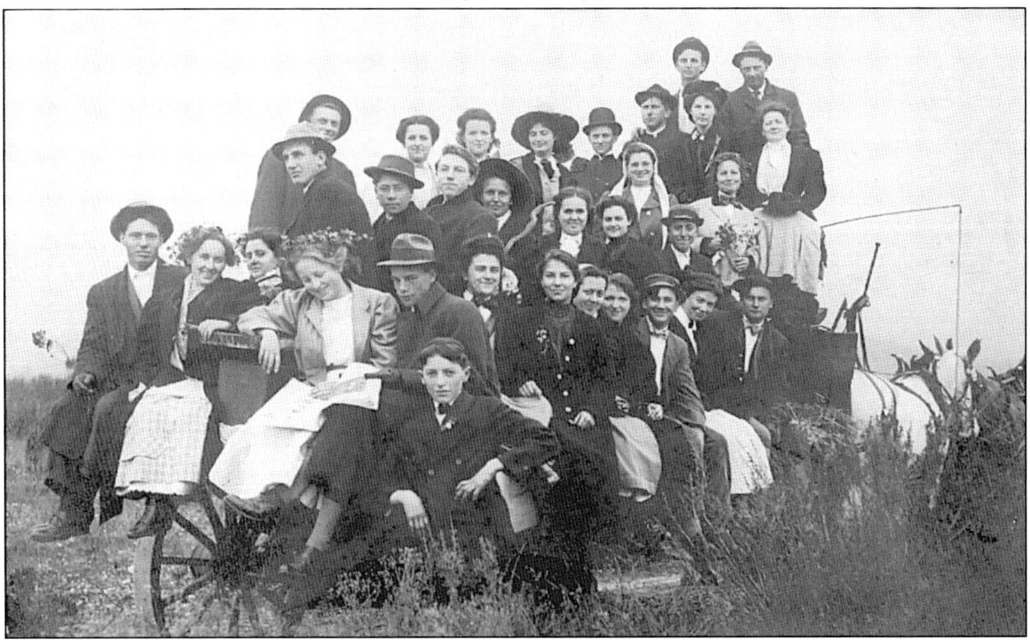

Leaving for College Picnic at Stoddards, 1910. The *Lordsburg Educator* of March 1910, reported, "Early in the morning of February 22, Washington's birthday, a party of about 35 students and three teachers boarded a big 'carry all' wagon and went to Stoddard's Canyon, about 15 miles away to spend the holiday and enjoy a grand picnic." (P/P: unknown; courtesy University of La Verne, Wilson Library Archives.)

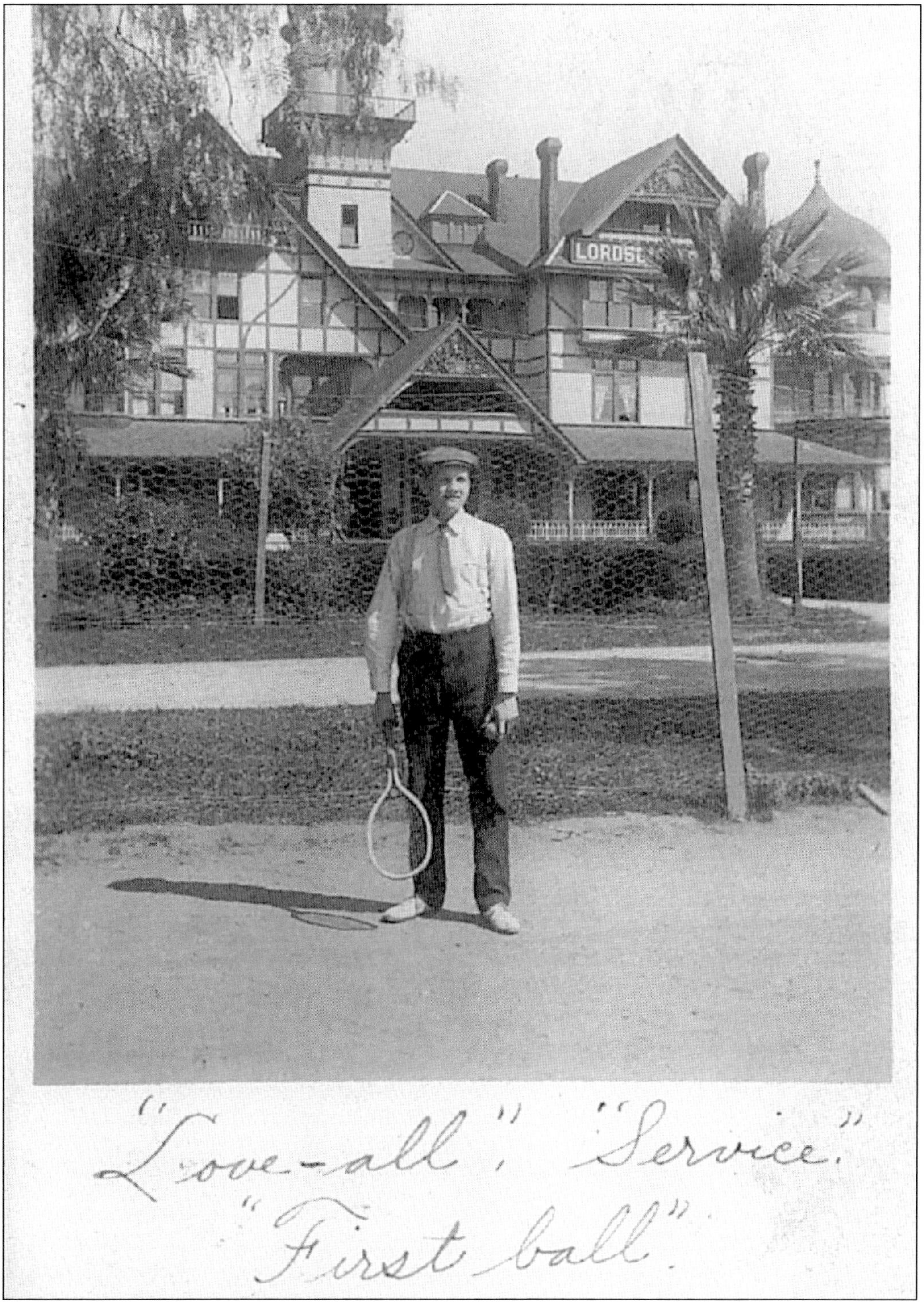

"Love All, Service, First Ball." Ernest G. Hoff plays tennis at the courts across the street from Lordsburg College. (P/P: unknown; postmark: March 17, 1909; courtesy Ernestine Hoff Emerick.)

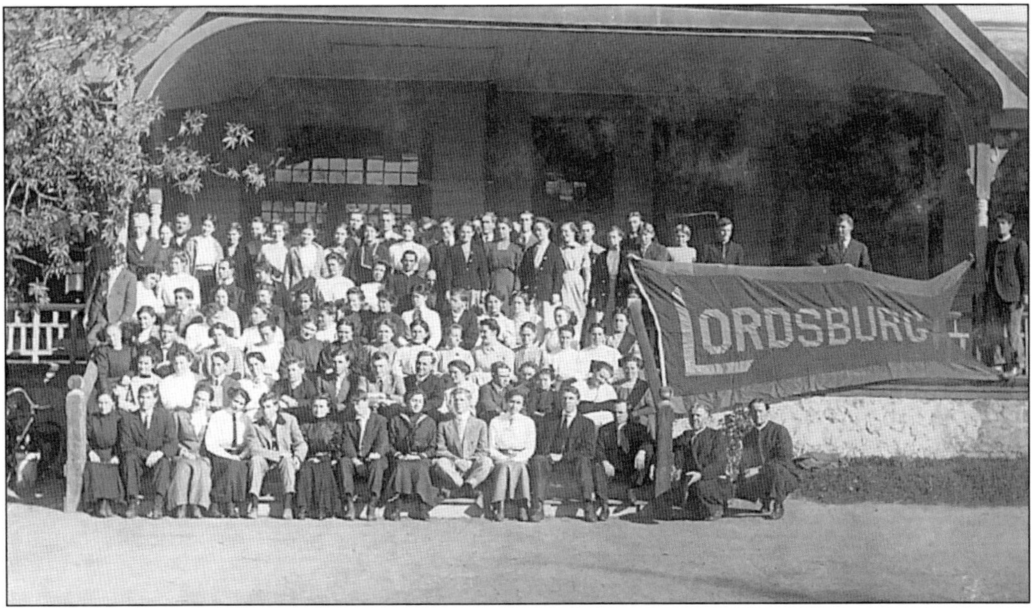

Lordsburg College Students and Faculty, 1911–12. This picture also appears in a 1912 issue of the *Palmerian*, a college publication. Pictured off to the right and below the Lordsburg banner are professors W.F. England and J.P. Dickey. (P/P: unknown; courtesy University of La Verne, Wilson Library Archives.)

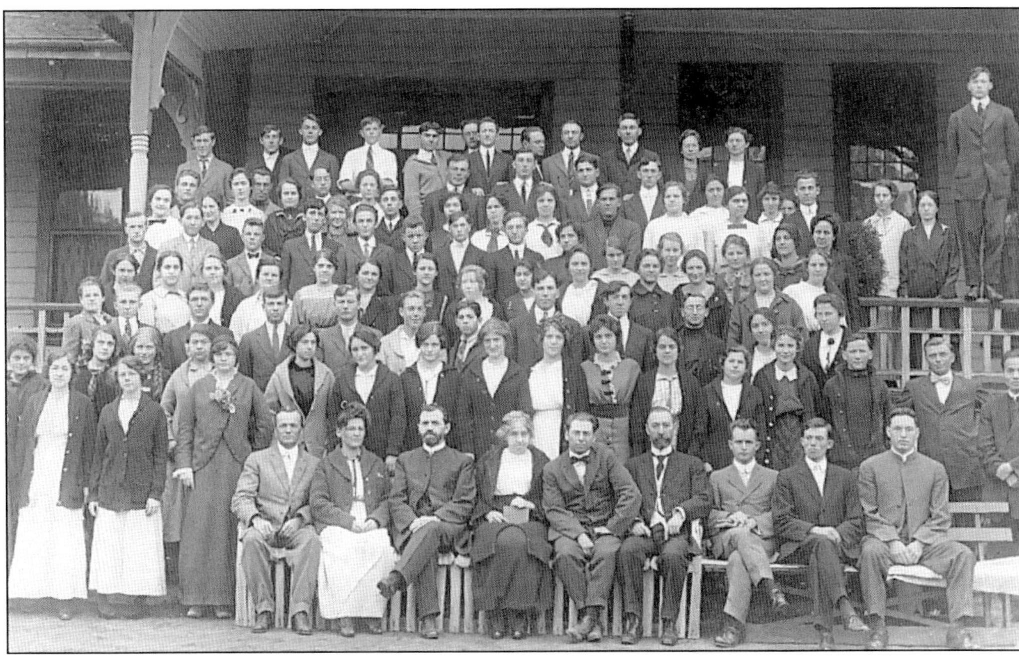

Lordsburg Academy, 1912–13. This is another view of the students and faculty of Lordsburg College. Since there was no yearbook in 1913, this is the only known picture of this group. (P/P: W.A. Jackson, Commercial Photographer, Alhambra, California; courtesy University of La Verne, Wilson Library Archives.)

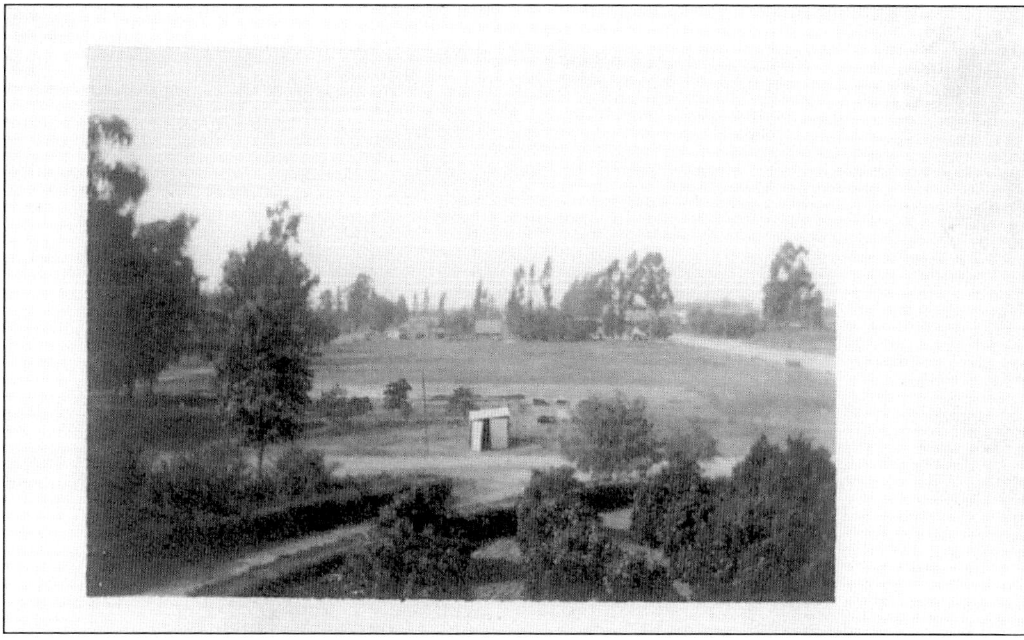

VIEW FROM SECOND-STORY WINDOW OF COLLEGE BUILDING, 1917. This view looking west shows the empty land that is the block where Miller Hall (1919), Founders Hall (1926), Davenport Dining Hall (1958), and the LaFetra/Mainiero Building (1969) were later built. (P/P: unknown; courtesy City of La Verne Planning Department.)

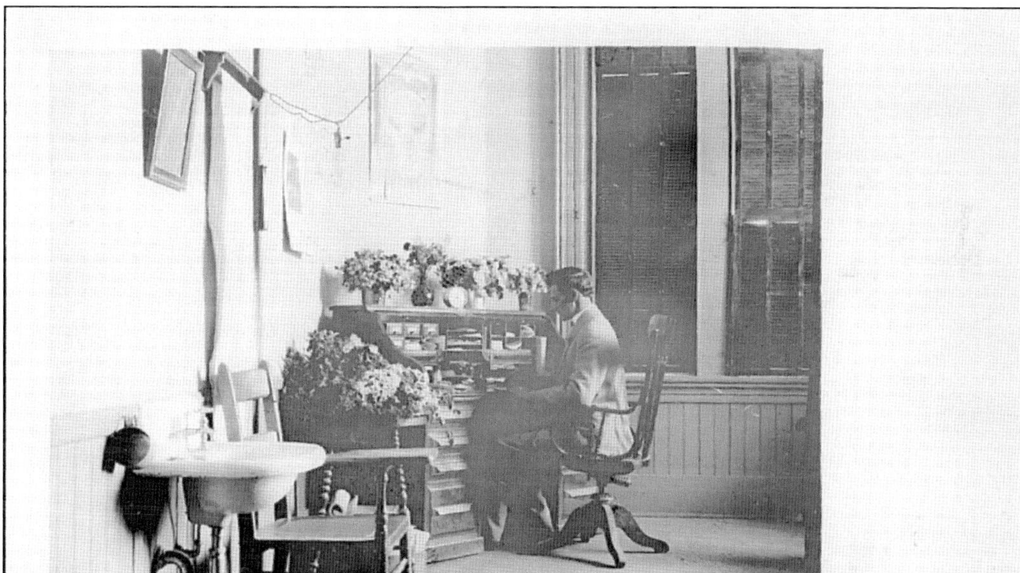

A LORDSBURG COLLEGE OFFICE. Since the building was built as a hotel, every room had a sink. This appears to have been an office for one of the faculty or administrators. Did the flowers designate a special day? The calendar on the wall appears to show December 1898. (P/P: unknown; courtesy University of La Verne, Wilson Library Archives.)

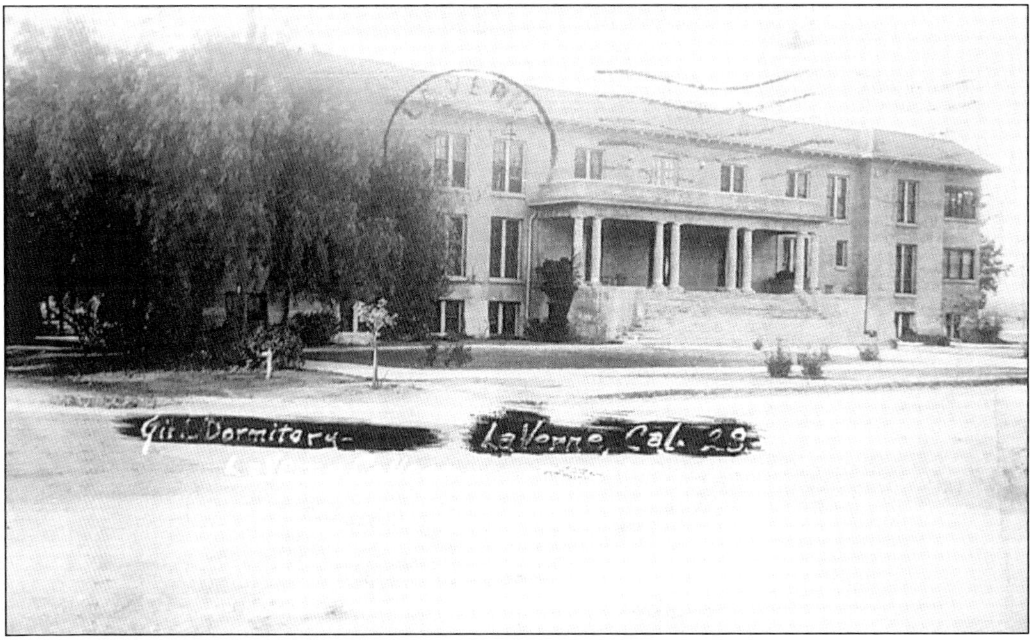

GIRL'S DORM, LA VERNE, 1929. The women's dormitory, Miller Hall, was constructed and dedicated in 1919, just as World War I had ended. (P/P: unknown; courtesy Jack McCaskill.)

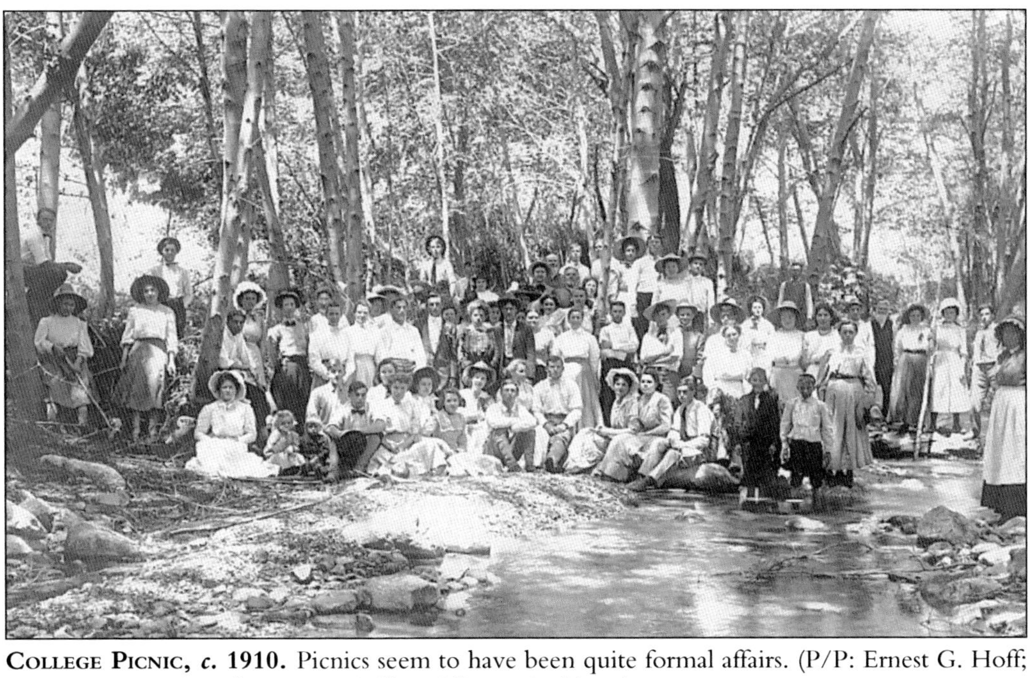

COLLEGE PICNIC, *c.* 1910. Picnics seem to have been quite formal affairs. (P/P: Ernest G. Hoff; courtesy University of La Verne, Wilson Library Archives.)

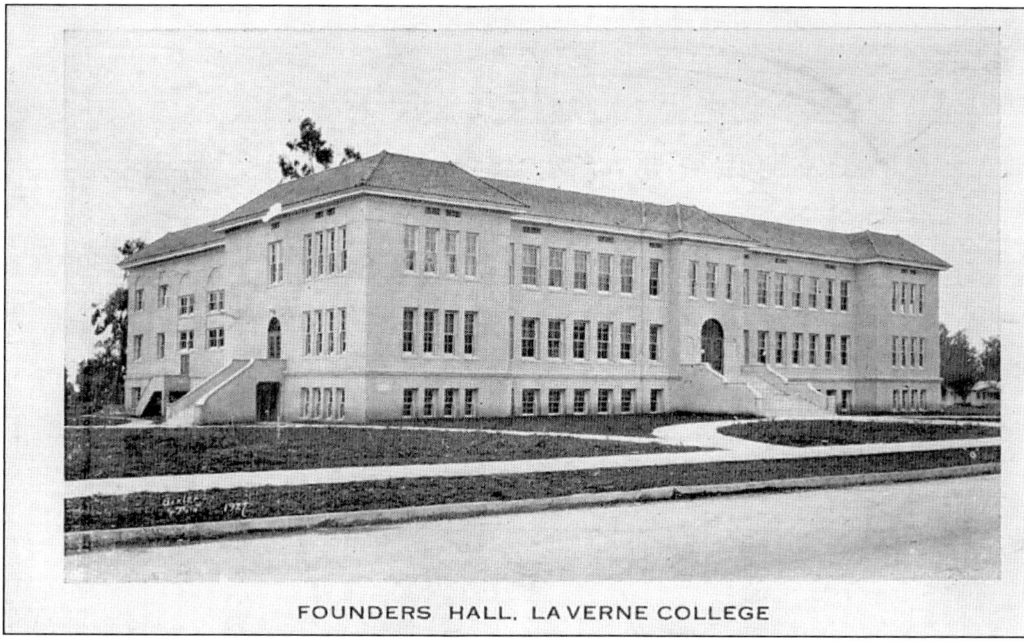

Founders Hall, La Verne College. This is an architect's rendering of Founders Hall, which was built in 1926 and dedicated February 13, 1927. Its floor space totaled 33,000 square feet, and the auditorium had a seating capacity of 600. The cost of building was $116,609.94. (P/P: Bixler Foto, 1927.)

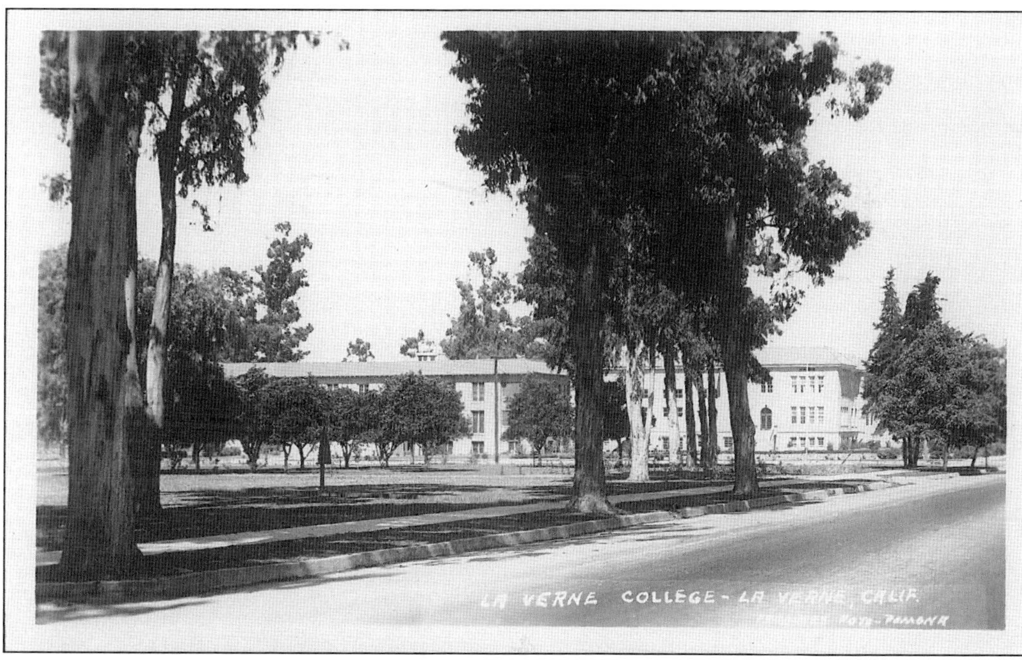

La Verne College, La Verne. This is the view of Miller Hall and Founders Hall as seen through College Park after the raising of the Hotel/College building in 1927. (P/P: Frasher, Pomona; courtesy University of La Verne, Wilson Library Archives.)

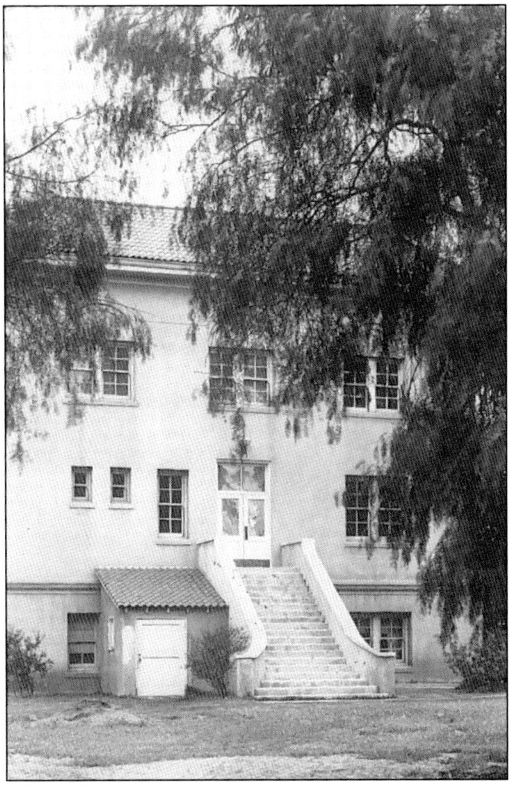

South View of Founders Auditorium. These are the south steps of the Founders Hall Auditorium wing. (P/P: unknown; courtesy University of La Verne, Wilson Library Archives.)

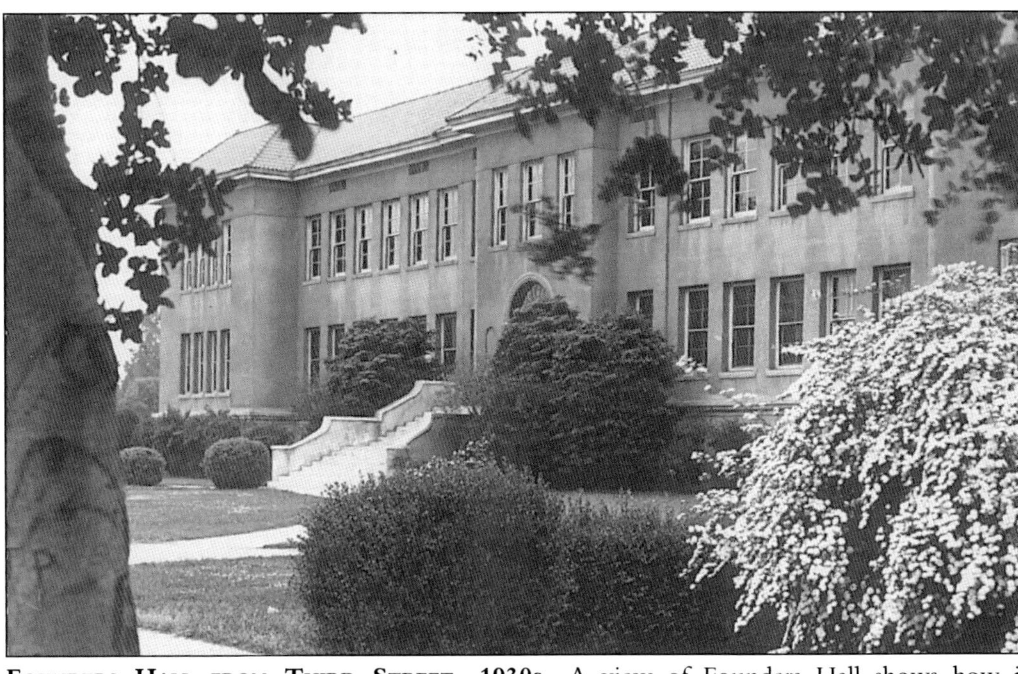

Founders Hall from Third Street, 1930s. A view of Founders Hall shows how it appeared after plantings had grown. (P/P: unknown; courtesy University of La Verne, Wilson Library Archives.)

Two

INSTITUTIONS: SCHOOLS, CHURCHES, AND THE ORPHANAGE

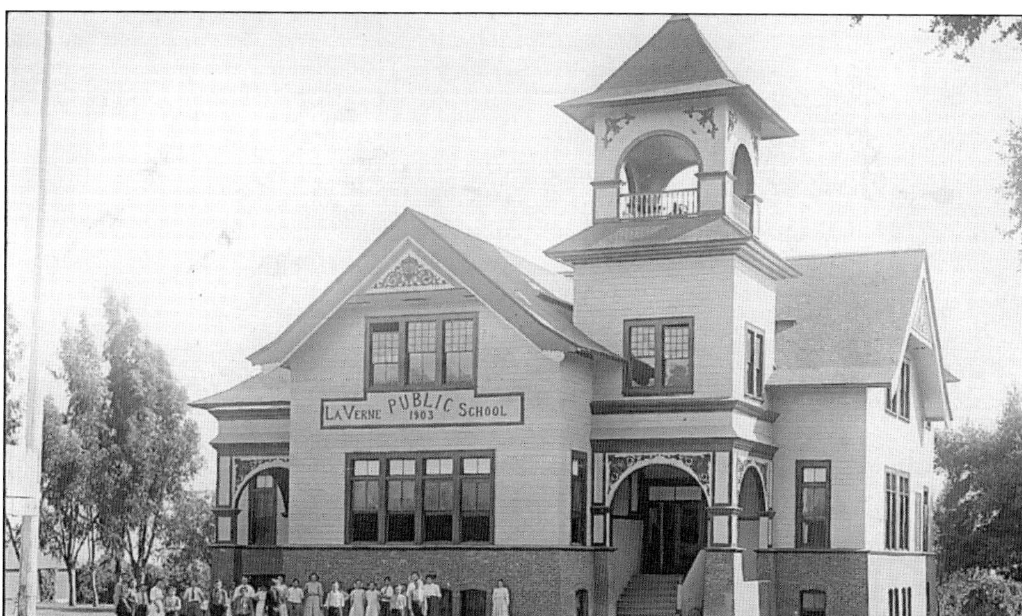

LA VERNE PUBLIC SCHOOL, 1903. Teachers and pupils appear in front of the La Verne Public School on the northern edge of Lordsburg. (P/P: unknown; postmark: November 1910.)

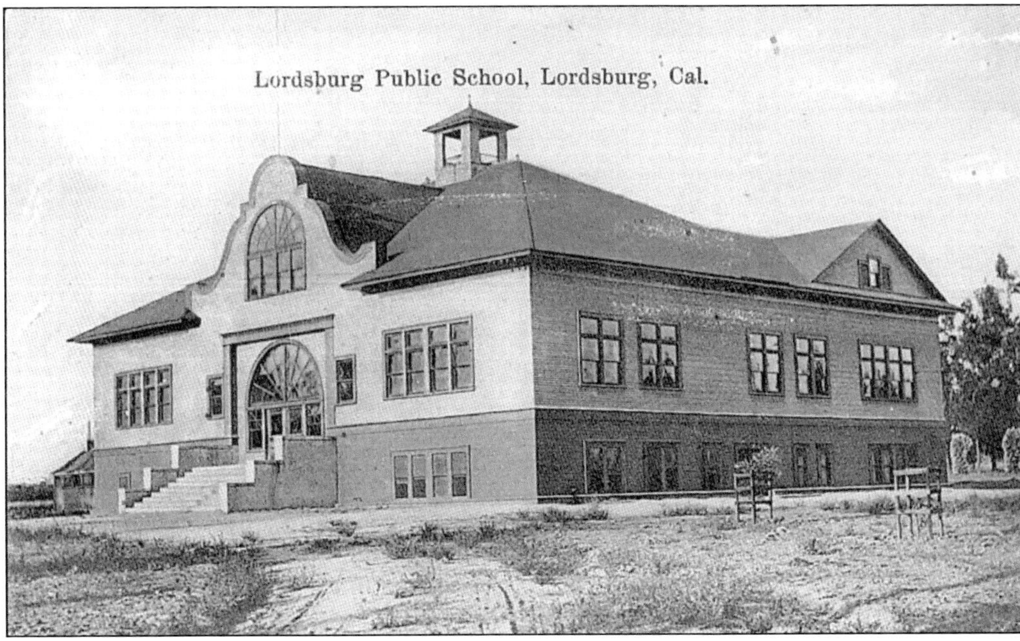

LORDSBURG PUBLIC SCHOOL. This building was built in 1907–1908, remodeled in 1926, and replaced in 1952. (P/P: published for W.H. Poston & Co., Lordsburg, by "Woods," Los Angeles, No. H-C-9; made in Germany.)

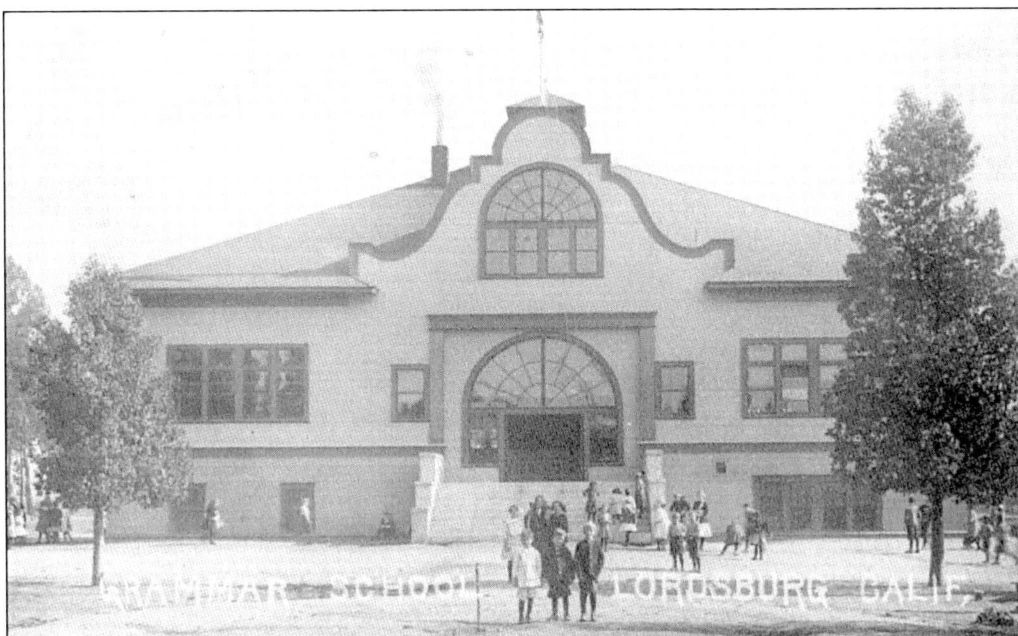

GRAMMAR SCHOOL, LORDSBURG. This building was located on the east side of D Street between Sixth and Eighth Streets. (P/P: unknown; courtesy Jack McCaskill.)

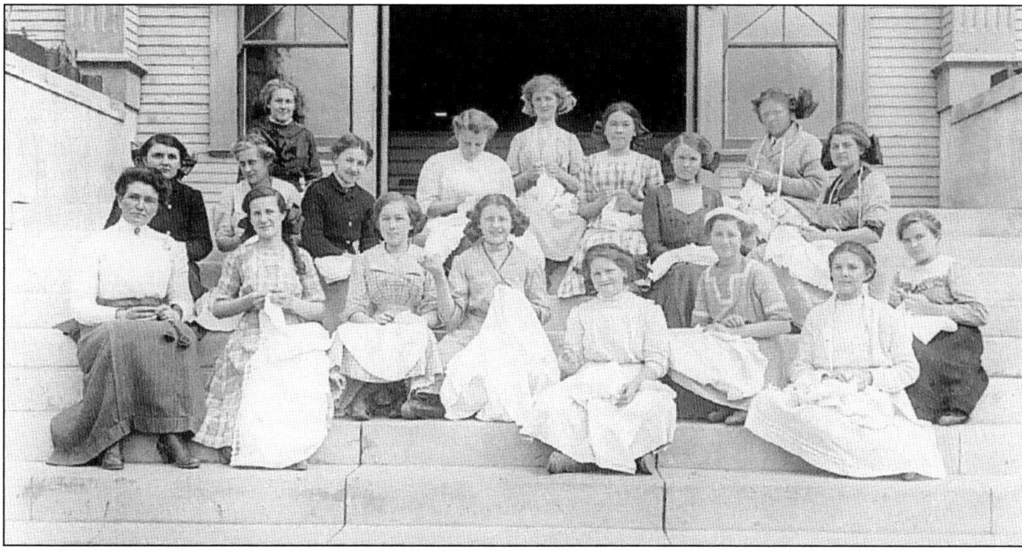

SEVENTH GRADE SEWING CLASS, LORDSBURG GRAMMAR SCHOOL, 1911. Mrs. Farley taught this class. Of the eighteen people pictured, fifteen have been identified: Olive Hesp, Willsie Mills, Fern Griggs, Azalea Sayce, Eleanor Roper, Ruth Barnhizer, Ella Henry, Mildred McClanahan, Gladdys Fesler, Oro Mills, Mattie Hubble, Jean Hubble, Hazel Weaver, Rhoda Price, and Mrs. Farley. (P/P: unknown; courtesy City of La Verne Planning Department.)

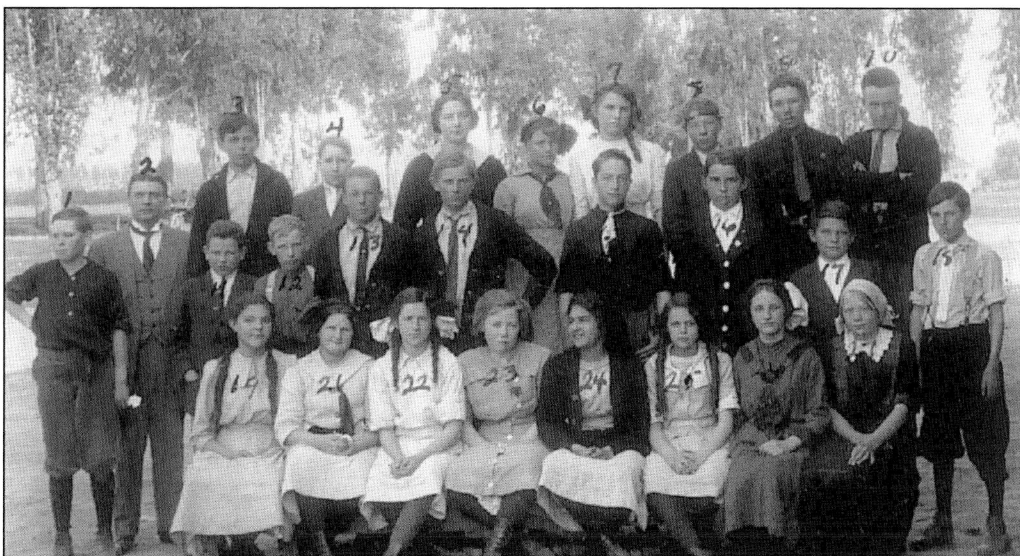

SEVENTH AND EIGHTH GRADES, LORDSBURG GRAMMAR SCHOOL, MARCH 1913. Mr. Sparks was the teacher of these students. The numbers are also on the back of the picture, but only initials are given. Using the yearbooks of Bonita High School and Lordsburg College, 7 of the 26 students have been identified: 1. F.C.; 2. C.R. Sparks (teacher); 3. Wellington Green; 4. O.L.; 5. K.A.; 6. O.M.; 7. N.L.; 8. W.C.; 9. F.C.; 10. Merrill Milne; 11. H.S.; 12. Earl Williams; 13. C.E.O.; 14. E.R.; 15. Roscoe Hoover; 16. I.S.; 17. J.P.; 18. R.S.; 19. Rhoda Price; 20. unidentified; 21. Jean Hubble; 22. Hilda Broad; 24. R.P.; 25. G.M.; 26. R.S.; 27. unidentified. (P/P: unknown; courtesy Roynon Family Album.)

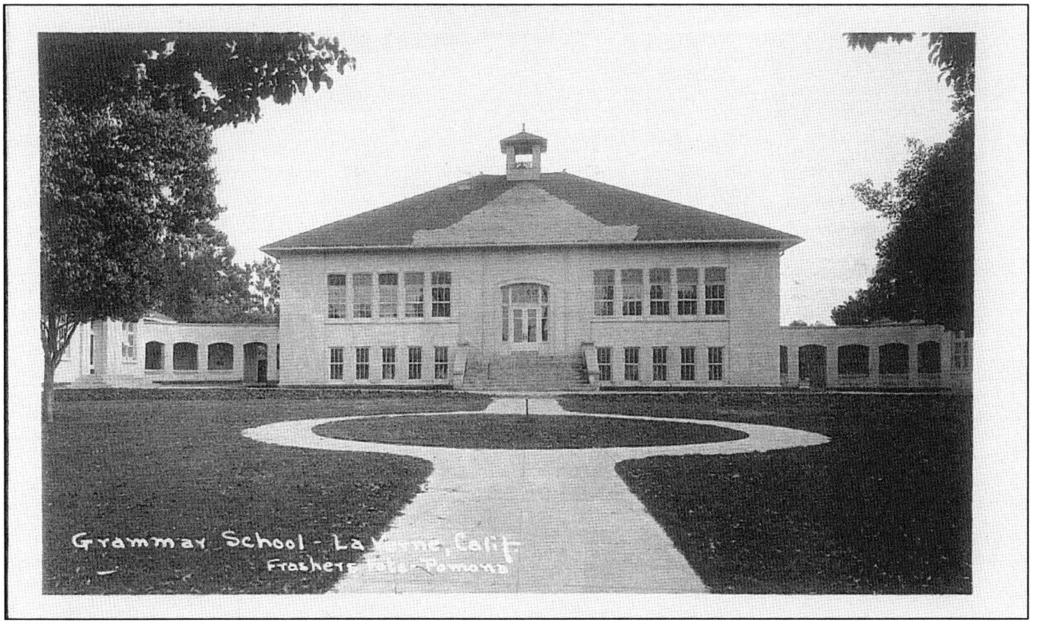

GRAMMAR SCHOOL, LA VERNE. This is the same building as the one pictured on the top of p. 24, but with the cupola removed. (P/P: Frashers, Pomona, California; courtesy Jack McCaskill.)

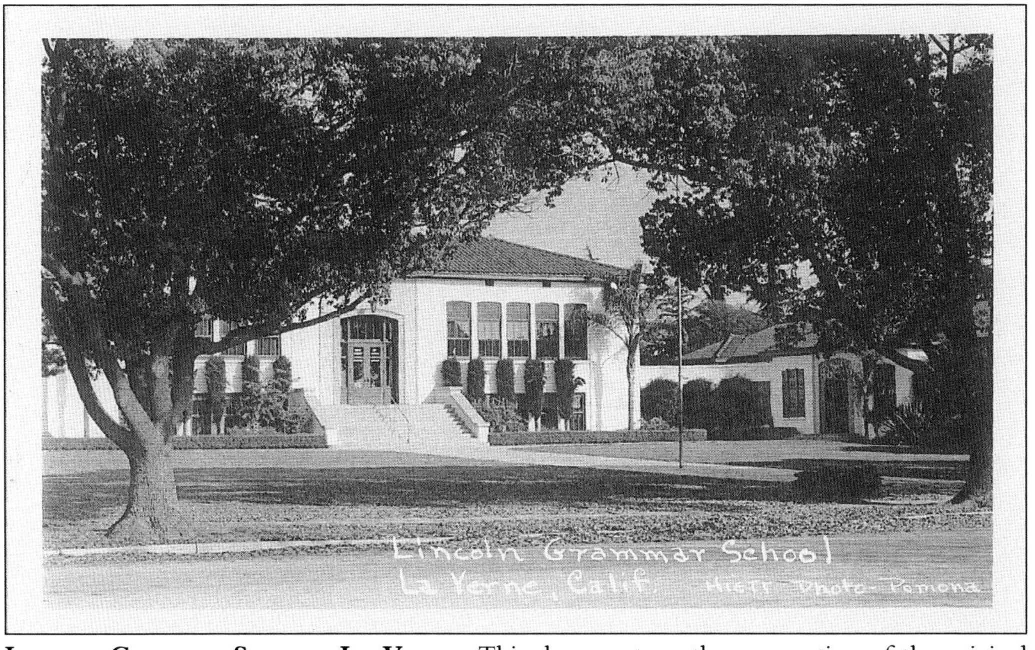

LINCOLN GRAMMAR SCHOOL, LA VERNE. This shows yet another renovation of the original building with tile added to the roof. (P/P: Hiett Photo, Pomona; postmark: September 1950; courtesy Jack McCaskill.)

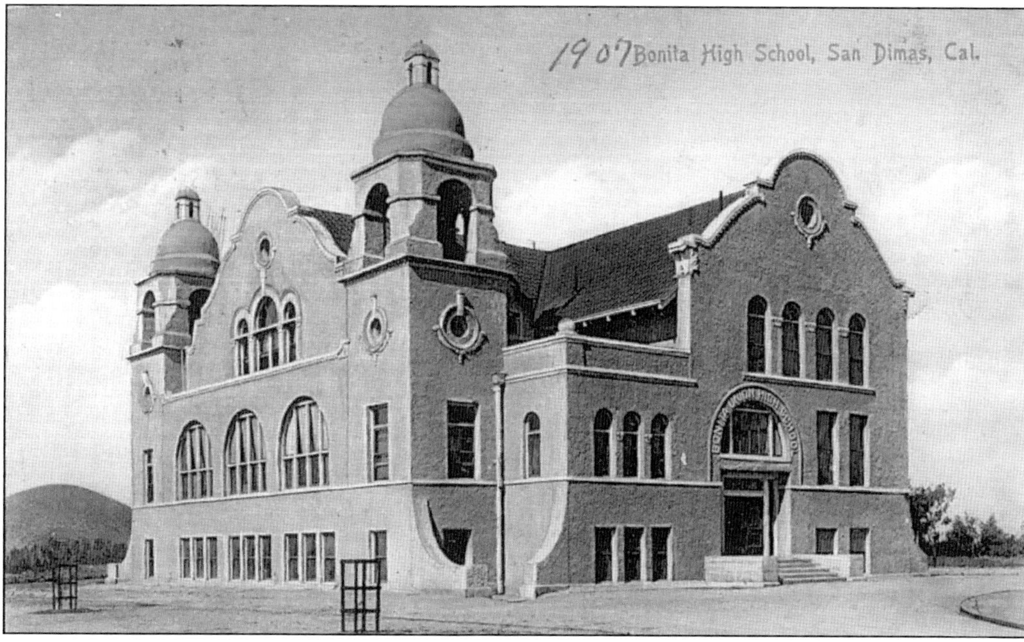

BONITA HIGH SCHOOL, SAN DIMAS. Bonita Union High School served the communities of San Dimas and Lordsburg until 1959, when a new building was built in La Verne. By 1970, each community had its own high school. (P/P: M. Rieder, Los Angeles, No. 7099; made in Germany; postmark: November 1907.)

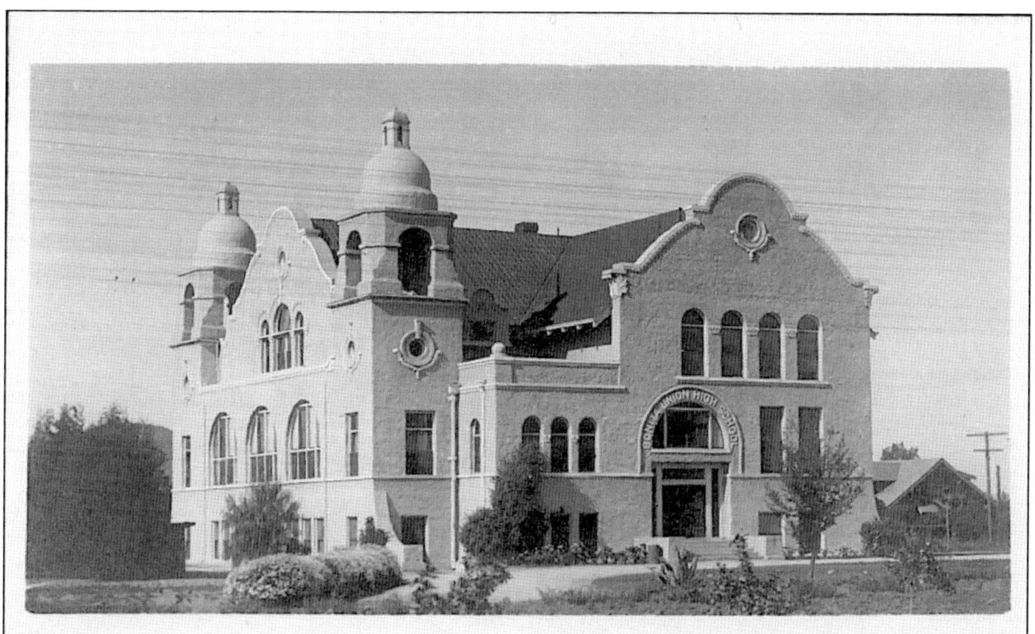

BONITA HIGH SCHOOL, 1910. This view shows the growth of plantings around the school. (P/P: unknown.)

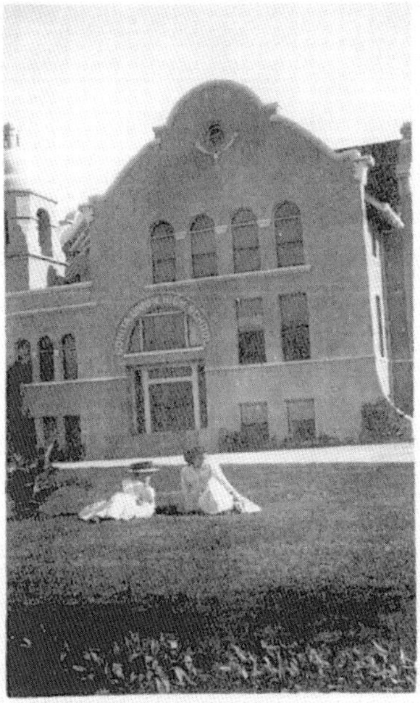

Bonita High School. Two unidentified women appear on the lawn in front of the building. (P/P: unknown; courtesy La Verne City Planning Department.)

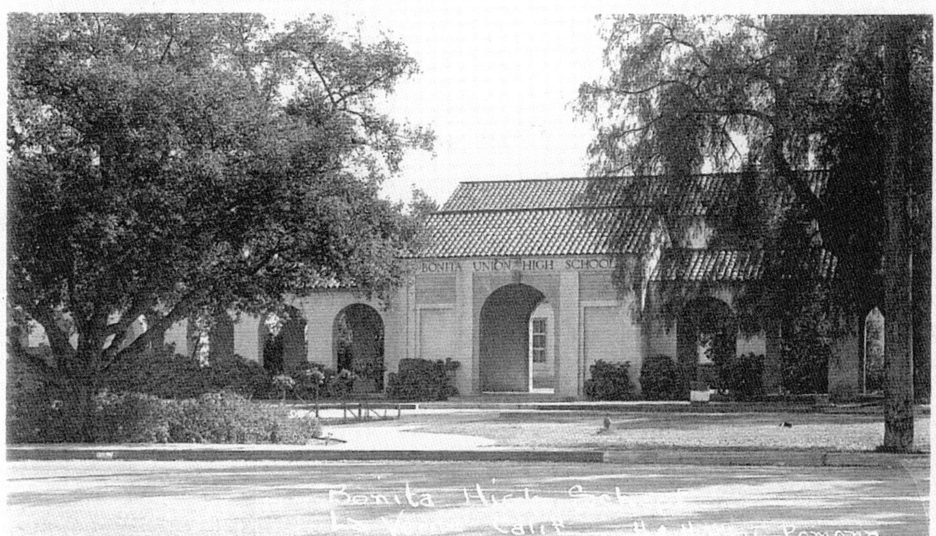

Bonita High School Addition. This addition to the original 1905 building was constructed in 1922. (P/P: H & H Photo, Pomona; courtesy Jack McCaskill.)

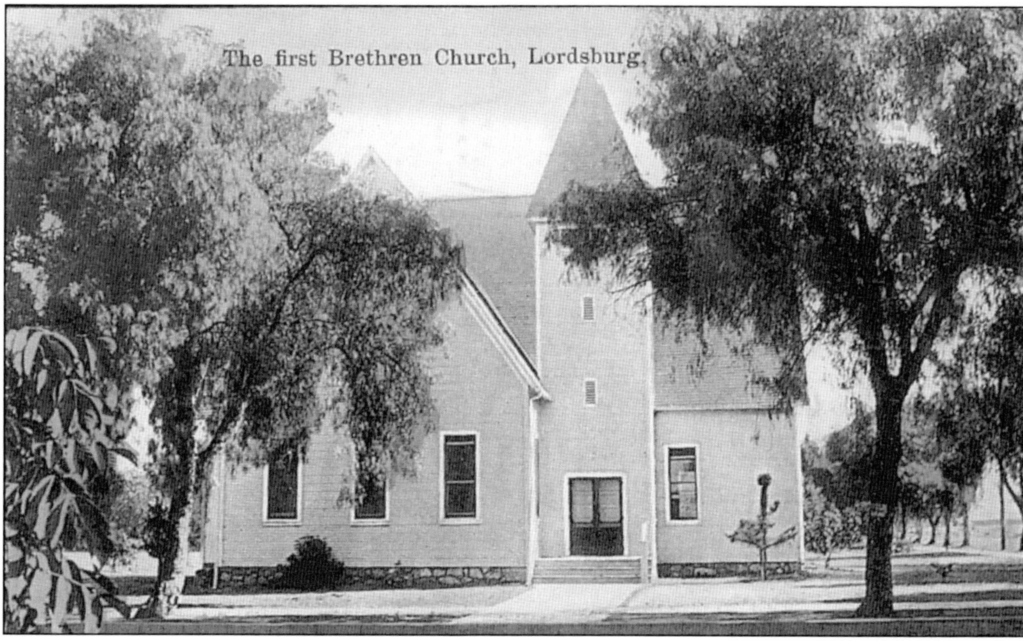

The First Brethren Church, Lordsburg. The Lordsburg German Baptist Brethren Church (Church of the Brethren), located on the corner of Fourth (Bonita) and E Streets, was built in 1901. (P/P: published for W.H. Poston & Co., Lordsburg, by "Woods," Los Angeles; postmark: July 1908.)

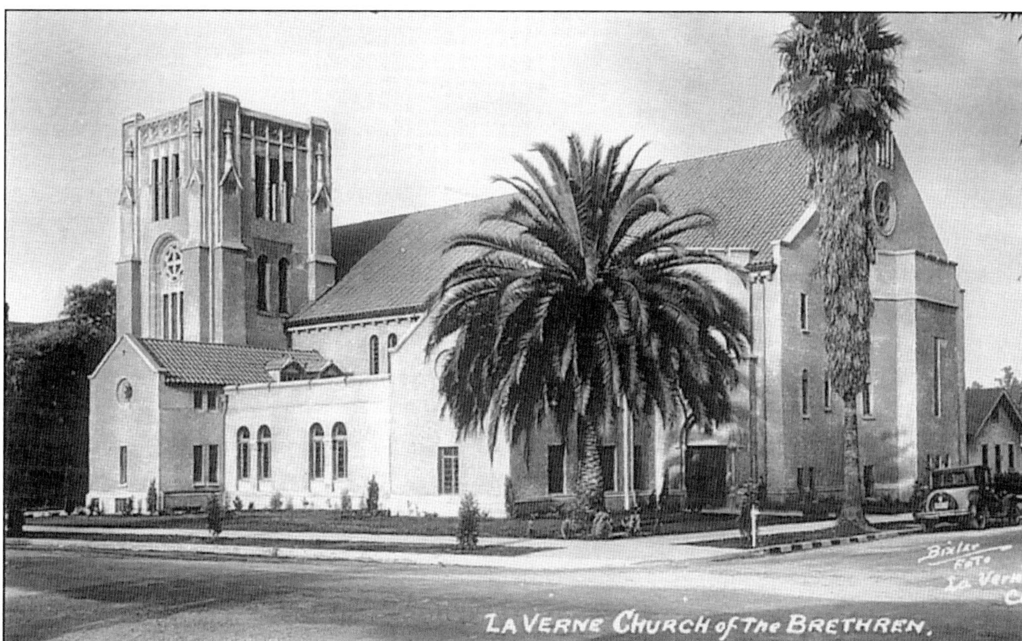

La Verne Church of the Brethren. This picture was taken at the time of the dedication of the current building, which was in September 1930. (P/P: Bixler Foto, La Verne; courtesy Jack McCaskill.)

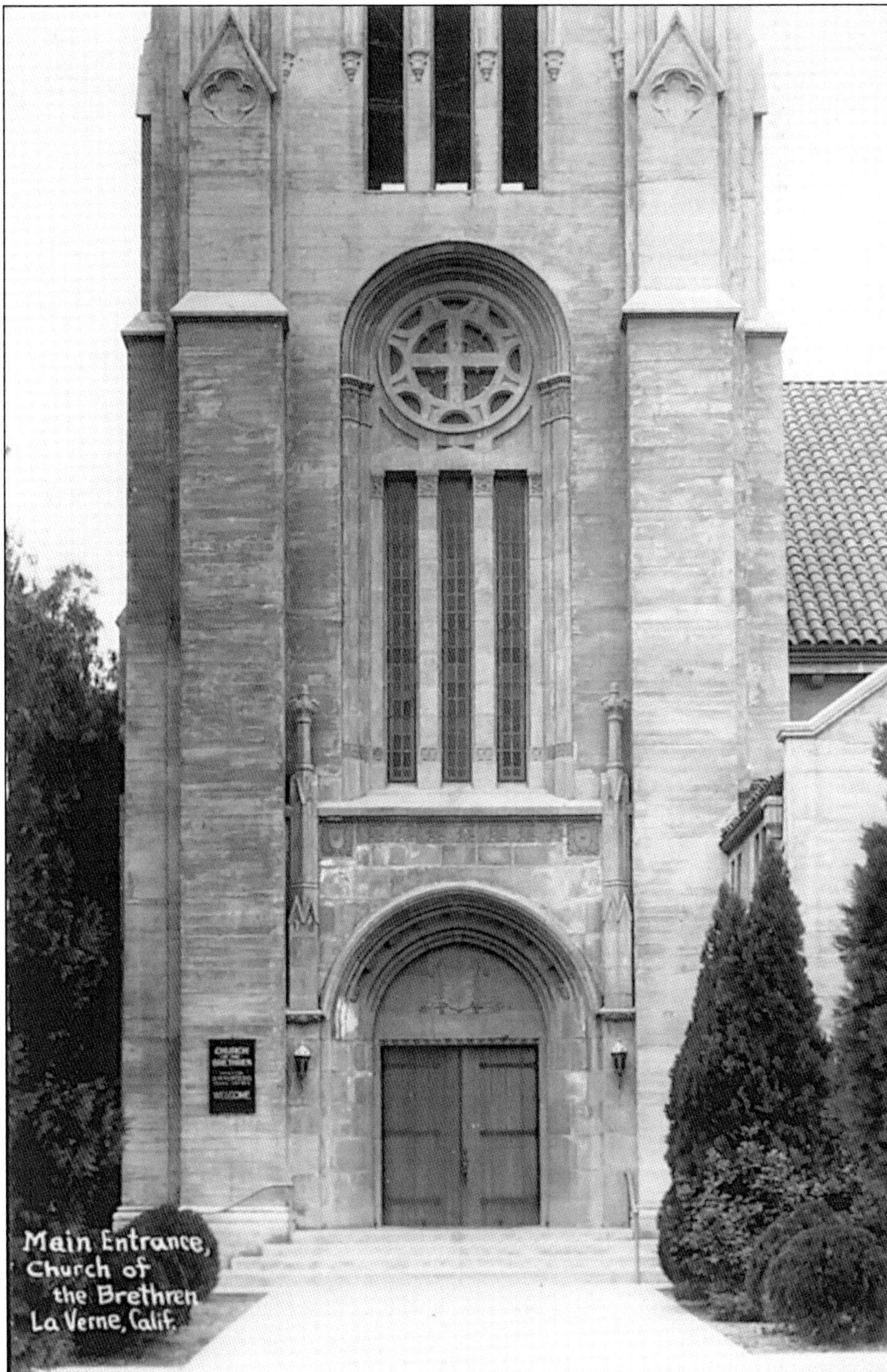

MAIN ENTRANCE, LA VERNE CHURCH OF THE BRETHREN. For many years, this was the largest congregation in town. Its sanctuary has hosted many community events across the decades. (P/P: unknown.)

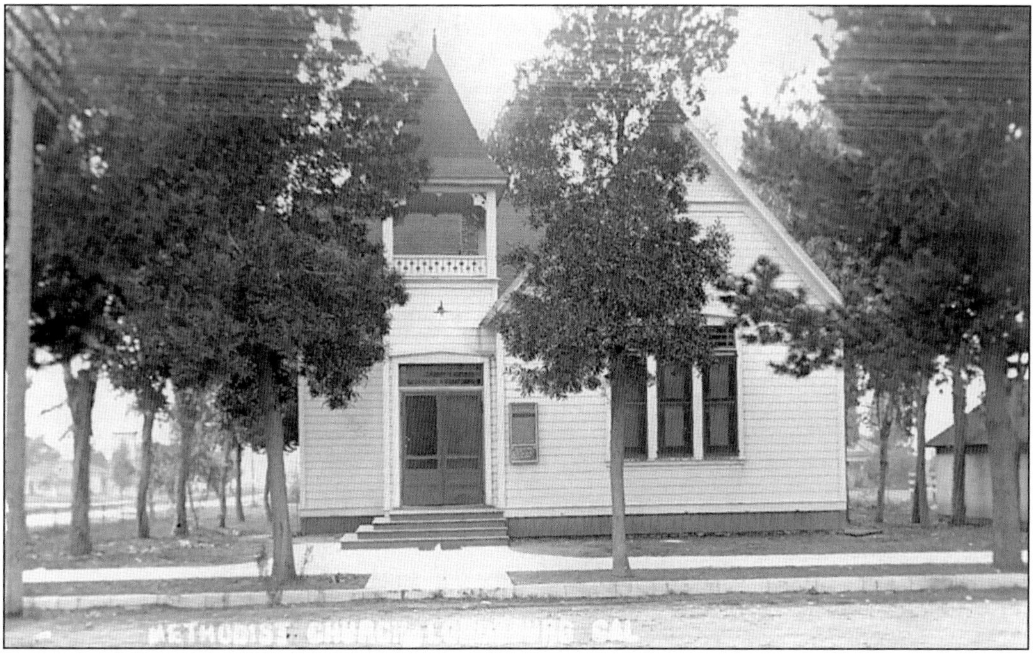

METHODIST CHURCH, LORDSBURG. This building was the first church the Lordsburg Methodists built, located on the corner of Third and F Streets in 1893. (P/P: unknown.)

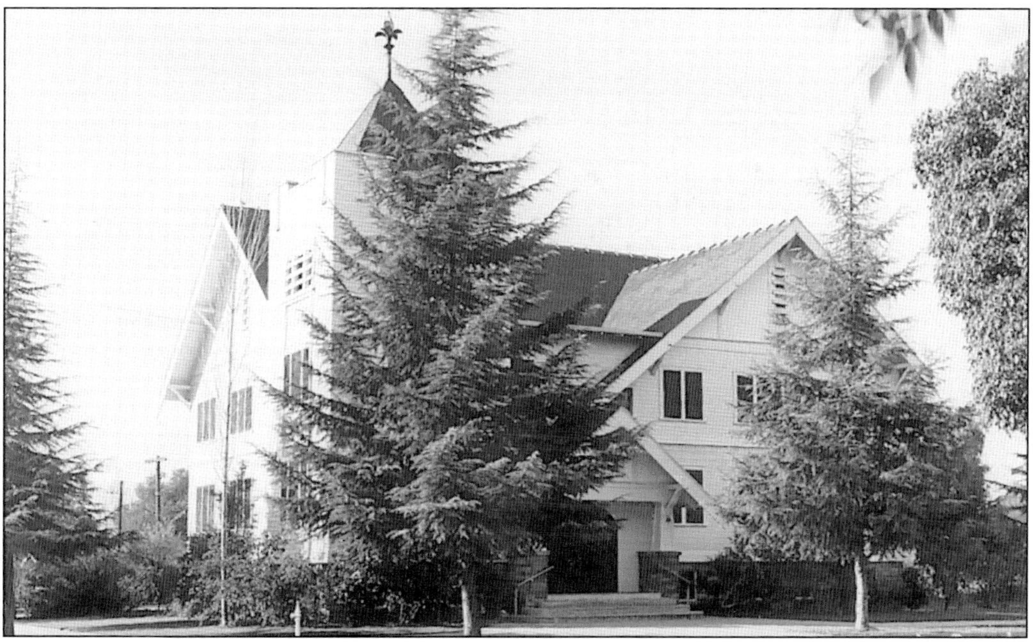

METHODIST CHURCH, LORDSBURG. This is the second building of the Methodists, located on the southwest corner of Third and F Streets in 1912. This building was used by the congregation until 1961, when the present church building was built on north D Street. (P/P: unknown; courtesy University of La Verne, Wilson Library Archives.)

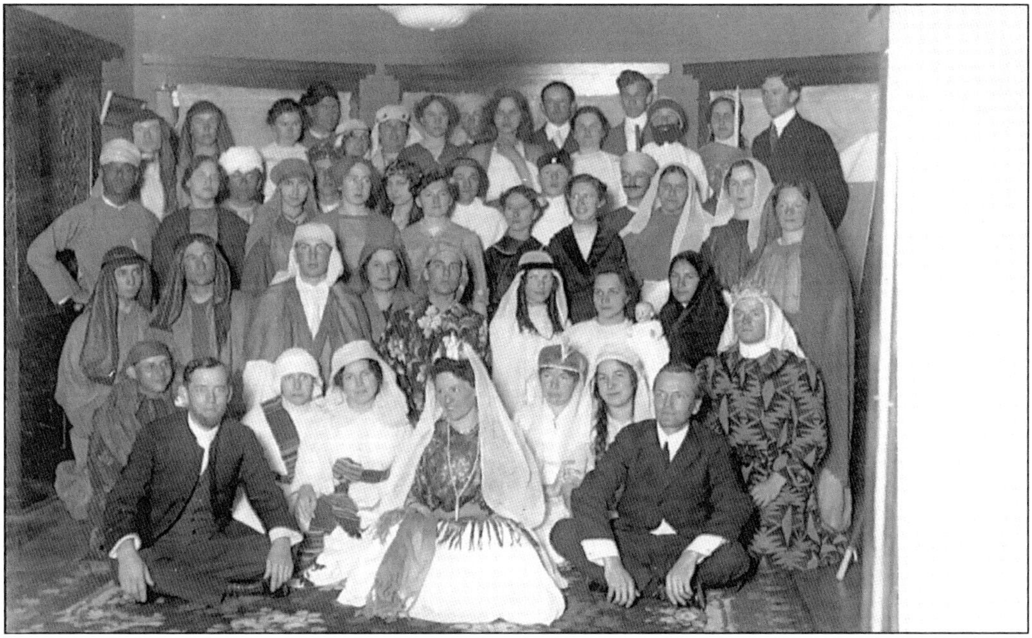

EXCELSIOR SUNDAY SCHOOL CLASS SOCIAL AT THE HAUGH'S. On February 26, 1914, this college-age Sunday school class met at the home of their teacher, Mrs. Laura Haugh. As it was an Oriental social, all were to come dressed in Oriental garb of Biblical times. (P/P: unknown; courtesy University of La Verne, Wilson Library Archives.)

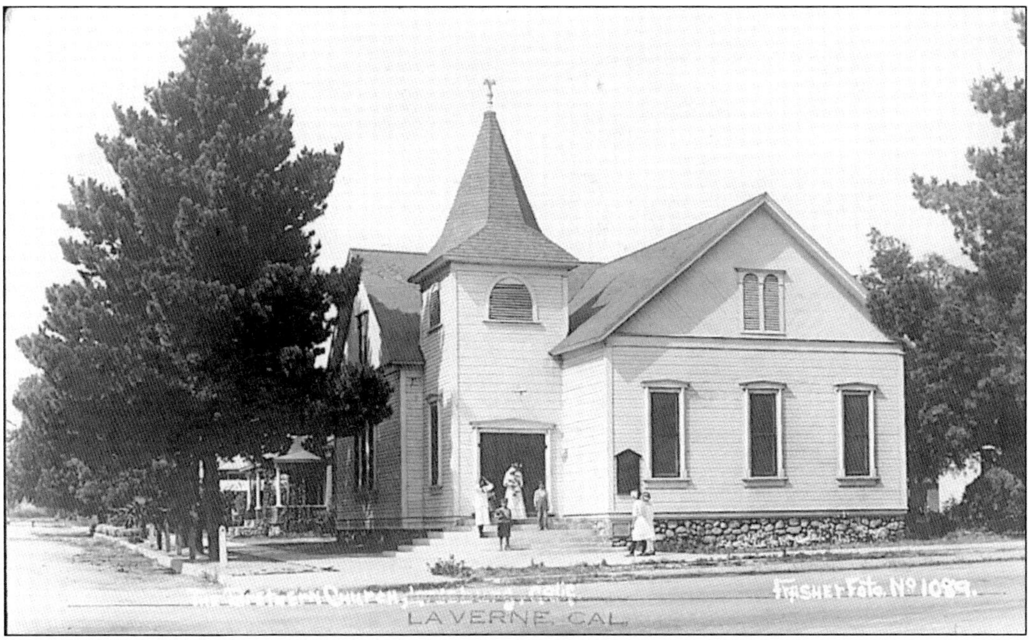

THE BRETHREN CHURCH, LORDSBURG. The Brethren Church (Progressive) was located on the northeast corner of Third and E Streets. The picture has La Verne stamped over Lordsburg, which would date the photo about 1917. (P/P: Frasher, No. 1089.)

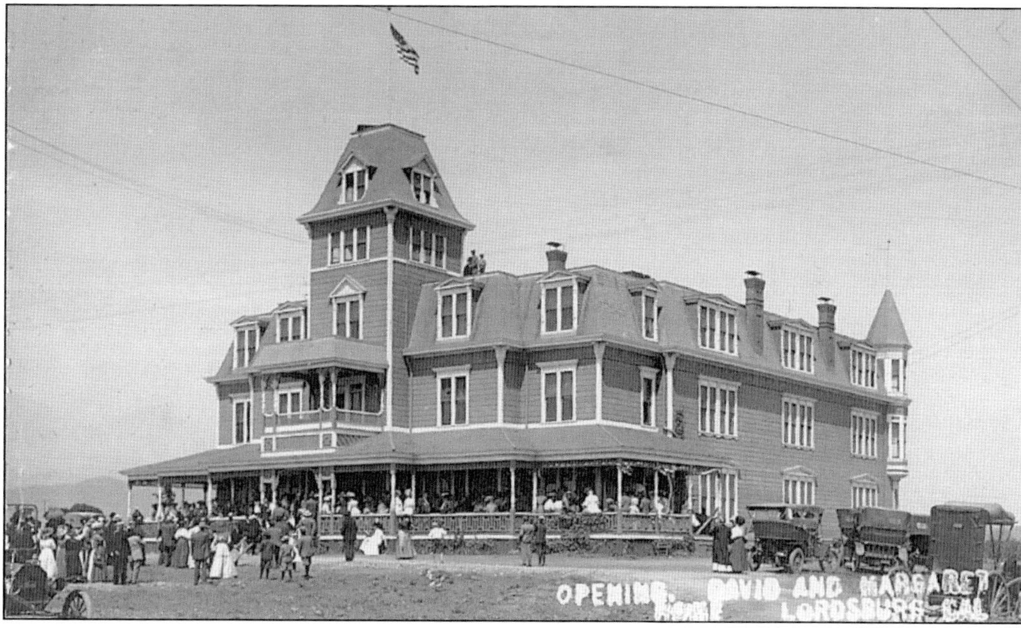

Opening of the David and Margaret Home. Henry L. Kuns, a founder of Lordsburg College, purchased the La Verne Hotel and donated the building and property to the Methodist Church in 1910 to use as an orphanage. The town of La Verne, northwest of Lordsburg, only lasted one year, 1887–88. (P/P: unknown.)

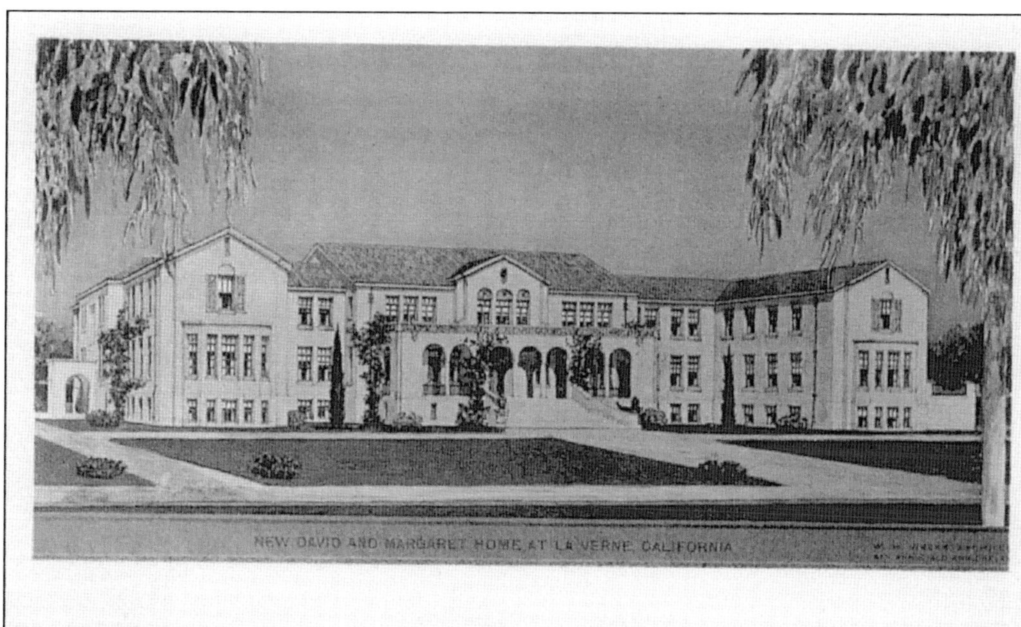

Architect's Rendering of the David and Margaret Home, 1926. The "new" David and Margaret Home opened at 1350 Third Street in La Verne in 1926. (P/P: unknown; courtesy City of La Verne Planning Department.)

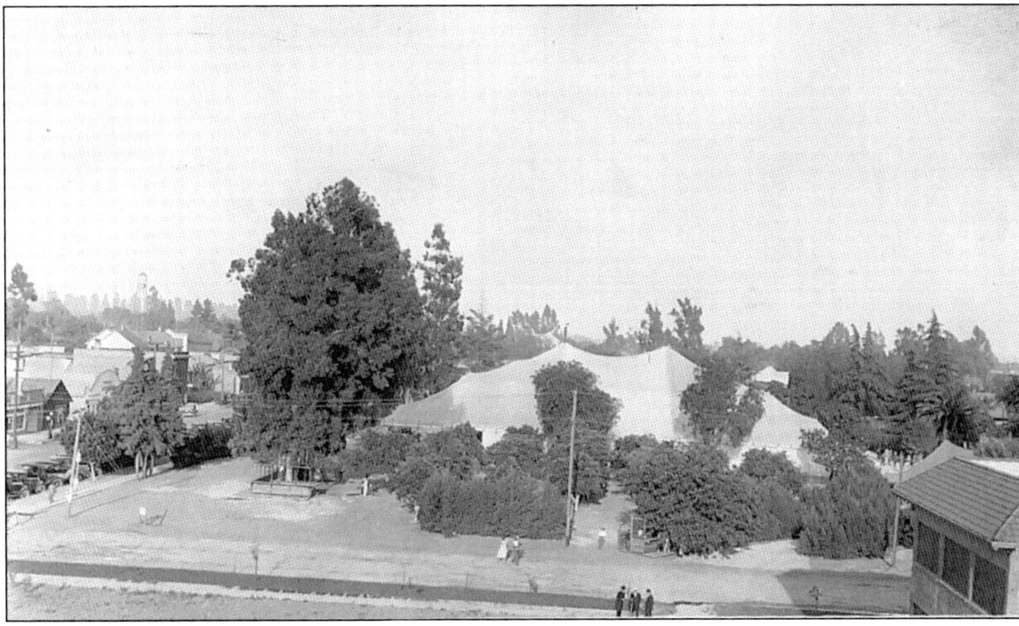

Church of the Brethren Annual Conference, La Verne, 1928. This national conference was held in a large tent in the city park from June 26 to July 3. More than 4,000 people were in attendance, and visitors were housed in tents and in people's houses. The meeting tent was 170 by 130 feet with side walls 12 feet high and center poles 50 feet high. (P/P: unknown.)

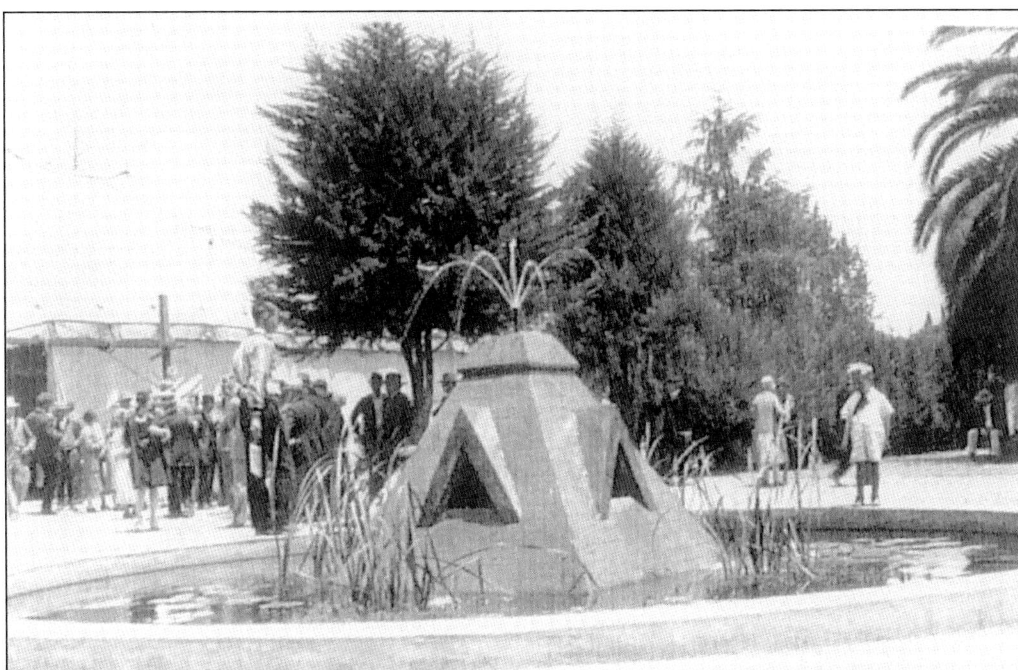

Church of the Brethren Annual Conference, La Verne, 1941. La Verne hosted the conference for a second time in a tent in the city park. The fountain in this view was in front of the original hotel/college building. (P/P: unknown; courtesy Charles and Dorothy Doyen.)

Three

Businesses, Homes, and People

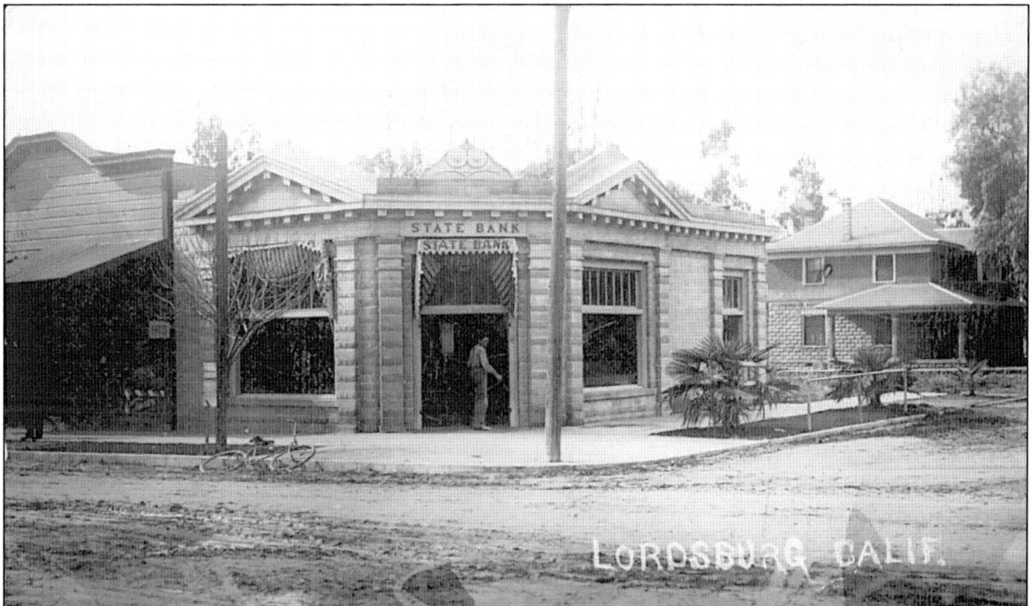

State Bank, Lordsburg. Built in 1909 on the southwest corner of D and Second Streets, this building served as the home of the First National Bank until it opened new quarters one block north in 1910. The State Bank of Pomona opened this branch office in 1910. (P/P: unknown.)

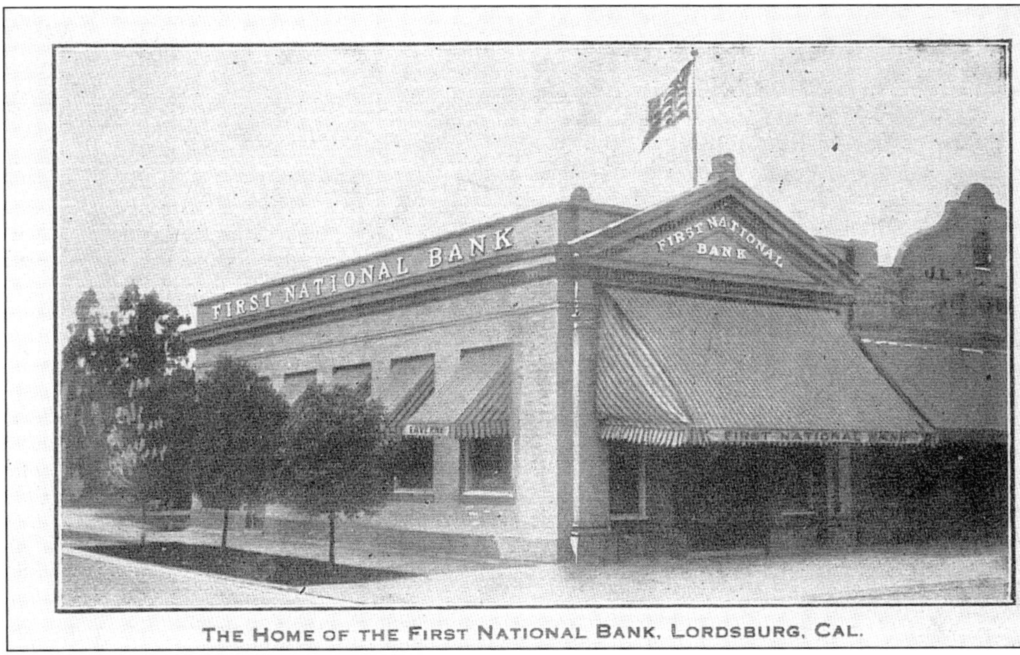

HOME OF THE FIRST NATIONAL BANK, LORDSBURG. On the northwest corner of D and Third Streets, this building served as home to the bank from 1910 until the mid-1950s. (P/P: unknown; courtesy Jack McCaskill.)

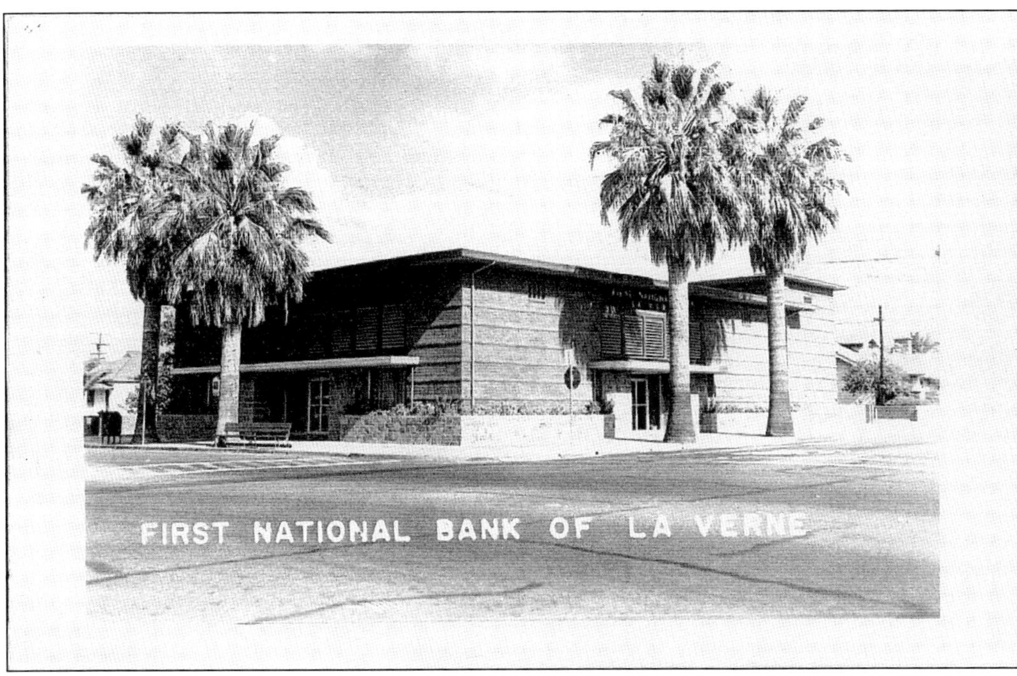

FIRST NATIONAL BANK, LA VERNE. Built in 1955, this bank building had several names over the next forty-some years before ceasing operation as a bank. The building opened in the fall of 1999 as the University of La Verne Bookstore and Some Crust Bakery. (P/P: unknown; courtesy Jack McCaskill.)

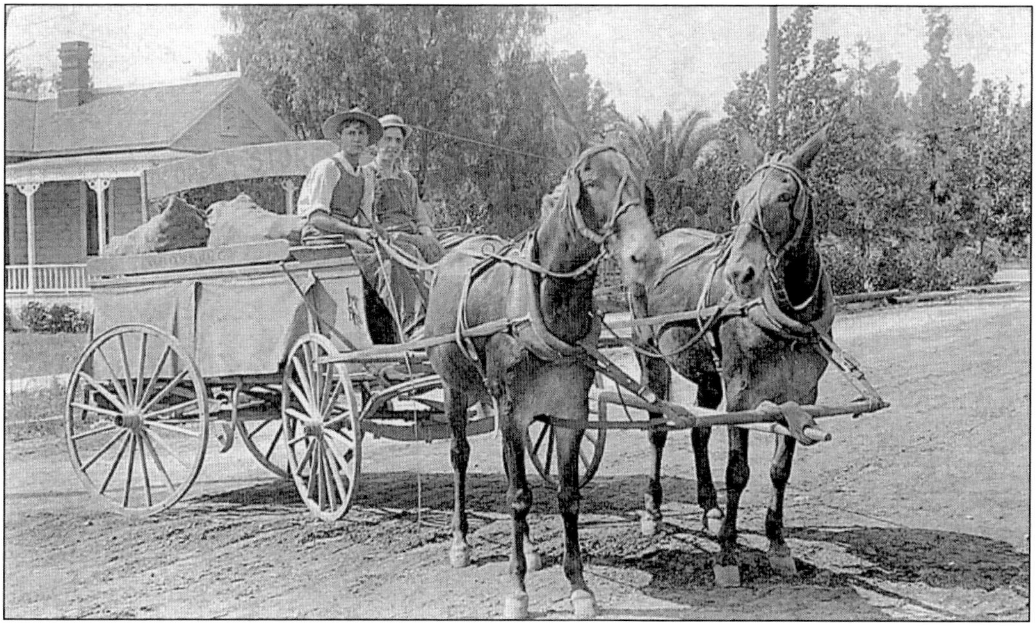

People's Store Delivery Wagon, Lordsburg. As shown in this postcard, groceries were delivered to homes by the People's Store delivery wagon. (P/P: unknown; postmark: August 1911; courtesy Jack McCaskill.)

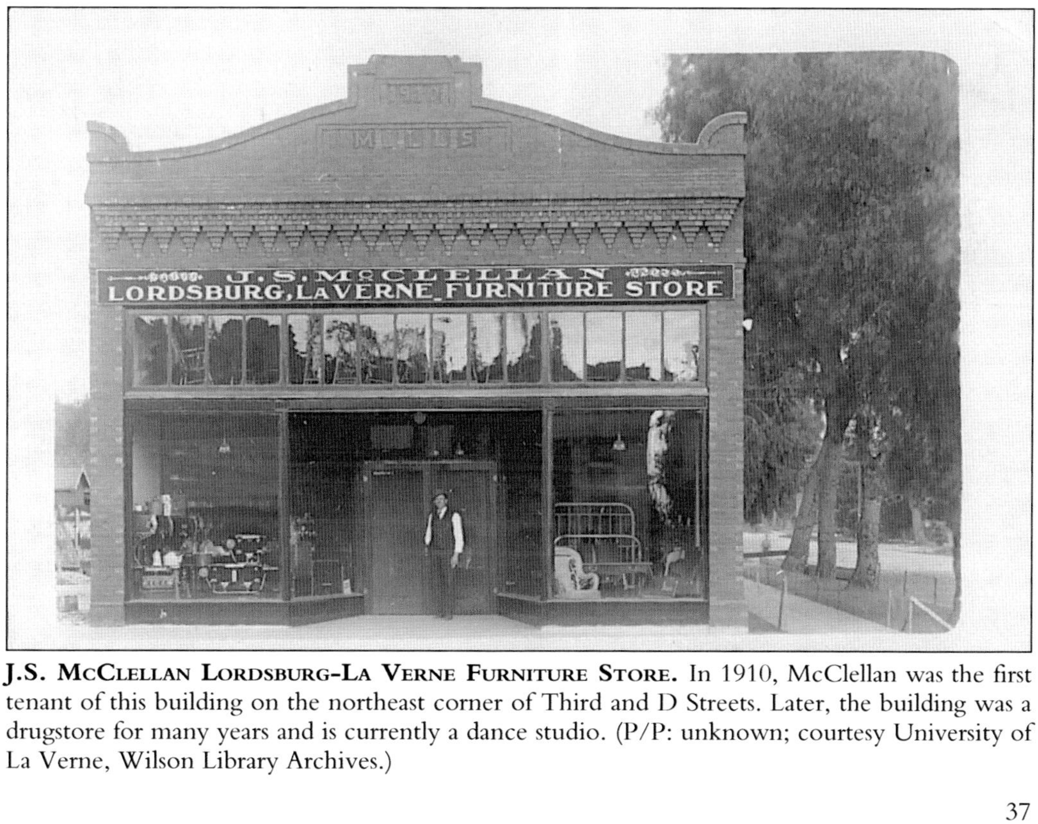

J.S. McClellan Lordsburg-La Verne Furniture Store. In 1910, McClellan was the first tenant of this building on the northeast corner of Third and D Streets. Later, the building was a drugstore for many years and is currently a dance studio. (P/P: unknown; courtesy University of La Verne, Wilson Library Archives.)

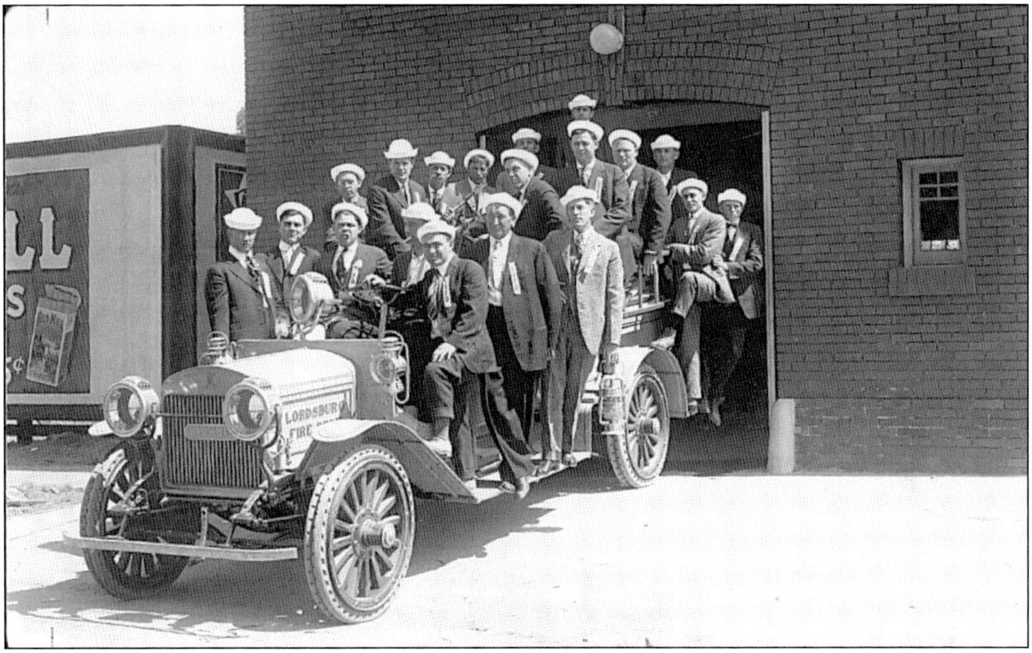

LORDSBURG VOLUNTEER FIRE DEPARTMENT, 1915. This picture was taken in front of the "new" fire station/city hall building. (P/P: Frasher Foto, Lordsburg; courtesy University of La Verne, Wilson Library Archives.)

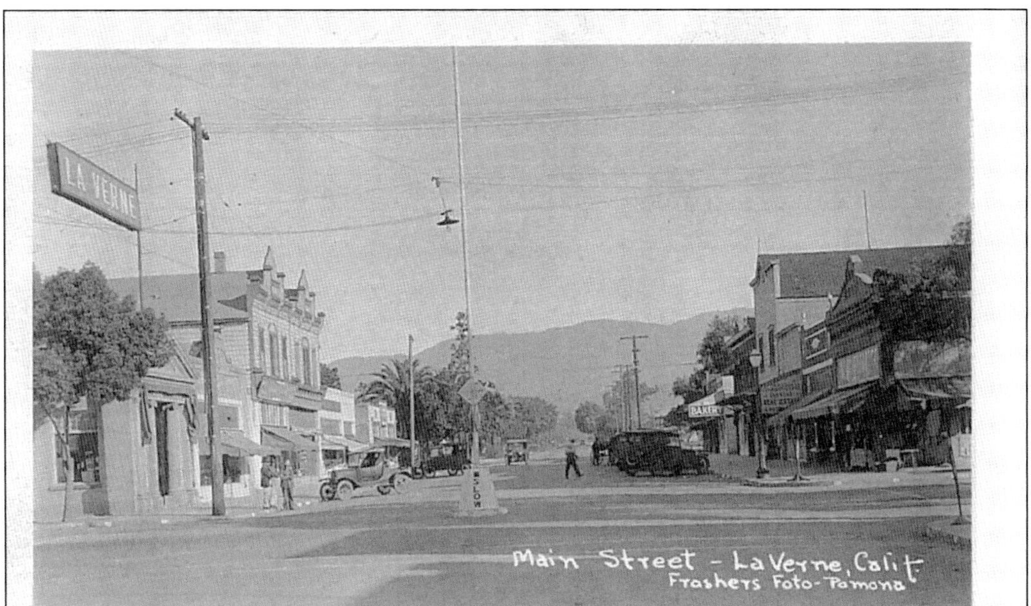

MAIN STREET, LA VERNE, CALIFORNIA. You are looking north from the intersection of Third and D Streets in the 1920s. (P/P: Frasher Foto, Pomona; courtesy Jack McCaskill.)

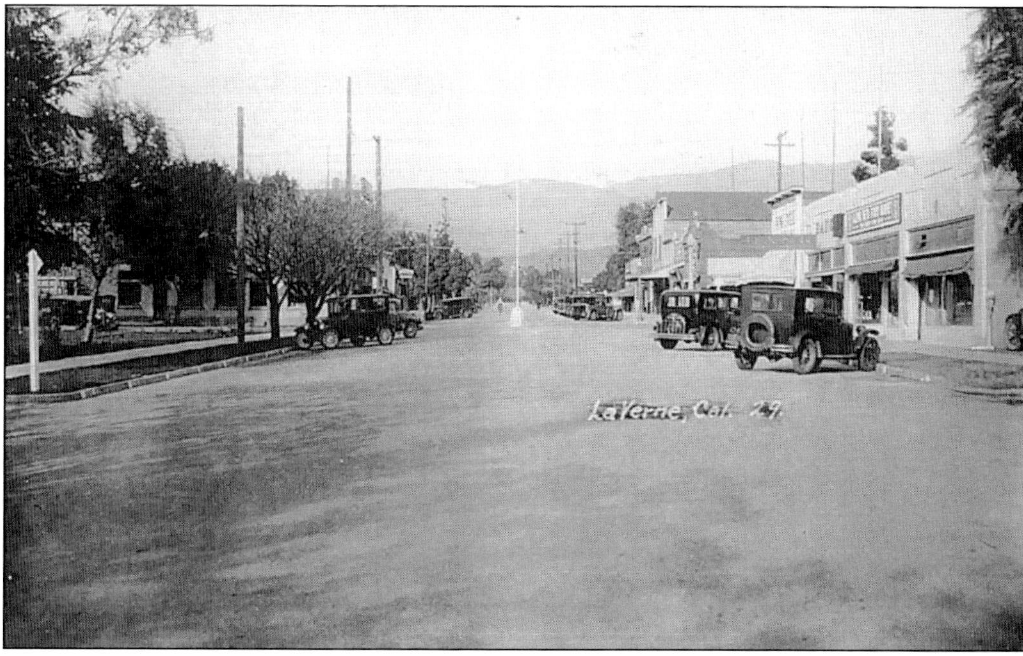

La Verne, 1929. This view of downtown was taken from the corner of D and Second Streets looking north into the business district. (P/P: unknown; courtesy Jack McCaskill.)

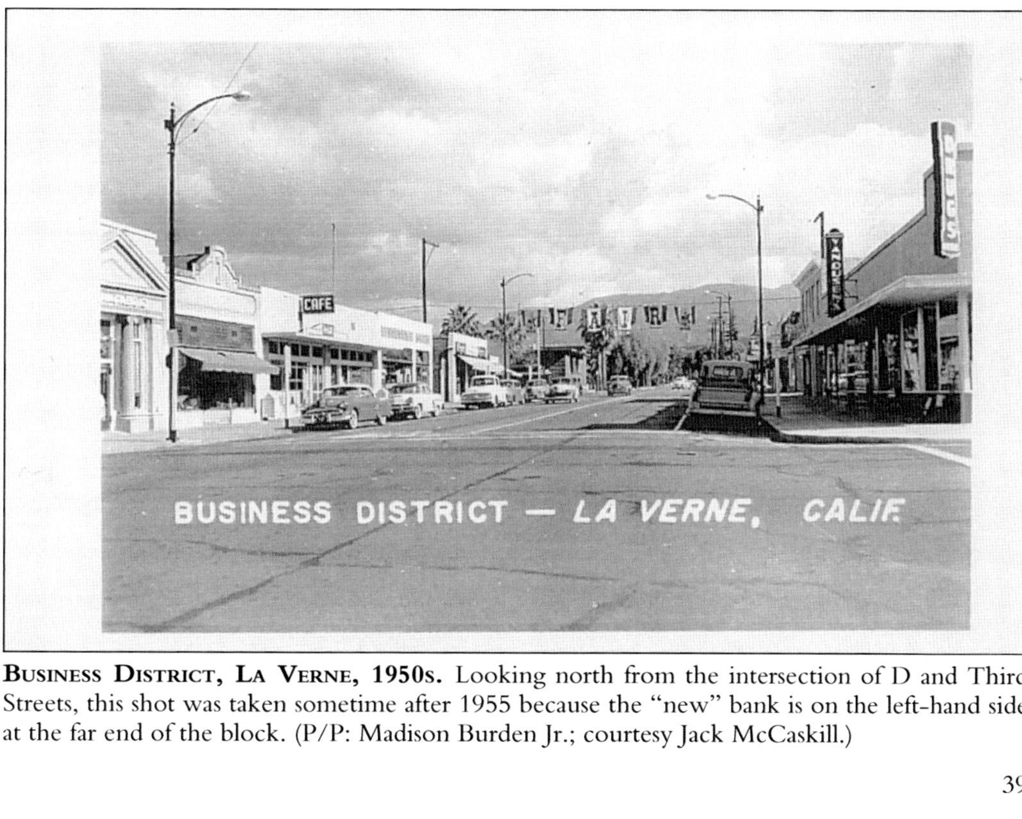

Business District, La Verne, 1950s. Looking north from the intersection of D and Third Streets, this shot was taken sometime after 1955 because the "new" bank is on the left-hand side at the far end of the block. (P/P: Madison Burden Jr.; courtesy Jack McCaskill.)

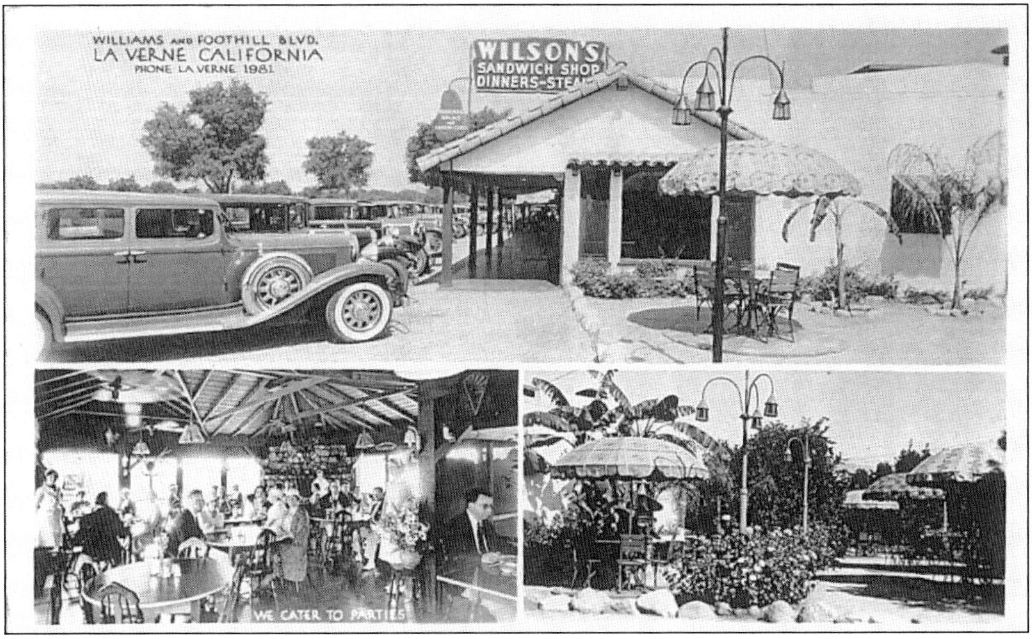

Wilson's Sandwich Shop, Foothill Boulevard, La Verne. A favorite eatery on U.S. Route 66 as it passed through La Verne, Wilson's served steak, chicken, rainbow trout, and regular dinners. Much of the original building remains today as a Mexican restaurant. (P/P: Douglas Calkins, Pomona; courtesy Jack McCaskill.)

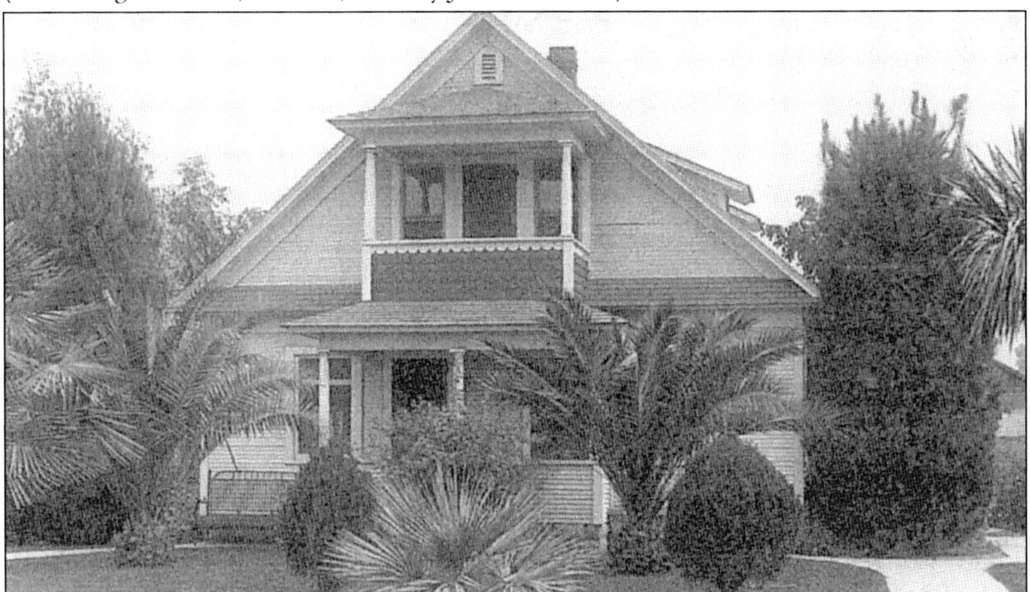

Noah Neher Home, 2219 Third Street. On May 9, 1909, this house hosted the triple wedding of three daughters of the Neher family. Clara Neher and Ira Vaniman, Susie Neher and Ernest Vaniman, and Lizzie Neher and Raymond Flory were married by the Rev. J.Z. Gilbert. A note on the card tells of the sender being one of thousands who saw President Taft in Pomona. A Pomona newspaper reported that a crowd of 10,000 people came to Pomona to see the President. (P/P: unknown; postmark: October 1911; courtesy Ernestine Hoff Emerick.)

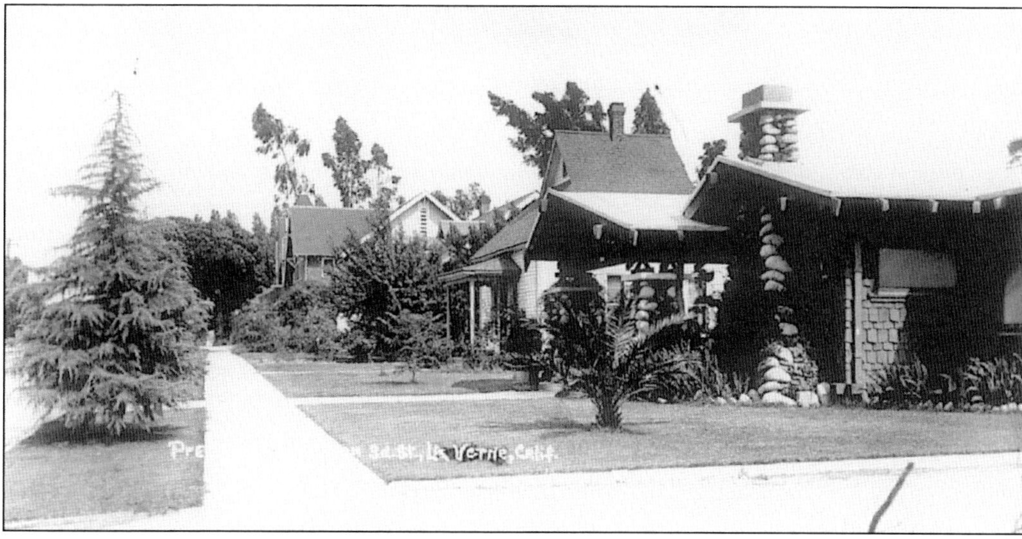

The Huigens' Home on Third Street. The home of Rex and Karen Huigens was located at 2236 Third Street. (P/P: Frasher; courtesy Rex and Karen Huigens.)

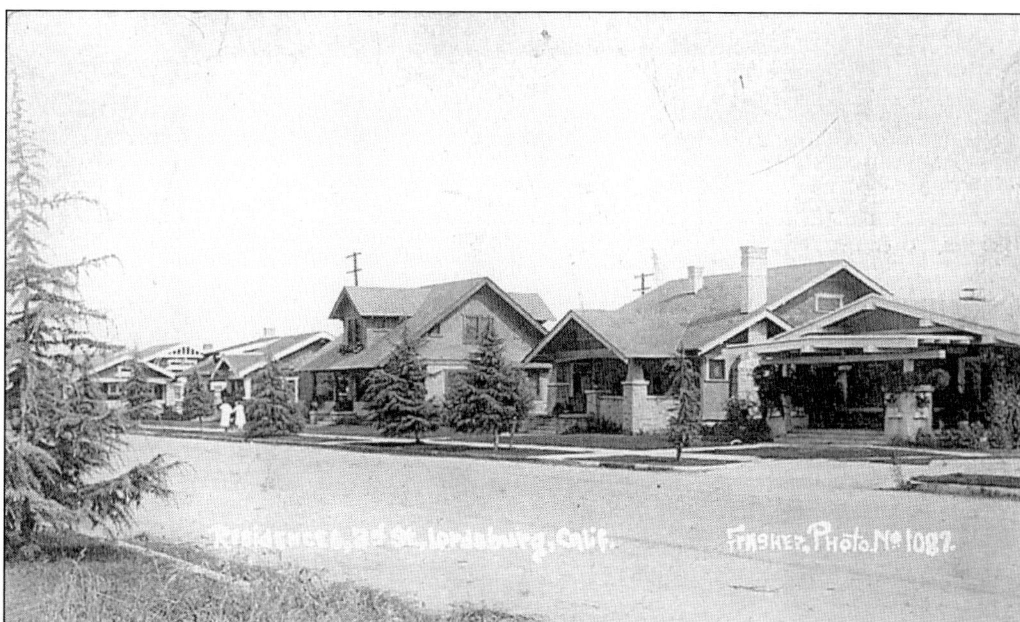

Residences on Third Street. These are the last four homes on the south side of the 2400 block of Third Street. The last home in the picture is situated across Lincoln Street (White Avenue). (P/P: Frasher, No. 1087; courtesy Jack McCaskill.)

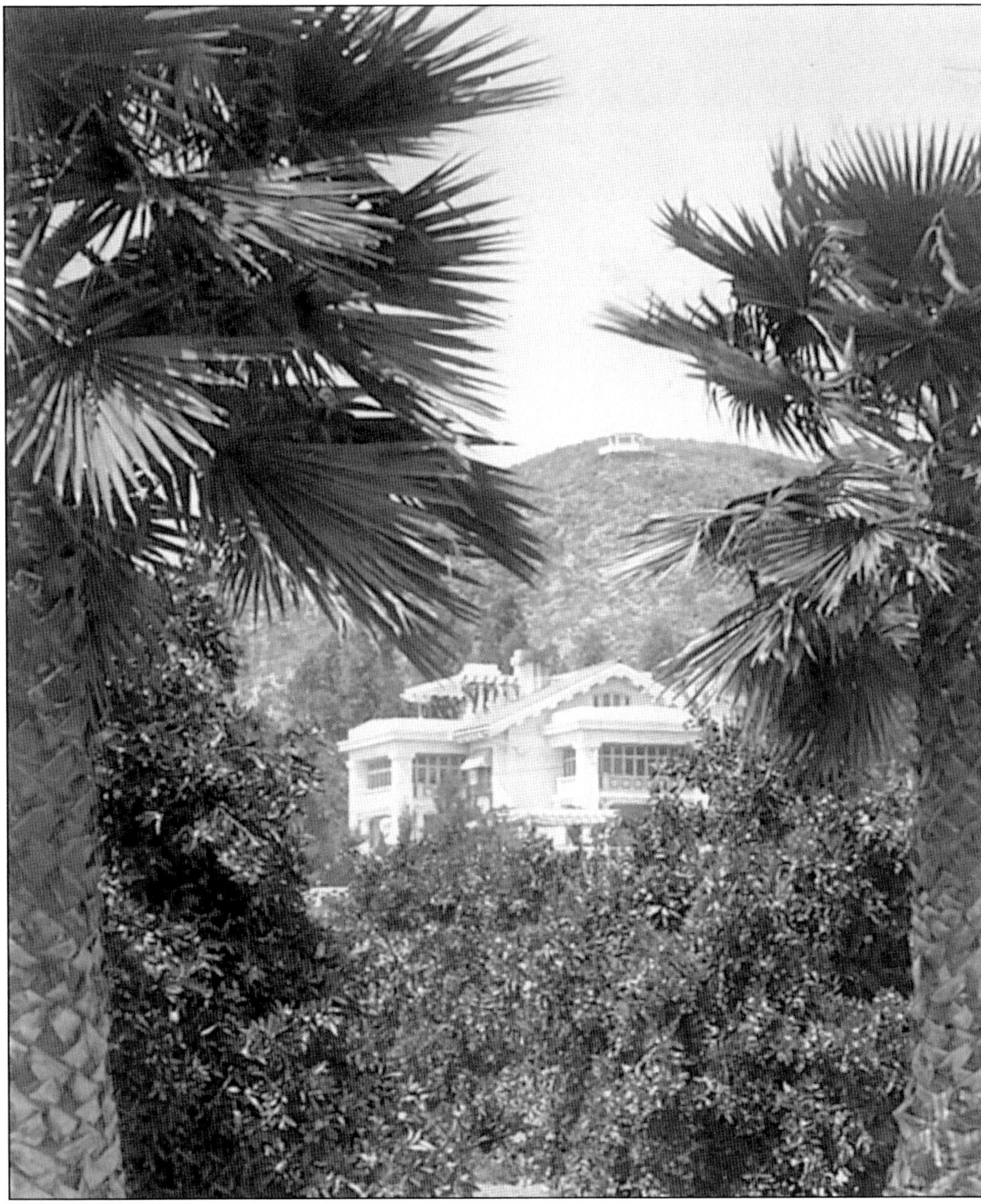

ELSBERY REYNOLDS HOME. Elsbery Reynolds, Chicago publisher of books by Harold Bell Wright, employed New York architect Paul F. Higgs to design this residence, which was built in 1913 a half-mile north of the Lordsburg city limits. The foothill home was three stories high and had a cellar. On the first floor were a 20-by-40-foot living room, a 20-by-30-foot dining room, a butler's pantry, a kitchen breakfast room, a reception room, and a den. On the second floor were six large bedrooms, six baths, and large screened porches. On the third floor were a 25-by-48-foot ballroom, servants' apartments, and three large decks overlooking the valley. The Colonial, grand staircase was 5 feet wide. The 25-by-50-foot garage had room for four cars and servants' quarters, and outside was a 50-by-75-foot swimming pool. The house is no longer standing. (P/P: Collinge & Harris Postcards, Pomona.)

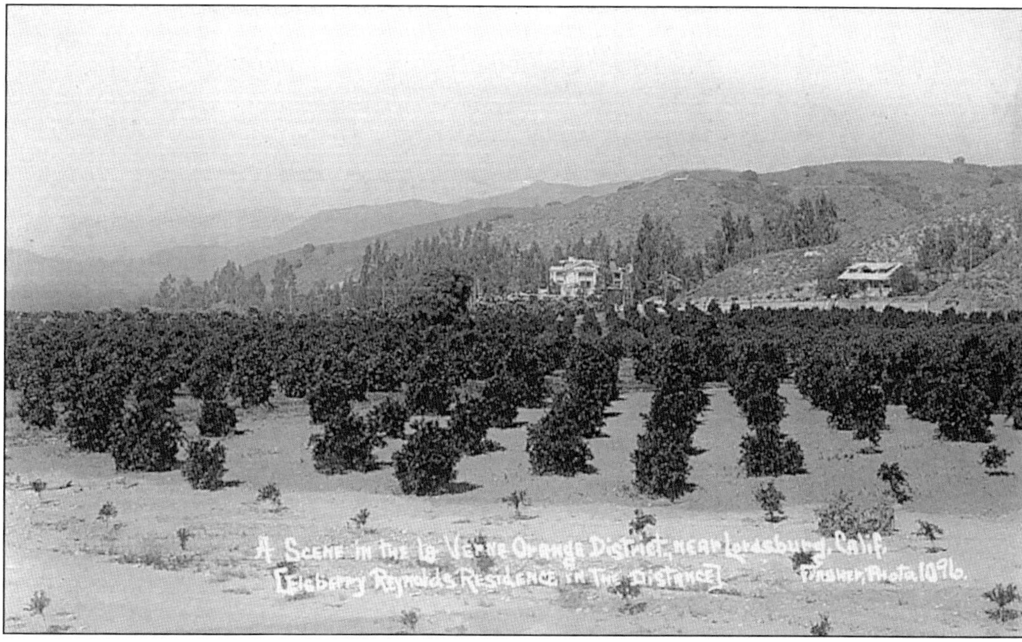

Scene in the La Verne Orange District near Lordsburg. This view of an orange grove, with younger trees in the foreground, shows the Elsbery Reynolds home in the distance. (P/P: Burton Frasher, photographer, Wapato, Washington, No. 1096; courtesy Jack McCaskill.)

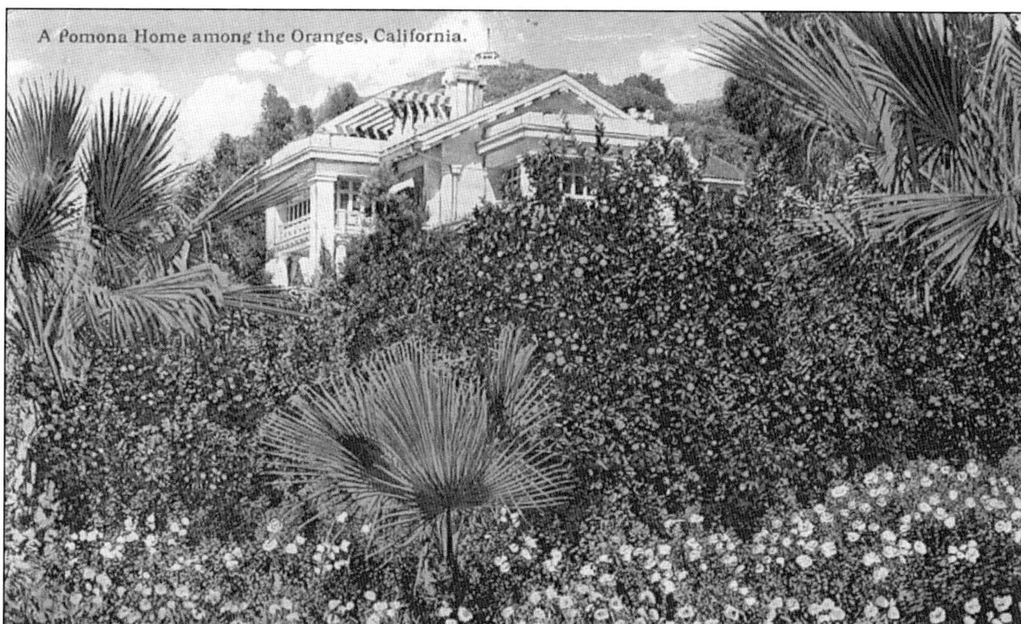

Pomona Home among the Oranges. With yet another view of the Reynolds home, listing Pomona as the address, this postcard was mailed to Hansen, Idaho, from Pomona. The sender wrote, "We had a nice trip and didn't find the roads so very bad—only a few places. Most of the way they were dry and dusty." (P/P: Julius Hecht; postmark: February 1920.)

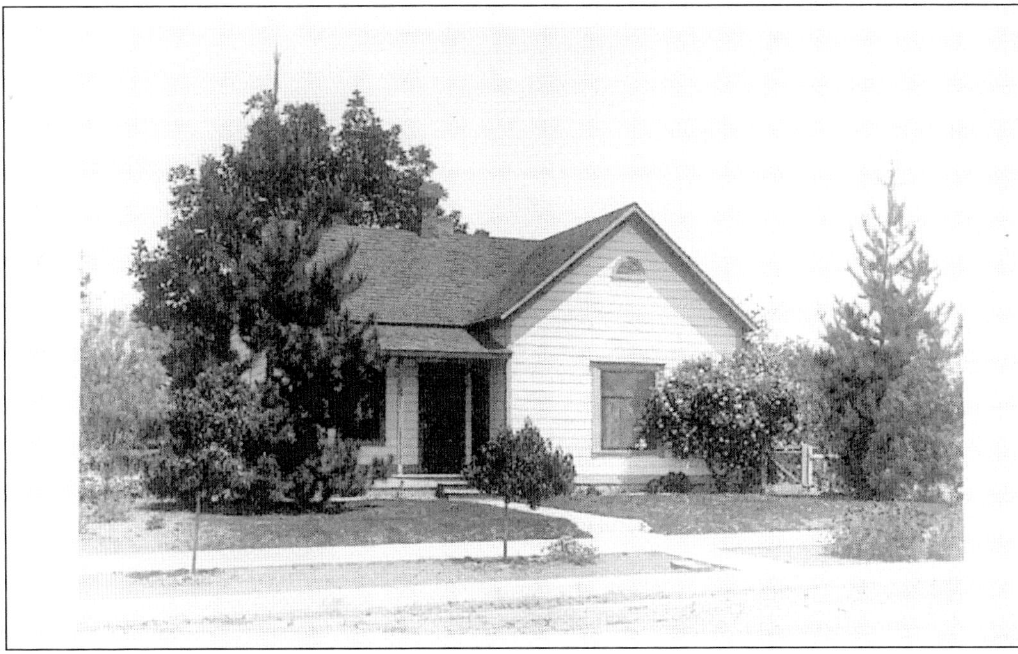

J.B. Hoff Home on Fourth Street (Bonita), Lordsburg. This house still stands at 2325 Bonita Street in La Verne. (P/P: E.G. Hoff; courtesy Ernestine Hoff Emerick.)

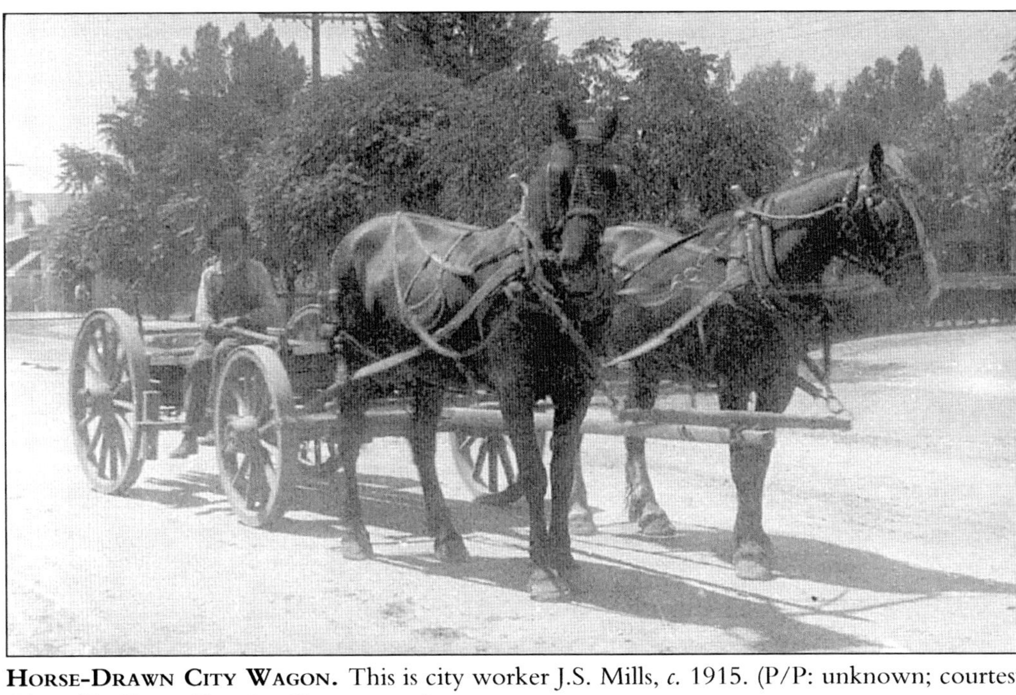

Horse-Drawn City Wagon. This is city worker J.S. Mills, *c.* 1915. (P/P: unknown; courtesy City of La Verne Planning Department.)

WILLIAMS BROTHERS, *c.* 1914. Ronald F. and Robert H. Williams appear here, probably in the family home on the southwest corner of E and Second Streets in Lordsburg. (P/P: unknown; courtesy Gary Williams.)

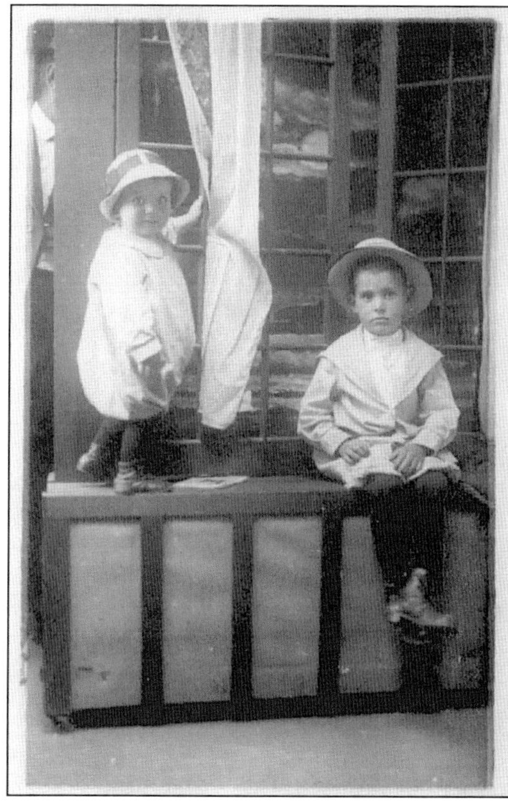

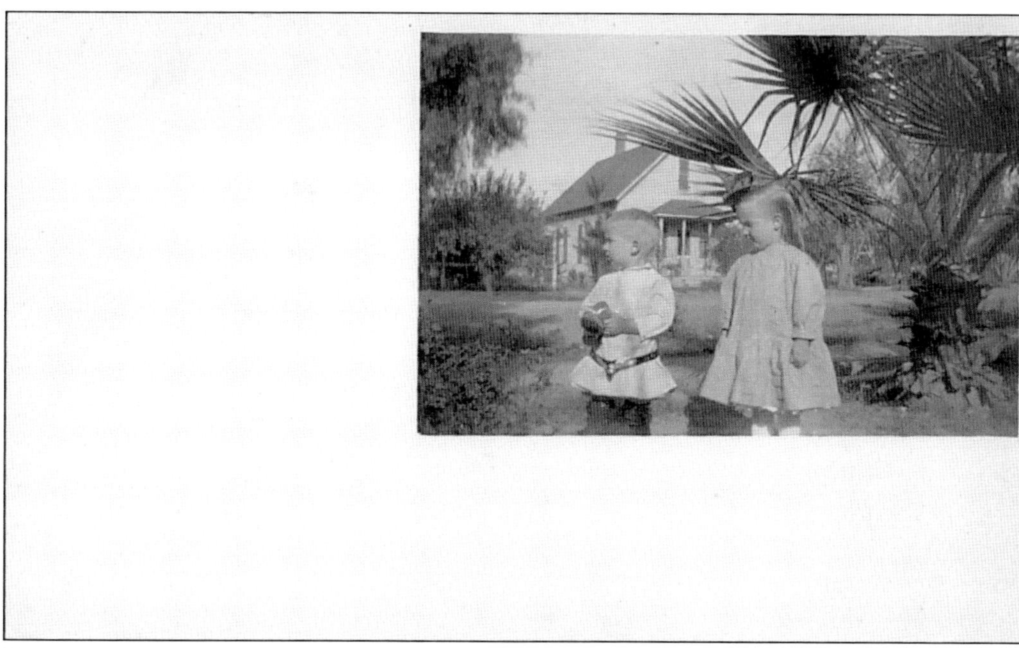

KENNETH EIKENBERRY AND MARY BLICKENSTAFF (BRUBAKER). This picture was taken in front of their home on the northwest corner of E and Third Streets in Lordsburg. (P/P: unknown.)

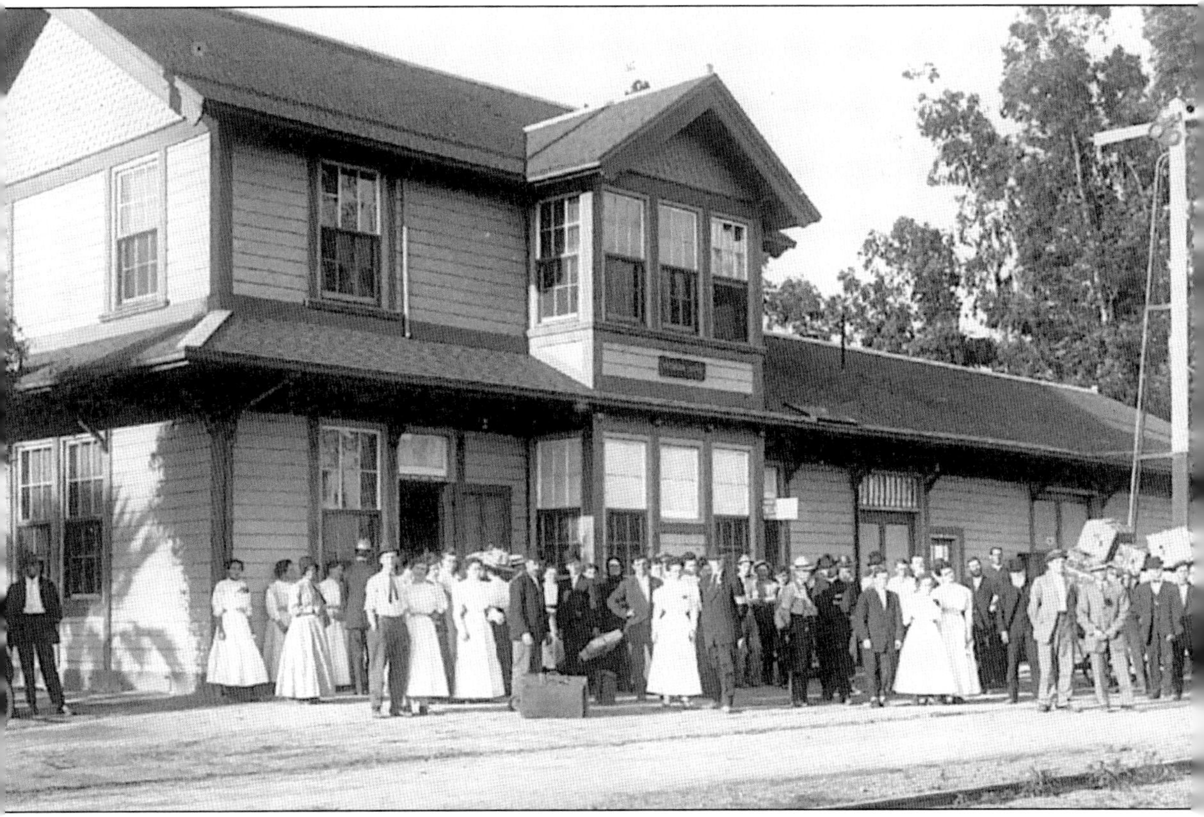

Ernest and Susie Neher Vaniman Leave for China, September 18, 1913. The Lordsburg College *Palmerian* for October 1913 reported, "A large delegation of friends and relatives were at the station to see them start. . . It was a very pathetic scene, yet Bro. & Sister Vaniman wore a bright smile and we all rejoiced to think that they were ready to do the great work in China." (P/P: unknown; courtesy Ernestine Hoff Emerick.)

Four

Heart of the Orange Empire

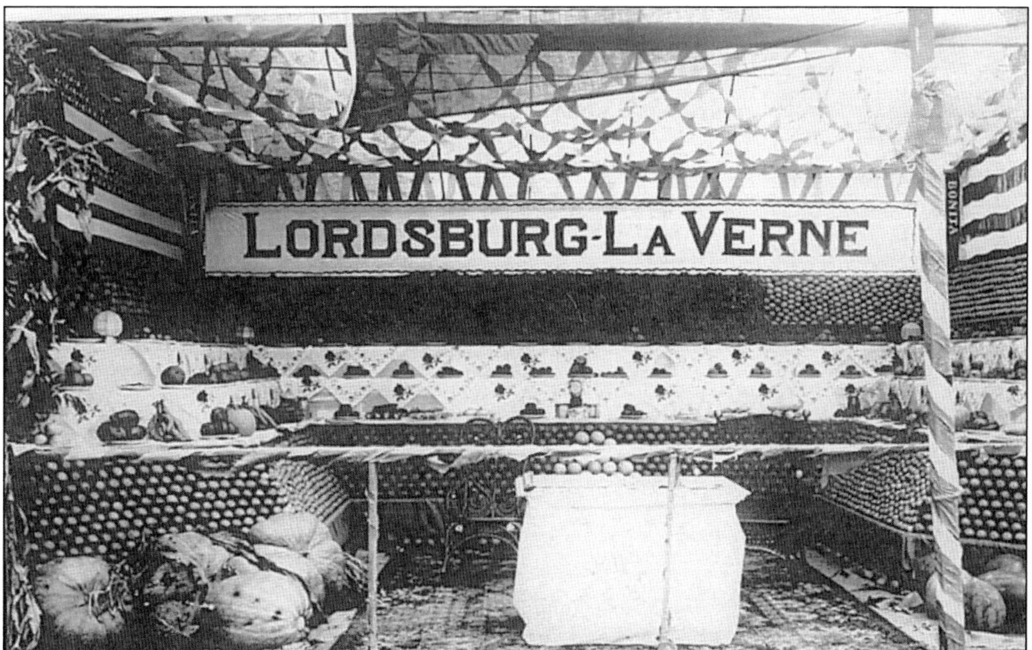

Lordsburg/La Verne Exhibit. This exhibit of fruit and vegetables was probably a Lordsburg/La Verne entry at the Los Angeles County Fair. (P/P: unknown; courtesy Jack McCaskill.)

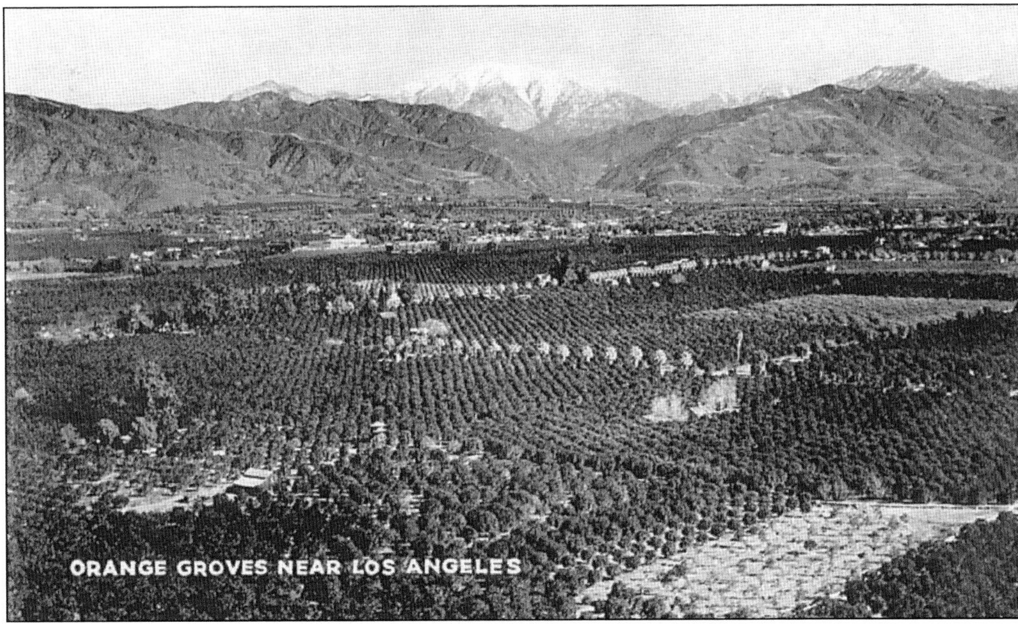

Orange Groves near Los Angeles. United Air Lines gave the following statistics on the back of this card: "Los Angeles is only 15 1/2 hours from Chicago and 20 1/2 hours from New York via UAL. A 2 hour flight from San Francisco and 8 hours from Seattle." (P/P: inflight with United Air Lines (UAL), No. 102.)

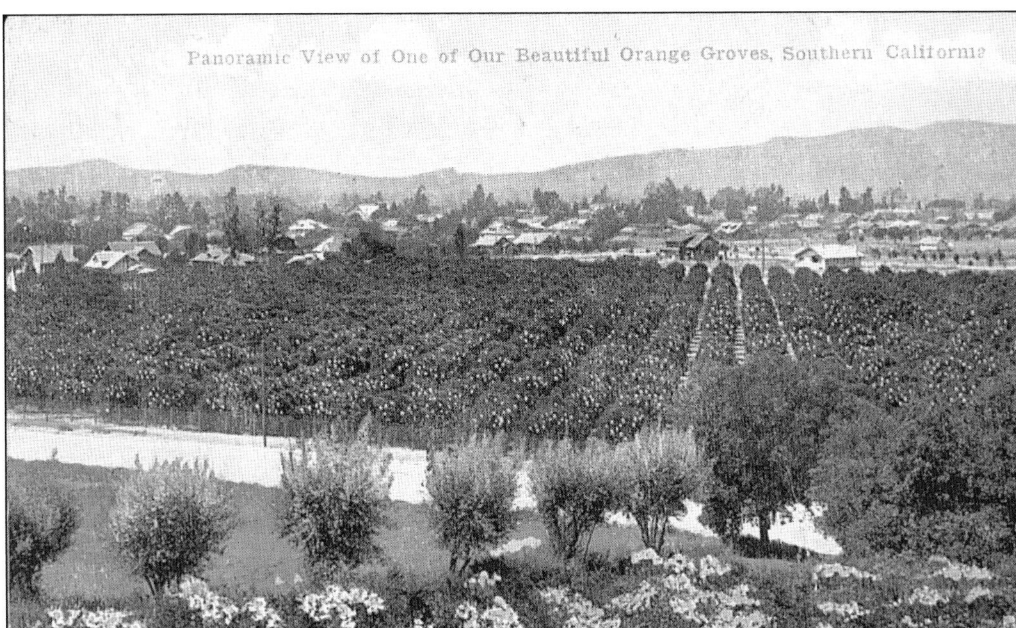

Panoramic View of One of Our Beautiful Orange Groves, Southern California. An article in the April-May 1907 issue of the *California Student* gave this description of the area: "Here amid the fragrance of some foothill ranch lurks Dame Nature with charming smile and healing zephyrs to woo back the reluctant color to the wan cheeks, and elasticity to the step." (P/P: Van Ornum Color Print Co., Los Angeles, No. 540.)

Navel Oranges, Claremont. This well-composed photo tells much more than words can convey. (P/P: Cooper Foto.)

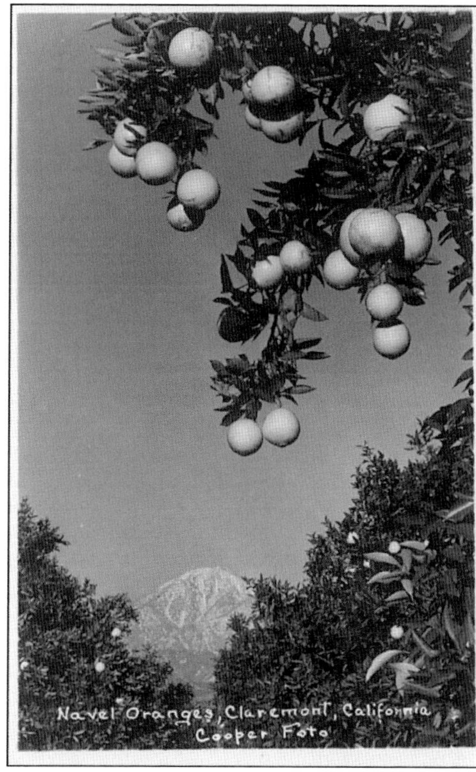

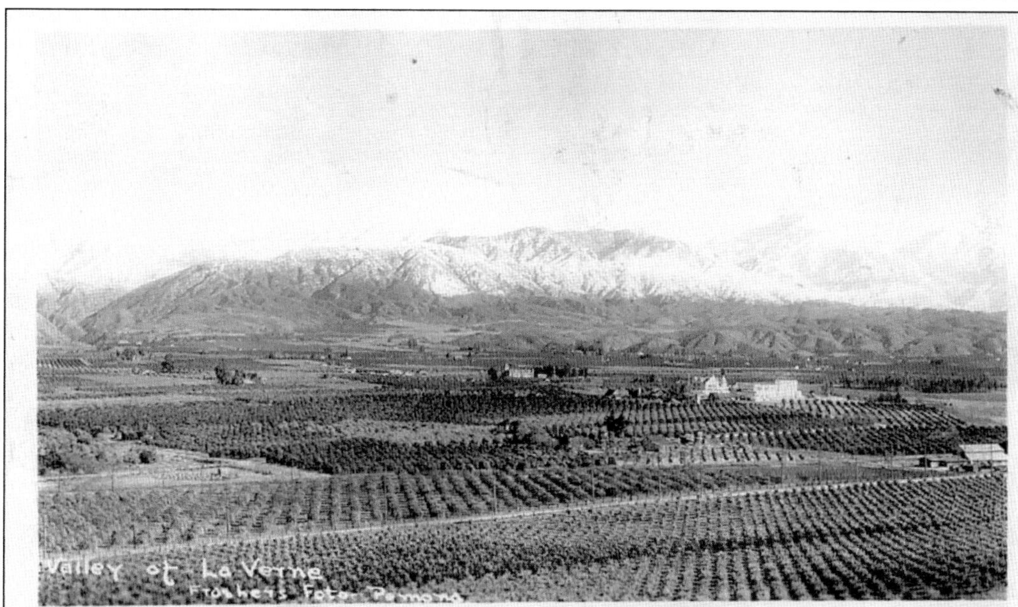

Valley of La Verne. La Verne lived up to its chamber of commerce slogan, "Heart of the Orange Empire." The large white building near the center of the photo is the original Bonita High School building. The written text on back reads, "Went for a drive yesterday and [saw] thousands of orange trees and [they] were loaded down." (P/P: Frashers, Pomona; postmarked: June 1928.)

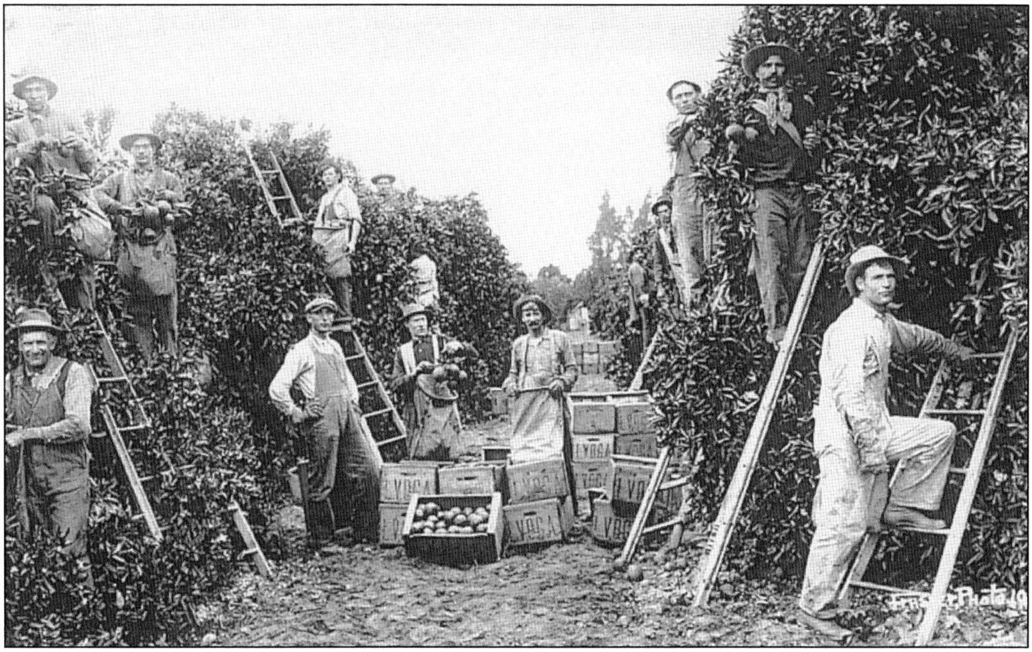

Orange Pickers in a Grove. All of the fruit was hand-picked. The boxes carry the mark of the LVOGA (La Verne Orange Growers Association). (P/P: Frasher; courtesy Jack McCaskill.)

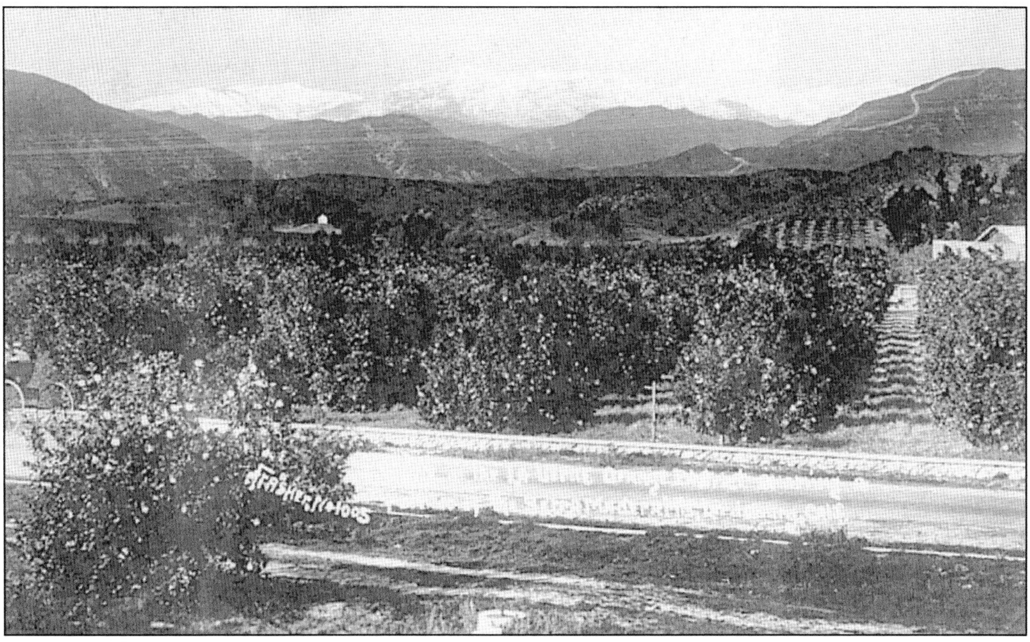

La Verne Orange District, Lordsburg. This scene shows a portion of the Sierra Madre Mountains. The area toward the mountains, north of Lordsburg, has always been known as La Verne. (P/P: Frasher, No. 1005; courtesy Jack McCaskill.)

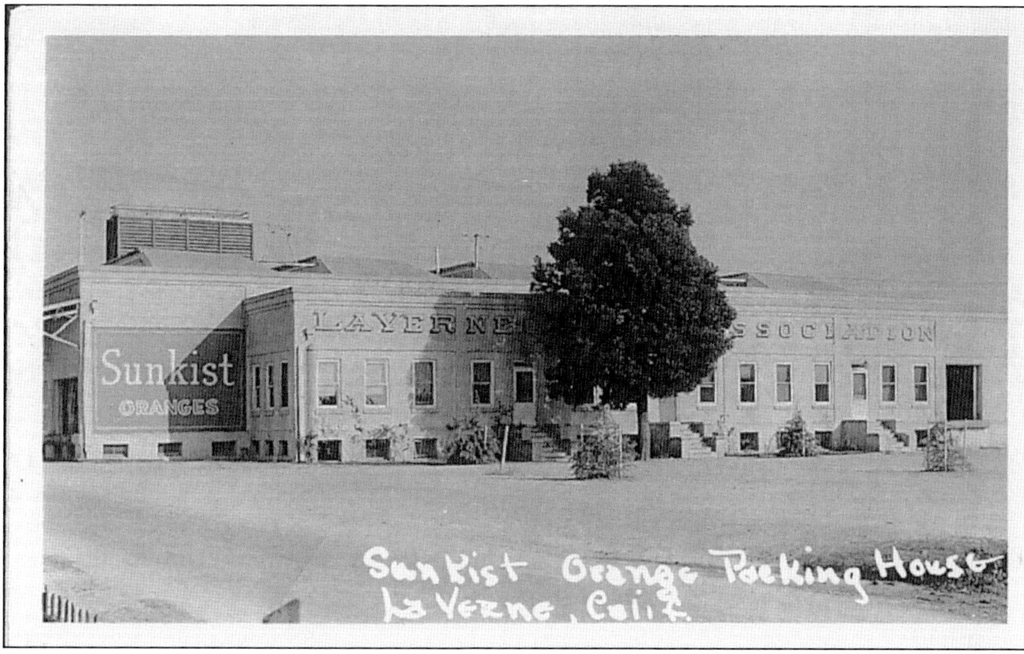

Sunkist Orange Packing House, La Verne. This is another one of the growers' cooperatives in La Verne. (P/P: unknown; courtesy Jack McCaskill.)

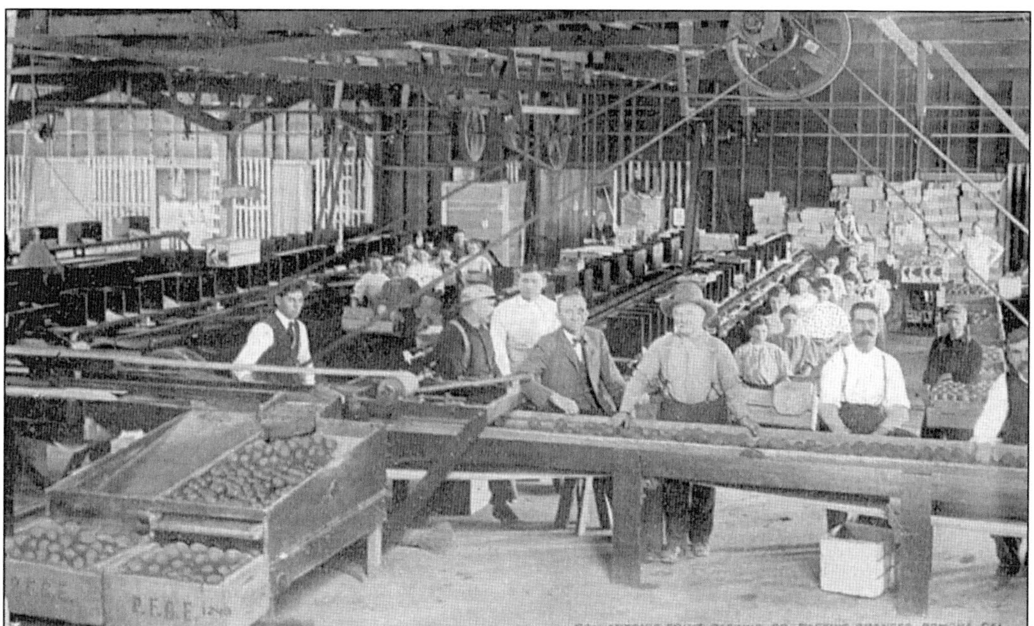

San Antonio Fruit Co., Packing Oranges. This postcard shows a packing house in a nearby community. The written text on back reads, "I just owe about 25 letters so I am answering all by postal cards. You know a great deal about this country so I know a postal card will please you more than a geography. . ." (P/P: Benham Co., Los Angeles; Neuner Calitype Process; made in America; postmark: February 1911.)

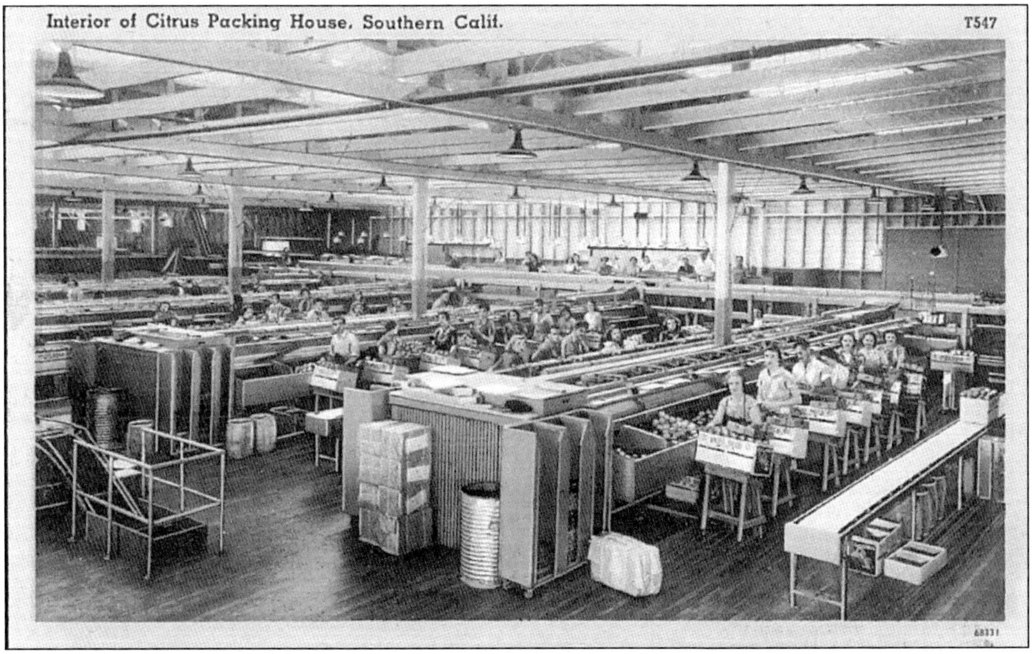

INTERIOR OF CITRUS PACKING HOUSE, SOUTHERN CALIFORNIA. This linen postcard shows a typical orange packing line. (P/P: Tichnor Art Co., Los Angeles, No. T547.)

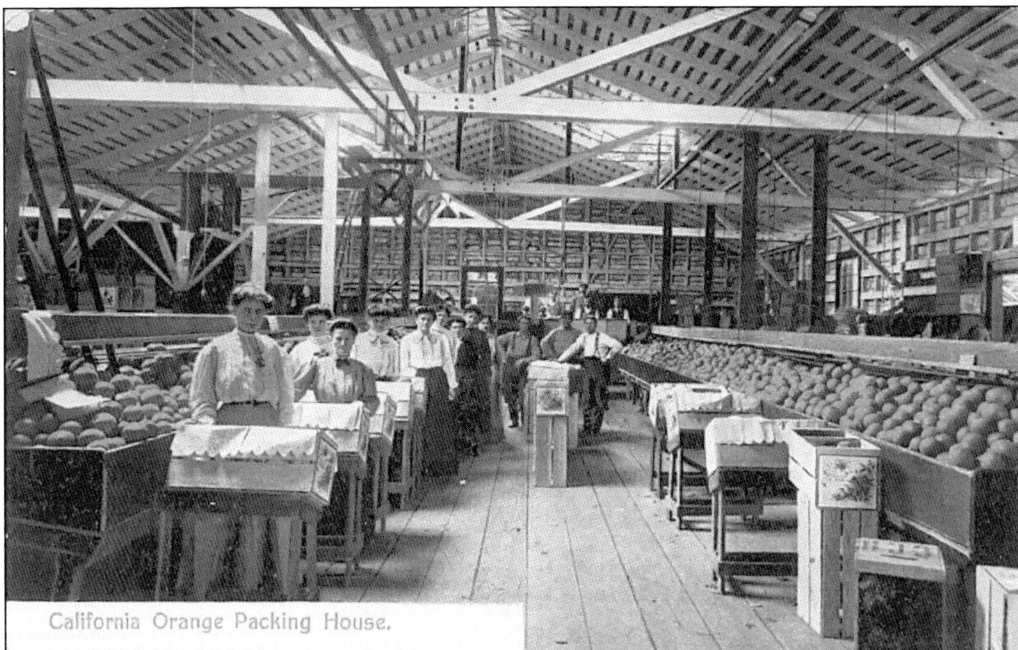

CALIFORNIA ORANGE PACKING HOUSE. The written text on the back reads, "This is a fine, cool climate. Good place for your business here and at the beaches. 50 cents round trip takes you to many of the beach resorts." (P/P: Newman Post Card Co., Los Angeles; made in Germany; postmark: July 1909.)

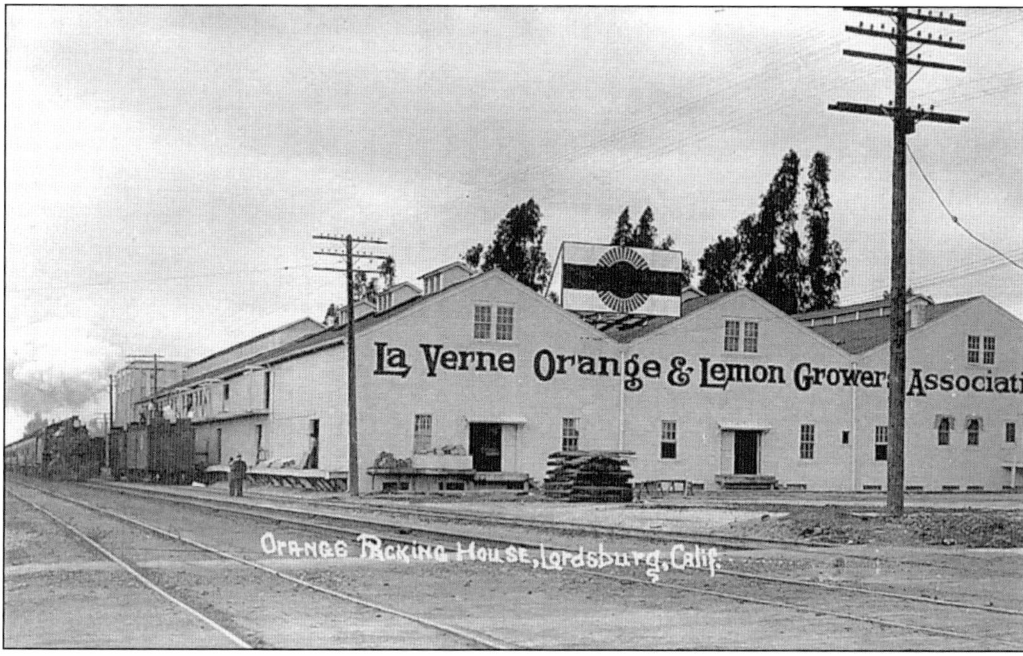

Orange Packing House, Lordsburg. This packing house of the La Verne Orange and Lemon Growers Association caught the interest of boxmaker and photographer, Burton Frasher Sr. A number of the images on the next several pages are interior shots of this packing house taken by Frasher. (P/P: Burton Frasher, Wapato, Washington; courtesy Jack McCaskill.)

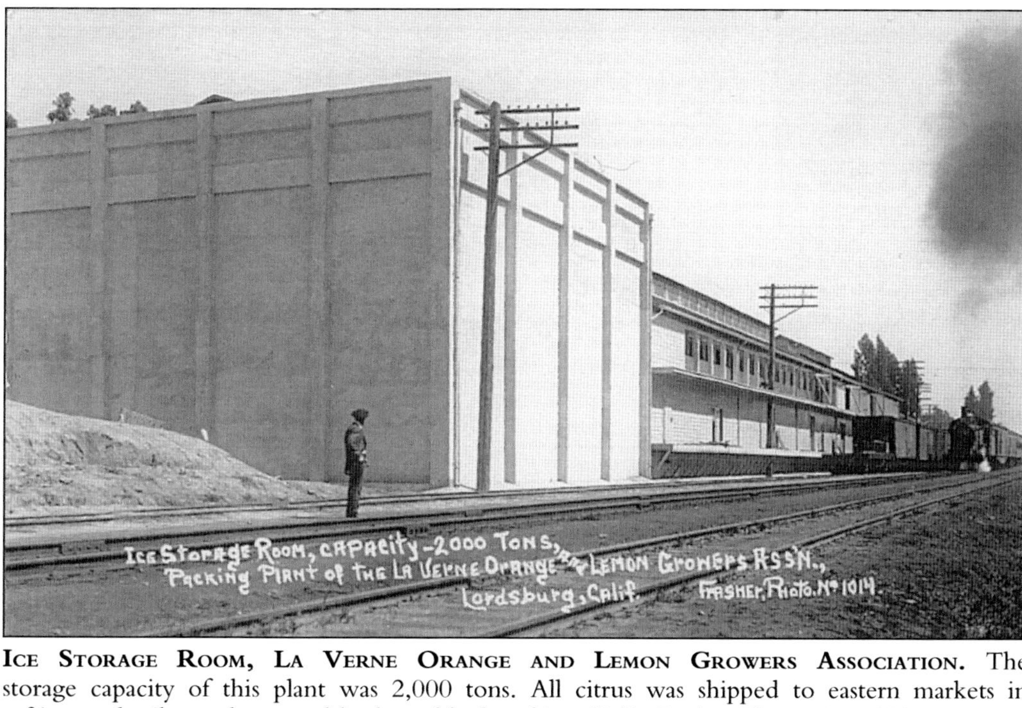

Ice Storage Room, La Verne Orange and Lemon Growers Association. The storage capacity of this plant was 2,000 tons. All citrus was shipped to eastern markets in refrigerated rail cars, kept cool by large blocks of ice. (P/P: Frasher Photo, No. 1014; courtesy Jack McCaskill.)

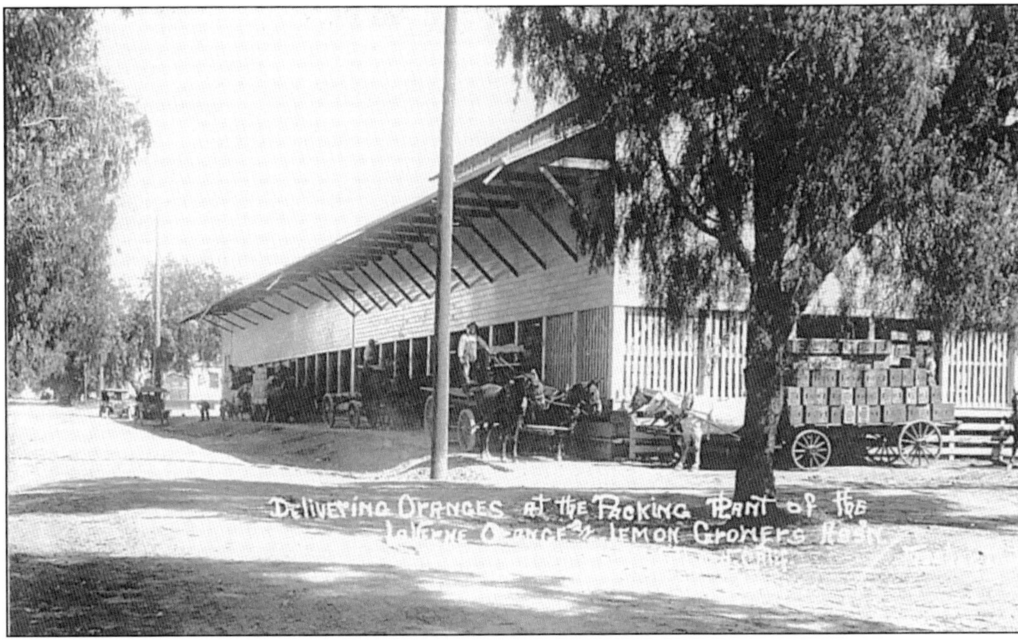

Delivering Oranges at the Packing Plant, La Verne Orange and Lemon Growers Association. Horse-drawn wagons bring oranges in from the field for processing and shipping. (P/P: Frasher Photo; courtesy Jack McCaskill.)

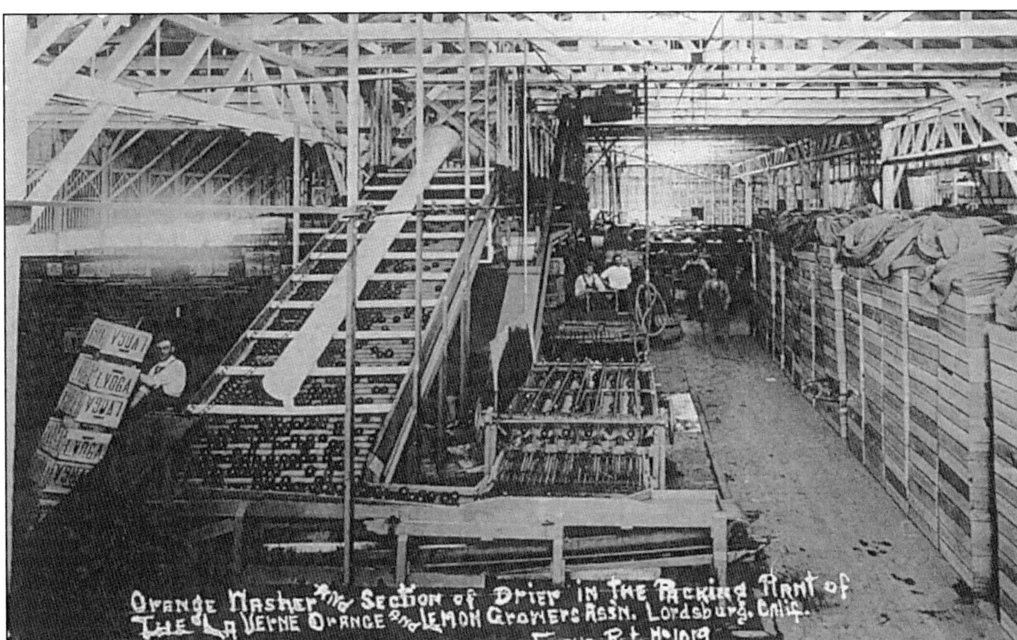

Orange Washer and Section of Drier, La Verne Orange and Lemon Growers Association. The cleaning process began as the fruit was brought in from the field. (P/P: Frasher Photo, No.1019; courtesy Jack McCaskill.)

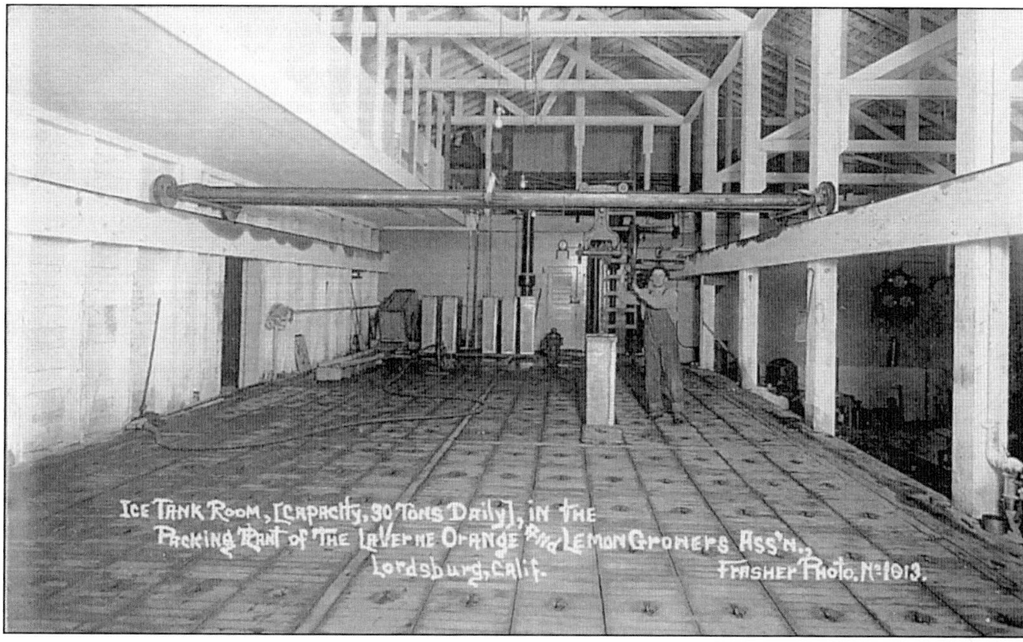

Ice Tank Room, La Verne Orange and Lemon Growers Association. The daily capacity of the ice tank room was 30 tons of ice. (P/P: Frasher Photo, No. 1013; courtesy, Jack McCaskill.)

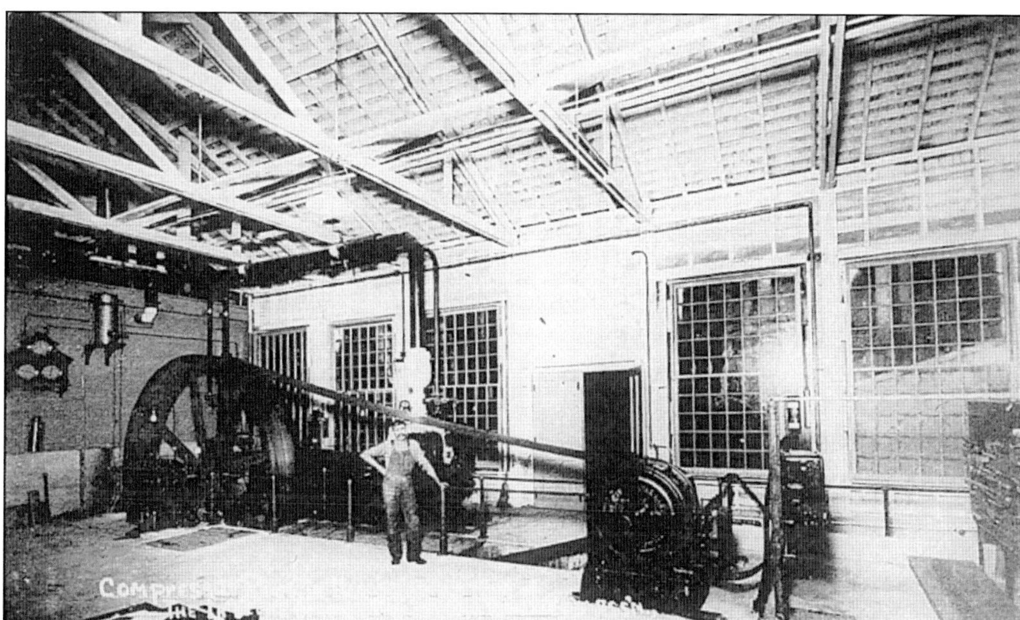

Compressor Room, La Verne Orange and Lemon Growers Association. This was the large machinery necessary to keep the plant operating. (P/P: Frasher Photo, No. 1015; courtesy Jack McCaskill.)

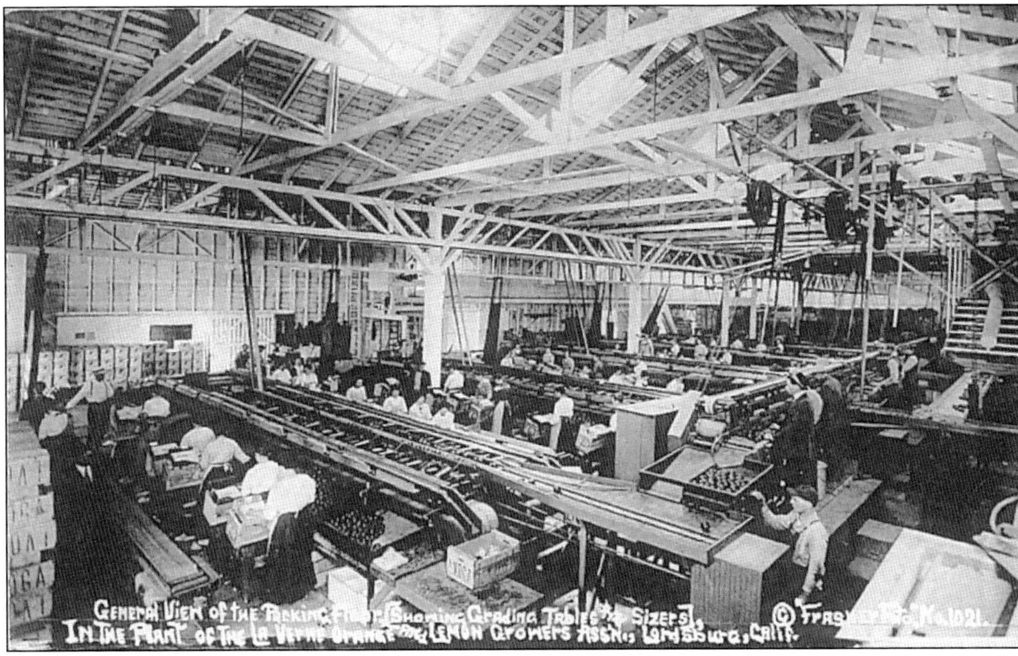

General View of the Packing Floor, La Verne Orange and Lemon Growers Association. This shows the grading tables and sizers and the boxes being packed for storage and shipment. (P/P: Frasher Photo, No. 1021; courtesy Jack McCaskill.)

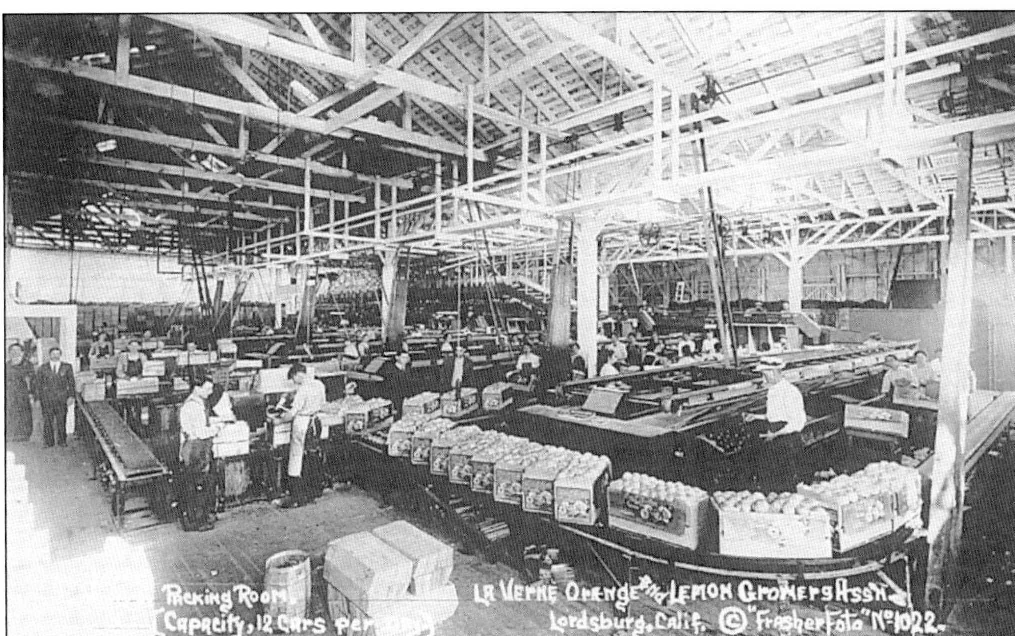

Packing Room, La Verne Orange and Lemon Growers Association. A view of the other side of the packing floor shows packed boxes with the Paul Neyron, La Verne label. The capacity of this floor was 12 cars per day. (P/P: Frasher Photo, No. 1022; courtesy Jack McCaskill.)

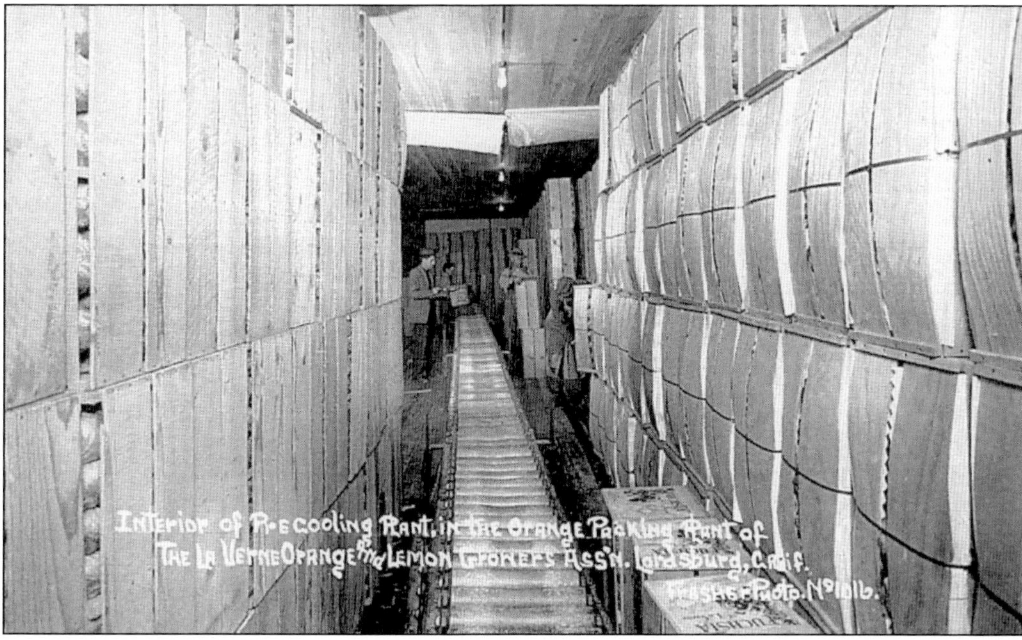

INTERIOR OF PRE-COOLING PLANT, LA VERNE ORANGE AND LEMON GROWERS ASSOCIATION. The packed boxes of oranges standing on end are being pre-cooled prior to shipment by refrigerated rail car. (P/P: Frasher Photo, No. 1016; courtesy Jack McCaskill.)

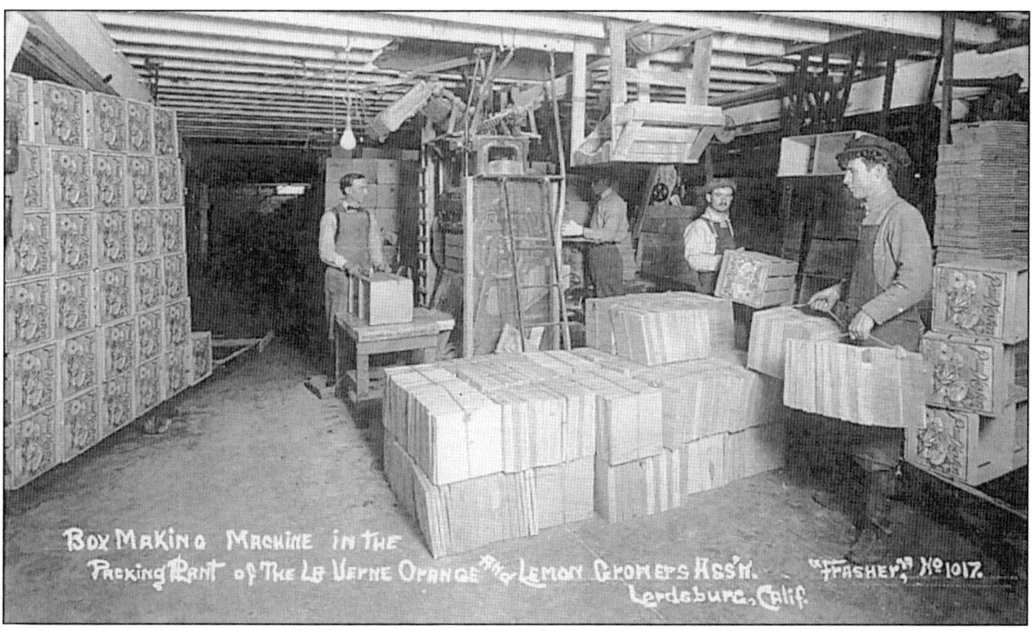

BOX-MAKING MACHINE, LA VERNE ORANGE AND LEMON GROWERS ASSOCIATION. This area of the plant was of particular interest to the photographer, Burton Frasher Sr. because he was also a California champion box maker. Frasher is the person at the center of the picture at the box making machine. (P/P: Frasher Photo, No. 1017; courtesy Jack McCaskill.)

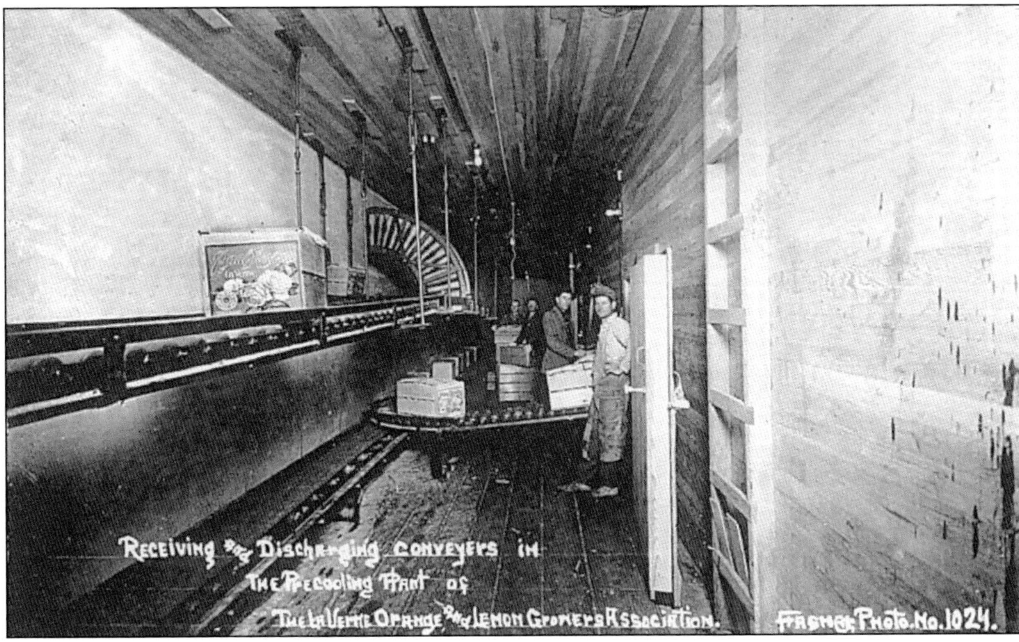

Receiving and Discharging Conveyors in Pre-cooling Plant, La Verne Orange and Lemon Growers Association. An extensive conveyor belt system moved the fruit through the packing house. Here is another view of the Paul Neyron label on the boxes. (P/P: Frasher Photo, No. 1024; courtesy Jack McCaskill.)

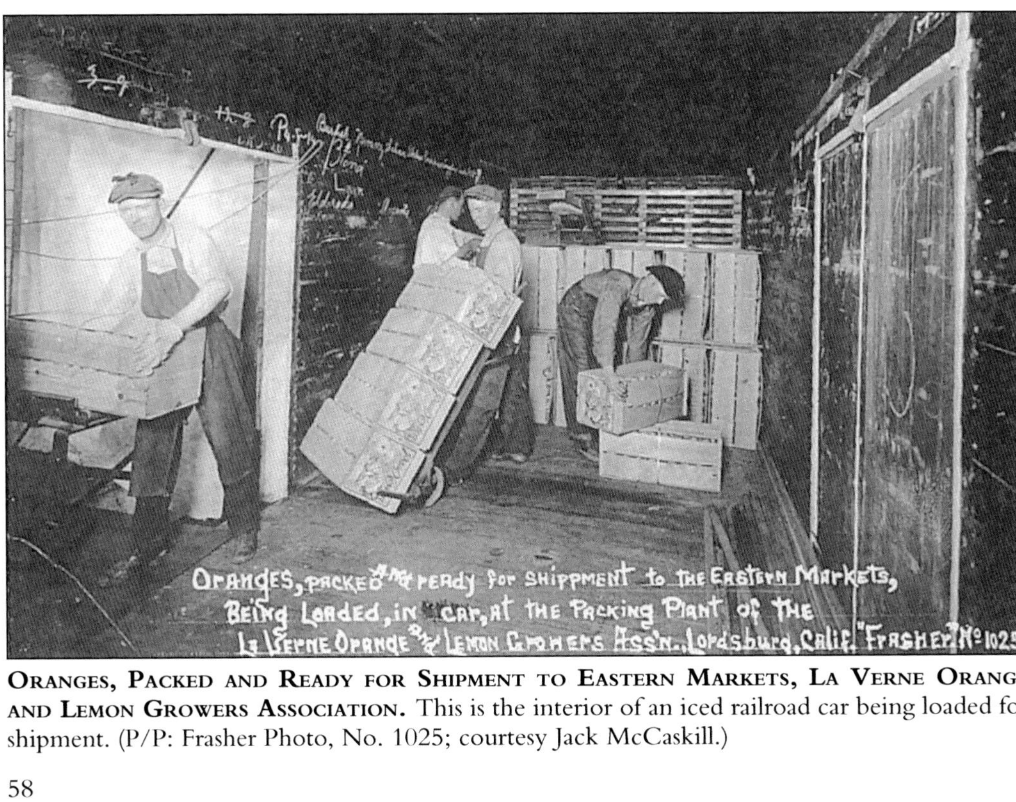

Oranges, Packed and Ready for Shipment to Eastern Markets, La Verne Orange and Lemon Growers Association. This is the interior of an iced railroad car being loaded for shipment. (P/P: Frasher Photo, No. 1025; courtesy Jack McCaskill.)

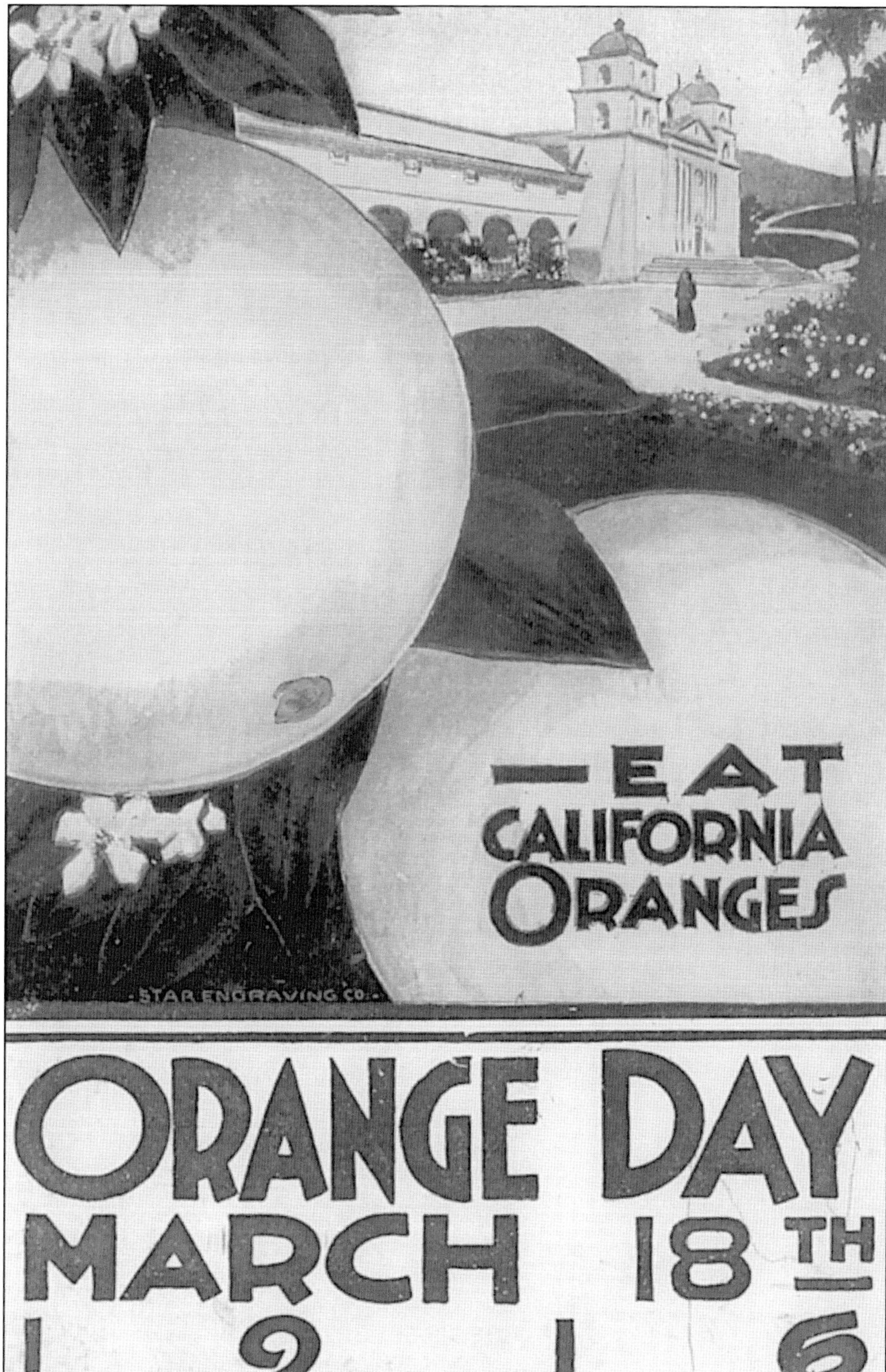

EAT CALIFORNIA ORANGES, ORANGE DAY, MARCH 18, 1916. A California Orange Day postcard advertised California fruit to the wider community. (P/P: W.F. Jefferies Co., Los Angeles.)

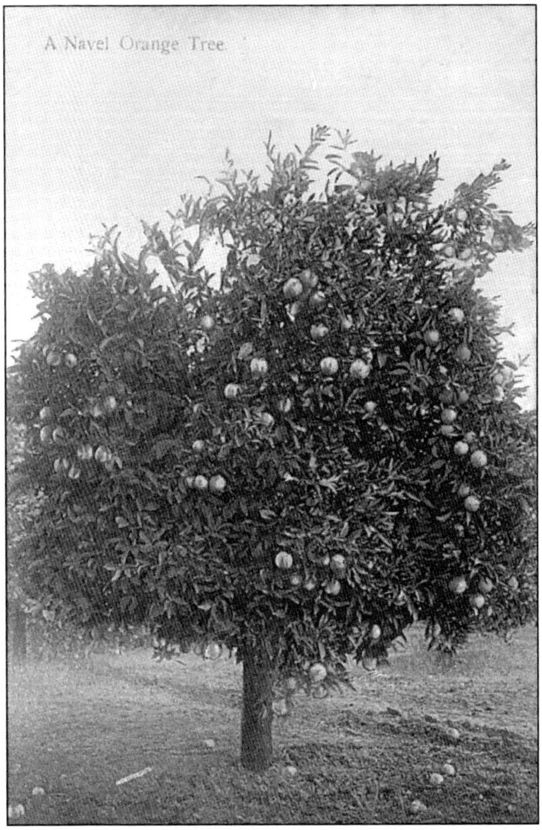

A Navel Orange Tree. This postcard shows a specimen of a Navel orange tree in a grove. (P/P: M. Rieder, Los Angeles, No. 3088; made in Germany; postmark: October 1908.)

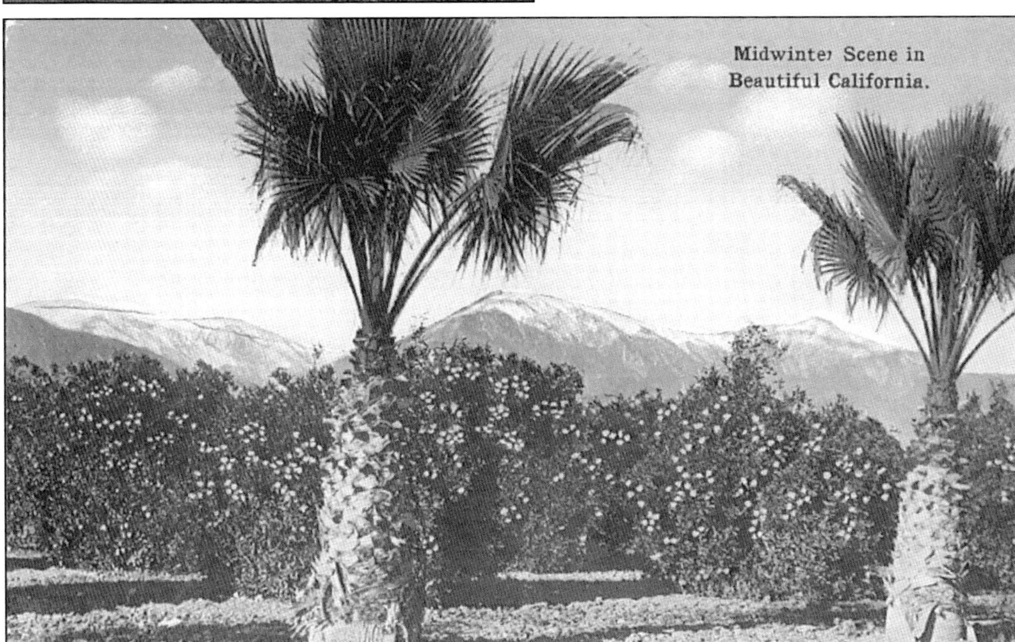

Midwinter Scene in Beautiful California. (P/P: Western Publishing & Novelty Co., Los Angeles.)

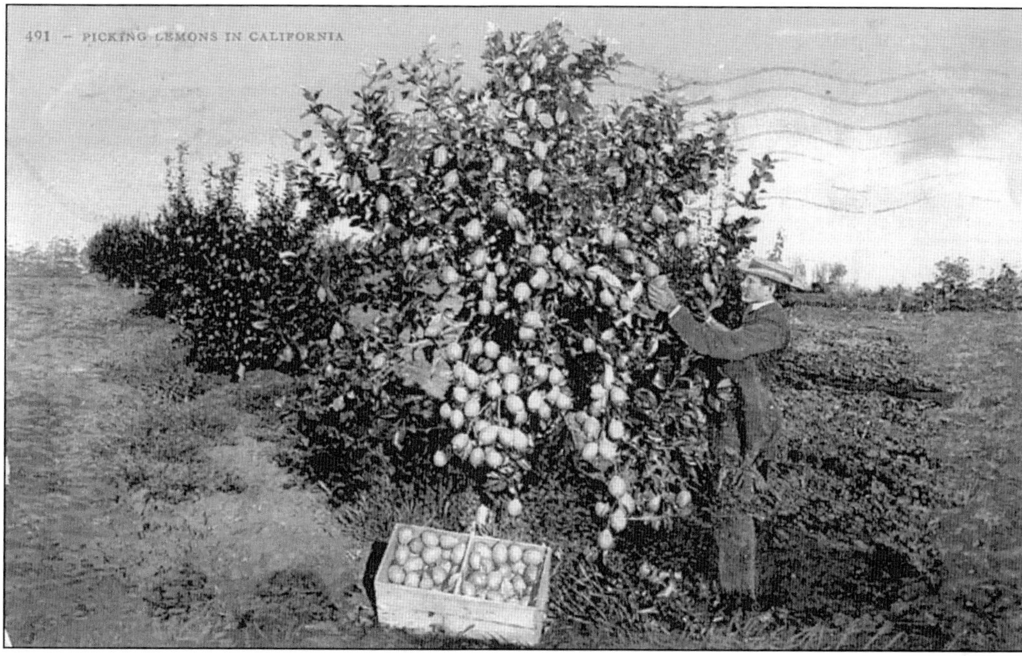

PICKING LEMONS IN CALIFORNIA. Although not as extensive as the orange crops, lemons also played an important part of Southern California's citrus industry. (P/P: Edward H. Mitchell, San Francisco, No. 491; postmark: December 1908.)

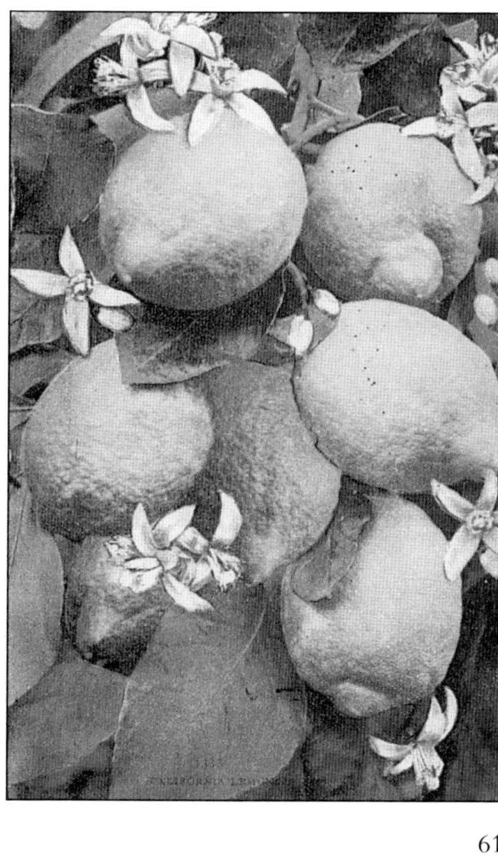

CALIFORNIA LEMONS. This is a beautiful portrayal of California lemons and blossoms. (P/P: Edward H. Mitchell, San Francisco, No. 1333; made in America.)

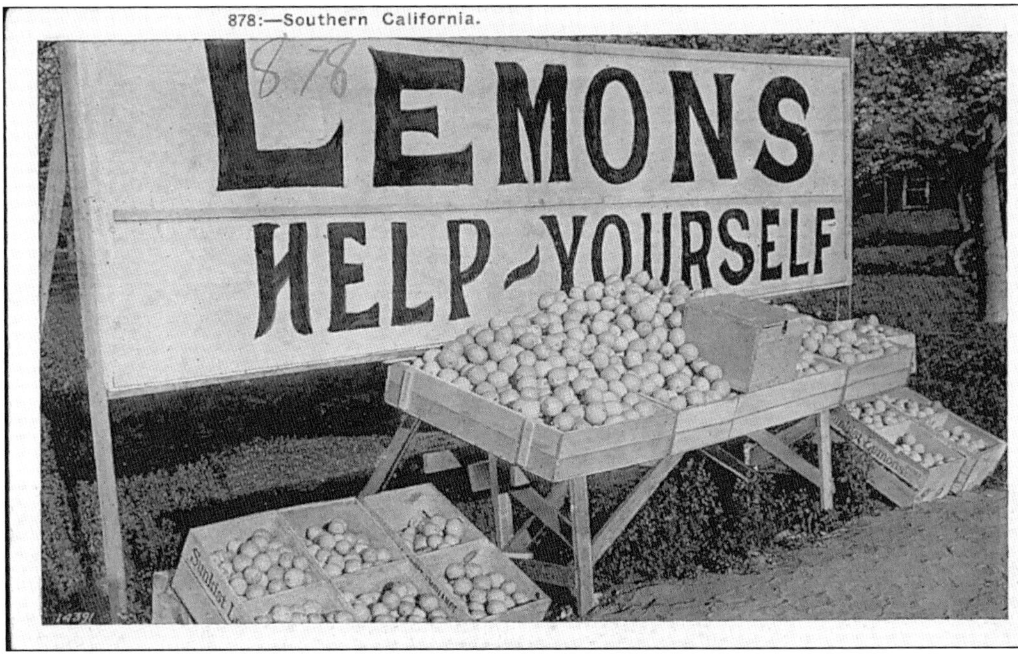

SOUTHERN CALIFORNIA. Lemons: Help-Yourself. This crop must have involved over-production or low prices! (P/P: M. Kashower Co., Los Angeles, No. 878.)

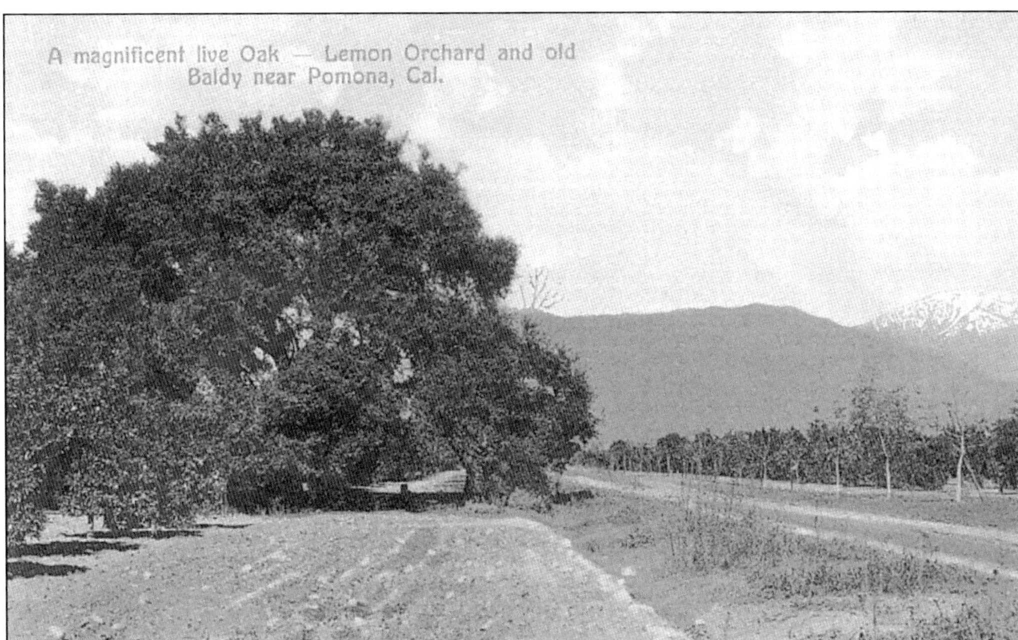

A MAGNIFICENT LIVE OAK/LEMON ORCHARD NEAR POMONA. This view, taken *c.* 1907, also shows "Old Baldy." The back side was for address only, no message permitted. (P/P: Newman Post Card Co., Los Angeles; made in Germany.)

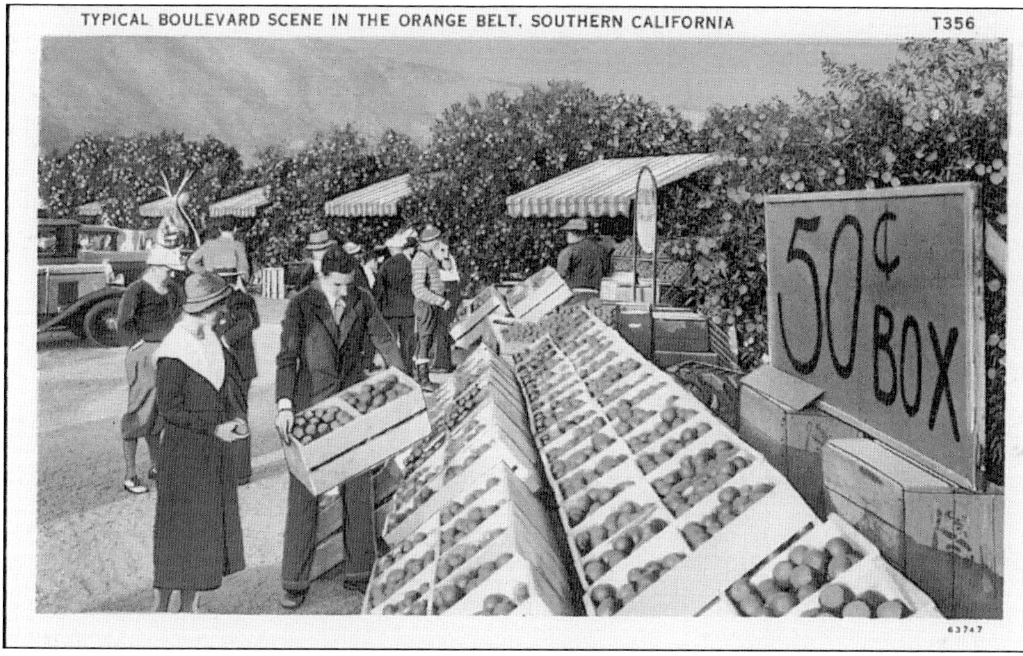

Typical Boulevard Scene in the Orange Belt, Southern California. Oranges for 50¢ a box must have been particularly interesting to anyone from out of state. (P/P: Tichnor Art Co., Los Angeles, No. T 356.)

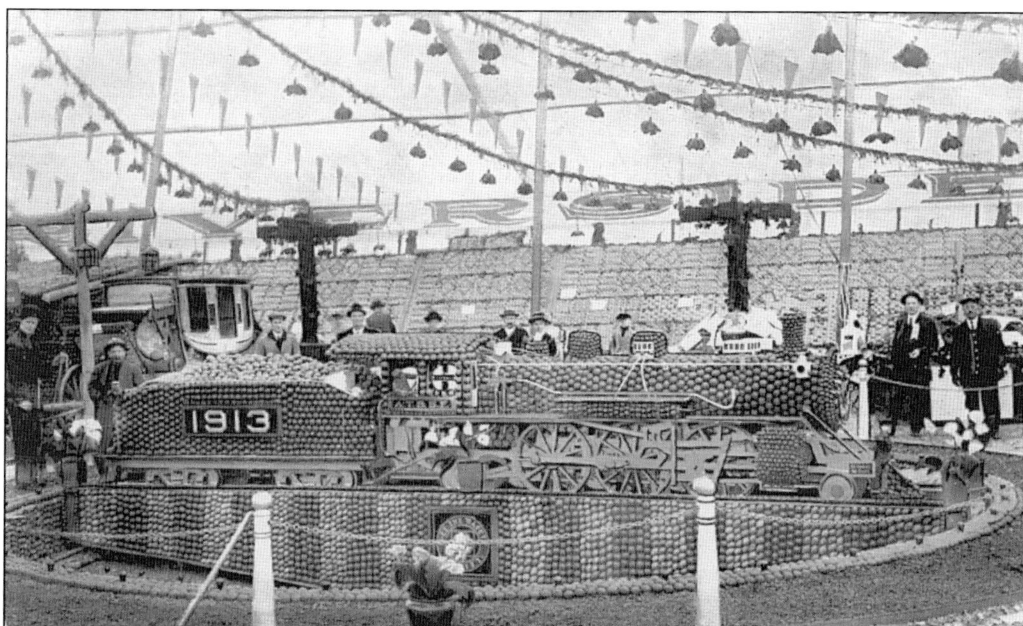

The Third National Orange Show, 1913. This is an interesting display of citrus fruit by the Santa Fe Railway at the National Orange Show in nearby San Bernardino. (P/P: Renfro-Haven Co., San Bernardino; Van Ornum Colorprint Co.)

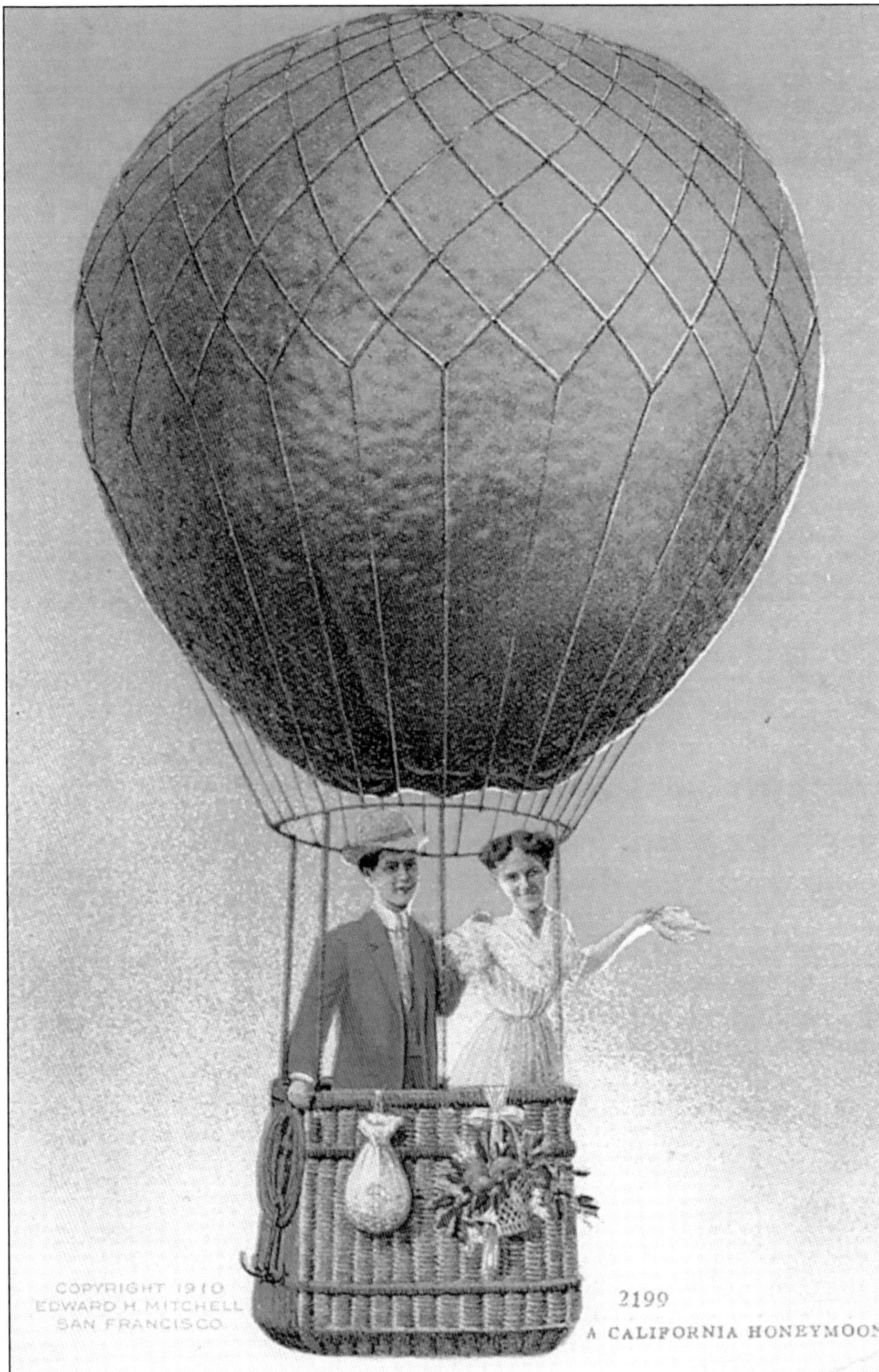

A California Honeymoon. Edward Mitchell published a series of "large fruit" postcards, which were popular to send to the folks back home. (P/P: Edward H. Mitchell, San Francisco; copyright 1910; No. 2199.)

Five

Mountain Vistas and Winter in California

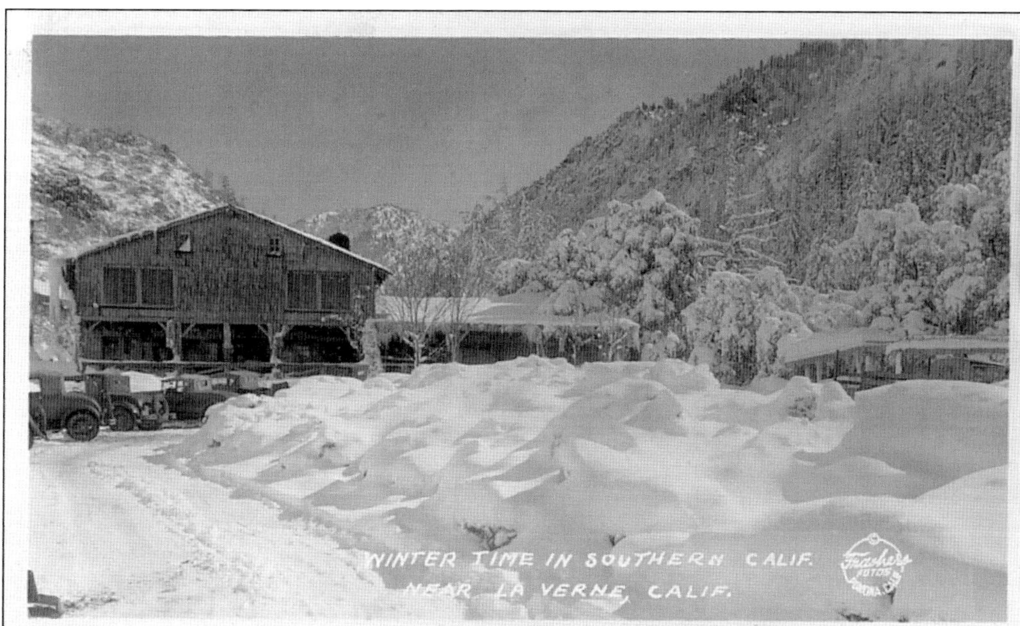

Winter Time in Southern California. This scene was captured near La Verne. California, does have "real" winter but one must go into the nearby mountains to find it. (P/P: Frasher, Pomona; courtesy University of La Verne, Wilson Library Archives.)

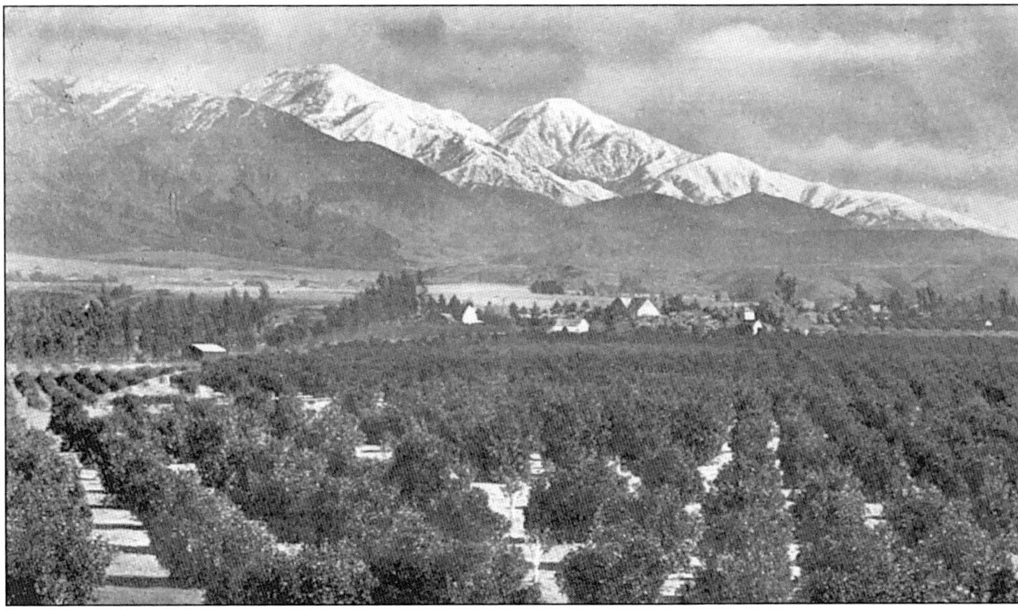

Snow and Oranges in Southern California. The written text on the back reads, "Here are the mtns. tho not just our view of them and the middle one is still capped with snow. There are hundreds of groves looking like this in this part of the state and the air is heavy with orange blossoms." (P/P: Edward H. Mitchell, San Francisco; "On the Road of a Thousand Wonders," No. 246; postmark: May 1911.)

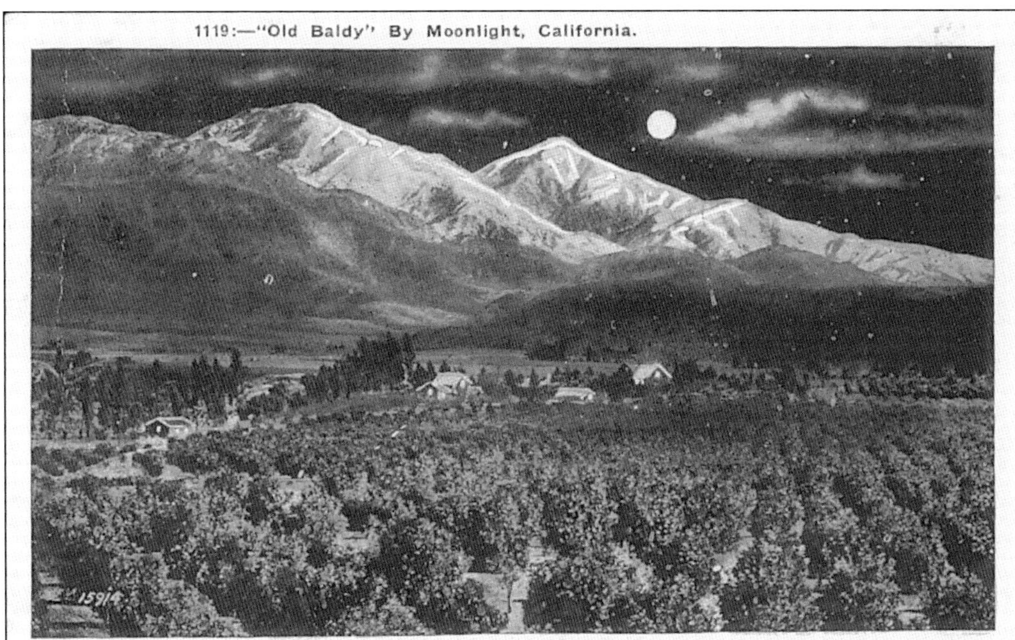

"Old Baldy" by Moonlight. Moonlight cards seemed to hold a fascination for buyers and this postcard of Mt. San Antonio, also known as "Old Baldy," was one of those views. (P/P: M. Kashower Co., Los Angeles, No. 15914; postmark: October 1924.)

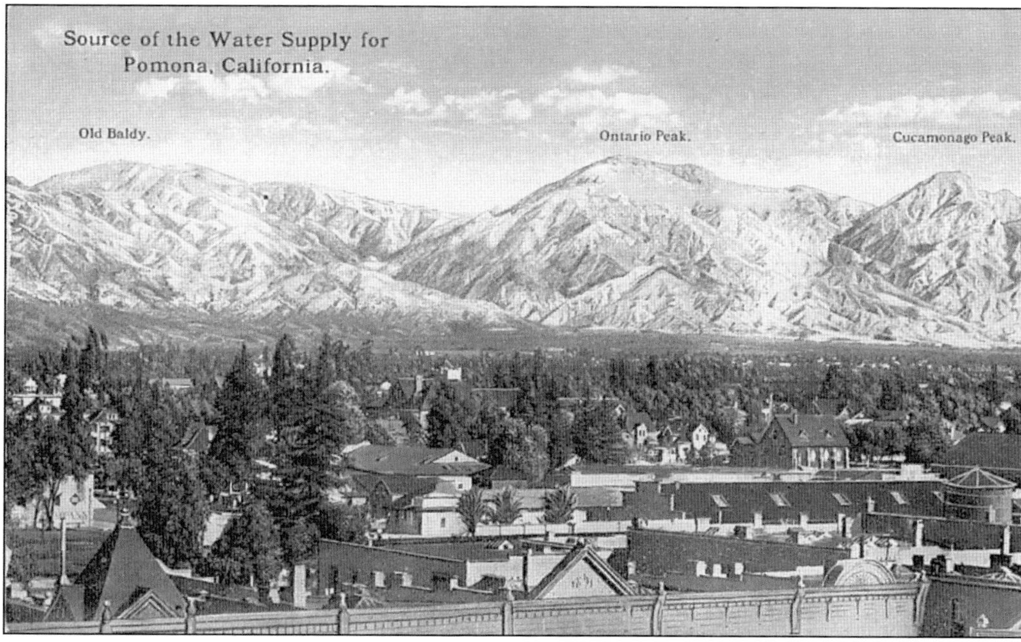

Source of Water Supply for Pomona. This postcard view shows the three peaks: "Old Baldy," Ontario Peak, and Cucamonga Peak. (P/P: Julius J. Hecht, Los Angeles, No. P-101; made in the U.S.A.)

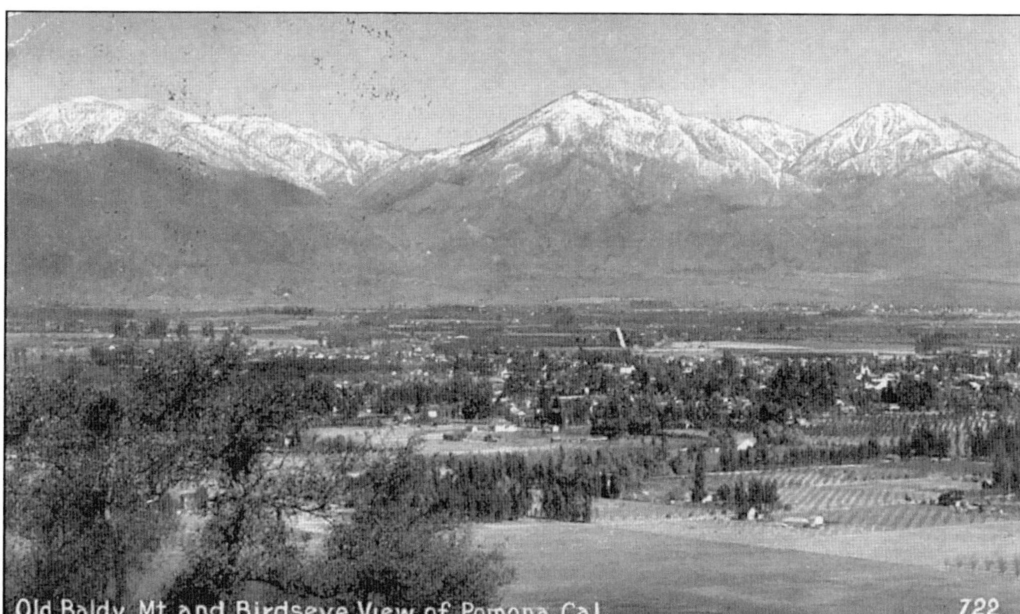

"Old Baldy" and Bird's-Eye View of Pomona. Although not postally used, this card had the following text written on the back: "Mama, Gee! but this place is like a cemetery. Work half a day. Hoop-La. Nothing to do until tomorrow. Gus." (P/P: Edward H. Mitchell, San Francisco; "On the Road of a Thousand Wonders," No. 722.)

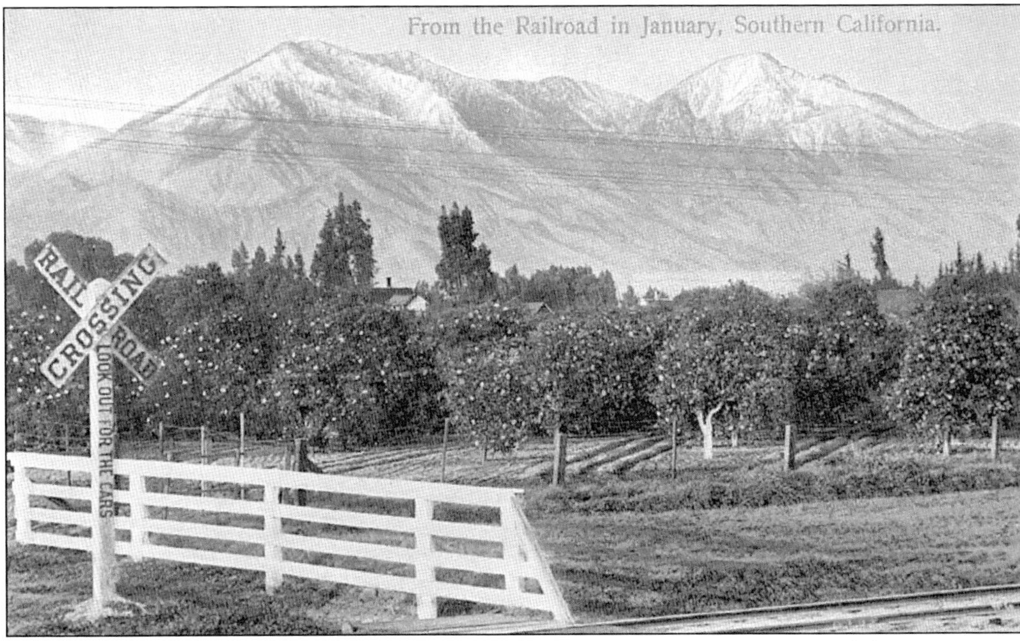

From the Railroad in January, Southern California. This view of the groves and mountains during the winter in Southern California always impressed train passengers from the east. (P/P: M. Rieder, Los Angeles, and Leipzig, No. 3547.)

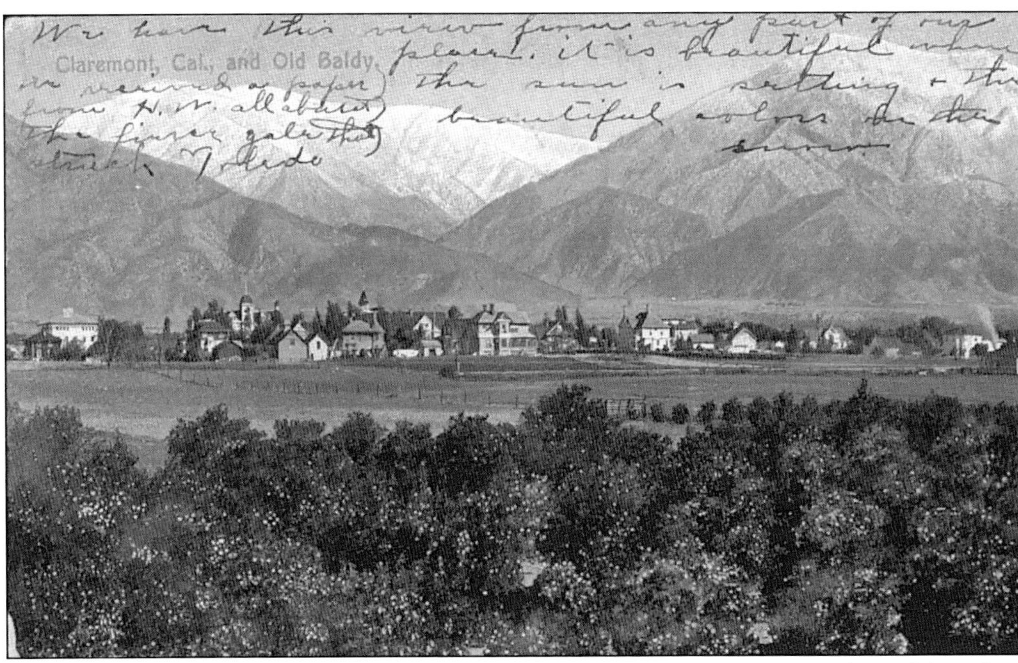

Claremont and "Old Baldy." The mountains are a part of Southern California life and are in constant view on the horizon. (P/P: Newman Post Card Co., Los Angeles, No. J 307; made in Germany; postmark: April 1909.)

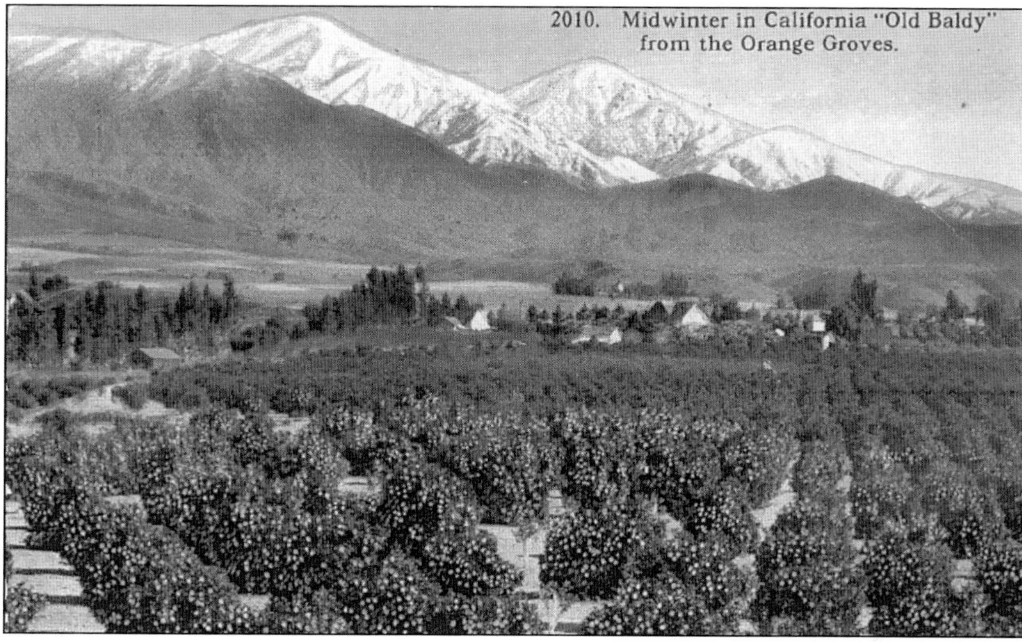

MID-WINTER IN CALIFORNIA. This scene shows "Old Baldy" from the orange groves. (P/P: Western Publishing & Novelty Co., Los Angeles, No. 1020; made in the U.S.A.)

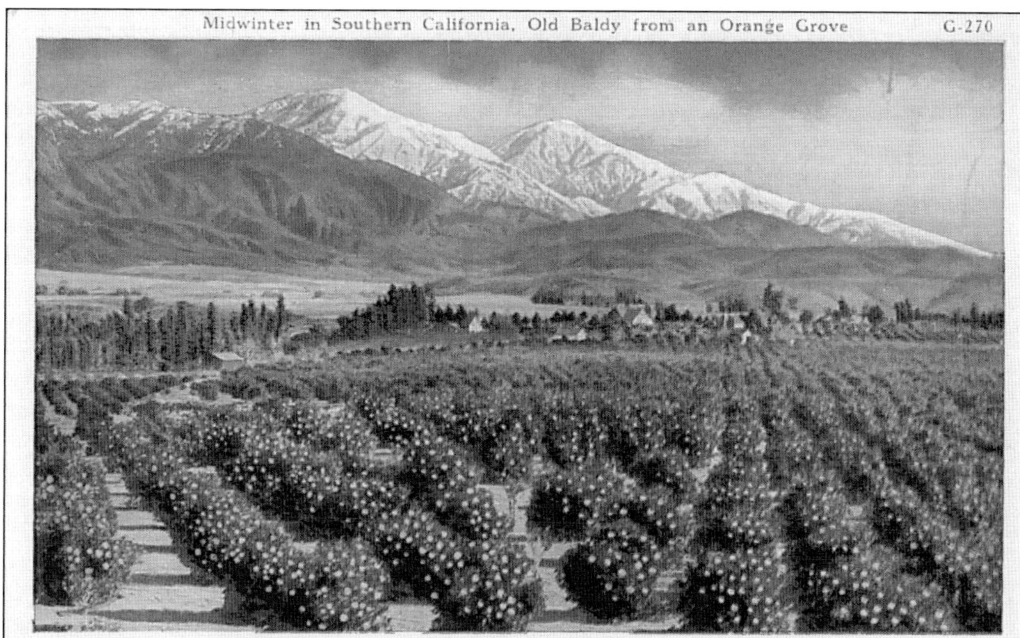

ANOTHER VIEW OF MID-WINTER IN SOUTHERN CALIFORNIA. This postcard also features a look at "Old Baldy" from an orange grove. Note that these two cards are the same view of "Baldy," as are the two cards on p. 66, and all four are by different publishers. (P/P: Pacific Novelty Co., San Francisco and Los Angeles, No. G270.)

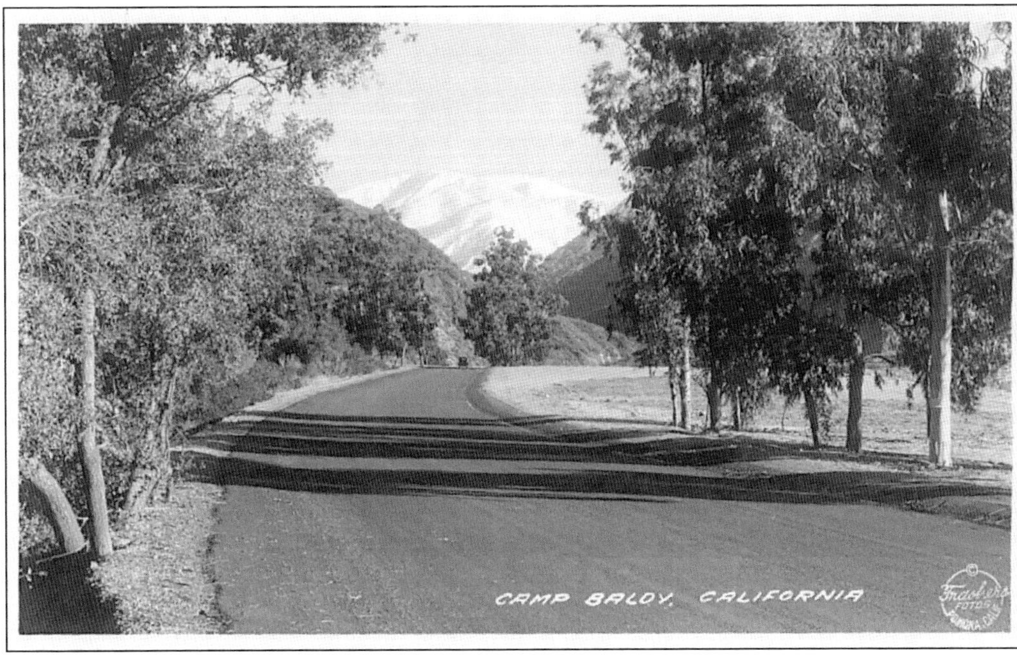

CAMP BALDY. Camp Baldy was a favorite camping spot for Southern Californians before it was washed away in a 1938 flood. (P/P: Frashers, Pomona.)

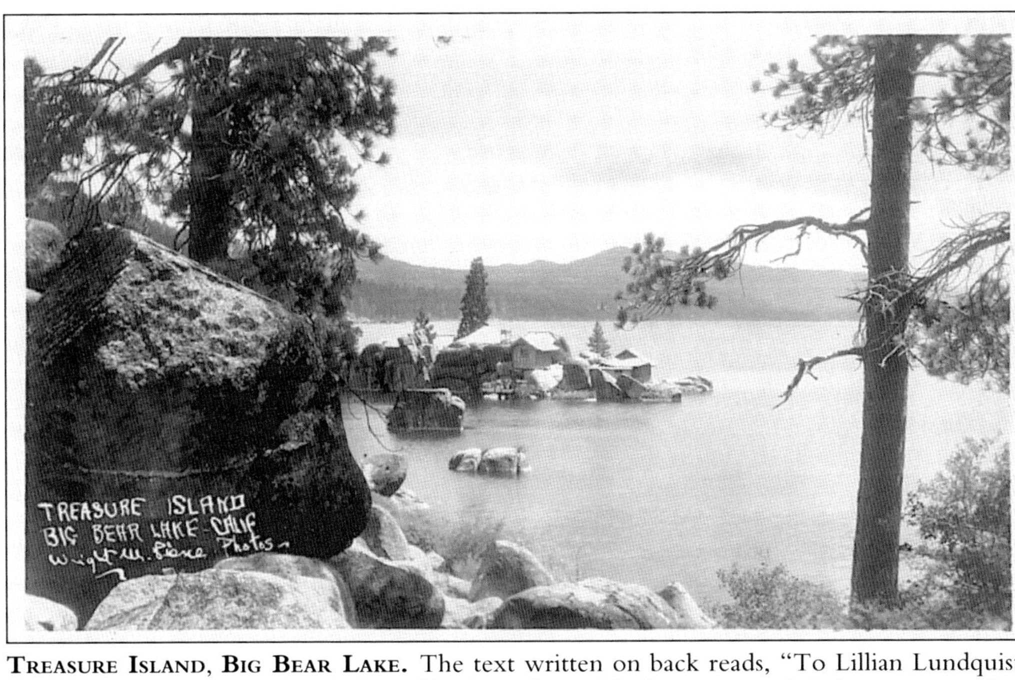

TREASURE ISLAND, BIG BEAR LAKE. The text written on back reads, "To Lillian Lundquist, Laurel, Neb., We have a lovely homelike log cabin with three rooms. It belongs to a patient of mine and we can stay as long as we like. Last night we toasted marshmallows in an immence [*sic*] fireplace. We take hikes everyday. . ." Jennie. (P/P: Wright Pierce, Photos; postmark: September 1923.)

CLIMBING MT. WILSON BY AUTO. Mountains and narrow, curving roads could not keep Californians and their cars at home. (P/P: Western Publishing & Novelty Co., Los Angeles, No. A85876; postmark: December 1924.)

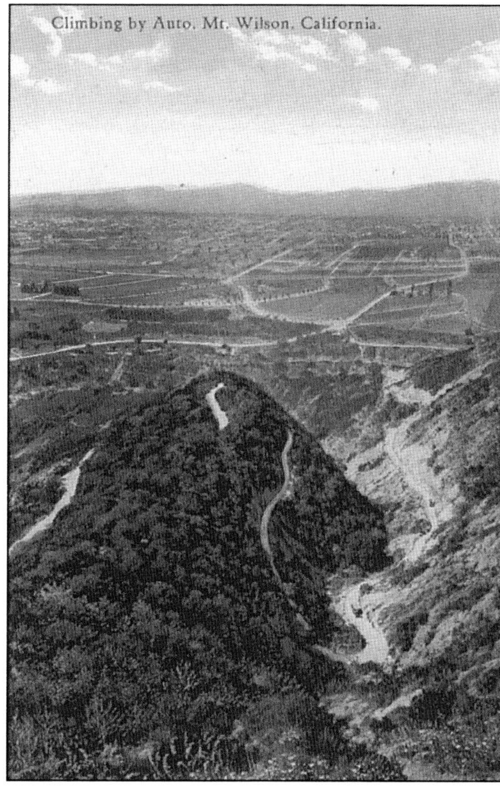

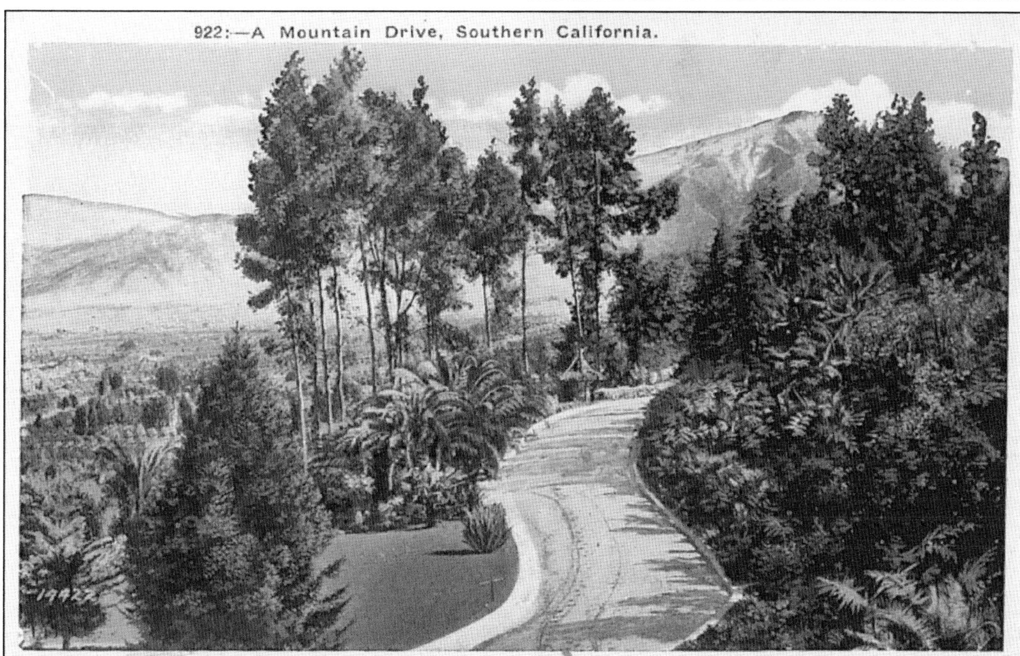

A MOUNTAIN DRIVE, SOUTHERN CALIFORNIA. A "Sunday drive" used to mean anywhere: to visit relatives in a nearby town, to go to the beach, the desert, or a special favorite—a mountain drive. (P/P: M. Kashower Co., Los Angeles, No. 922; postmark: October 1929.)

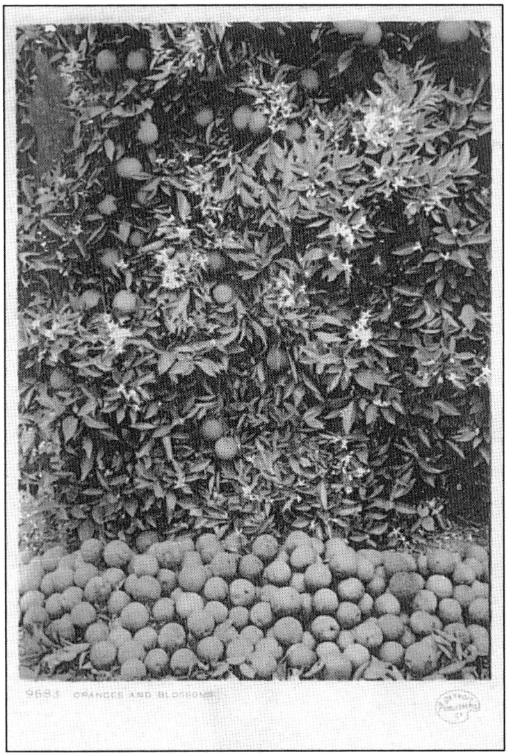

Oranges and Blossoms. To Southern Californians and especially their relatives and friends in the "east," winter time meant oranges and blossoms. (P/P: Detroit Publishing Co., No. 9638.)

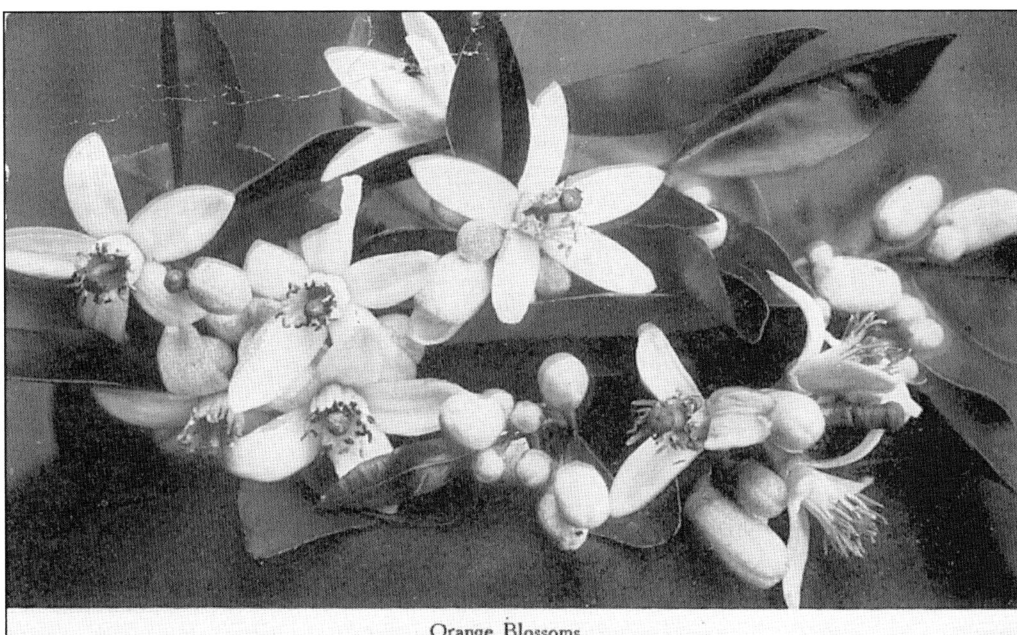

More Orange Blossoms. The beautiful wax-like look of the orange blossoms was a beauty to behold. (P/P: Benham Co., Los Angeles, No. 13755.)

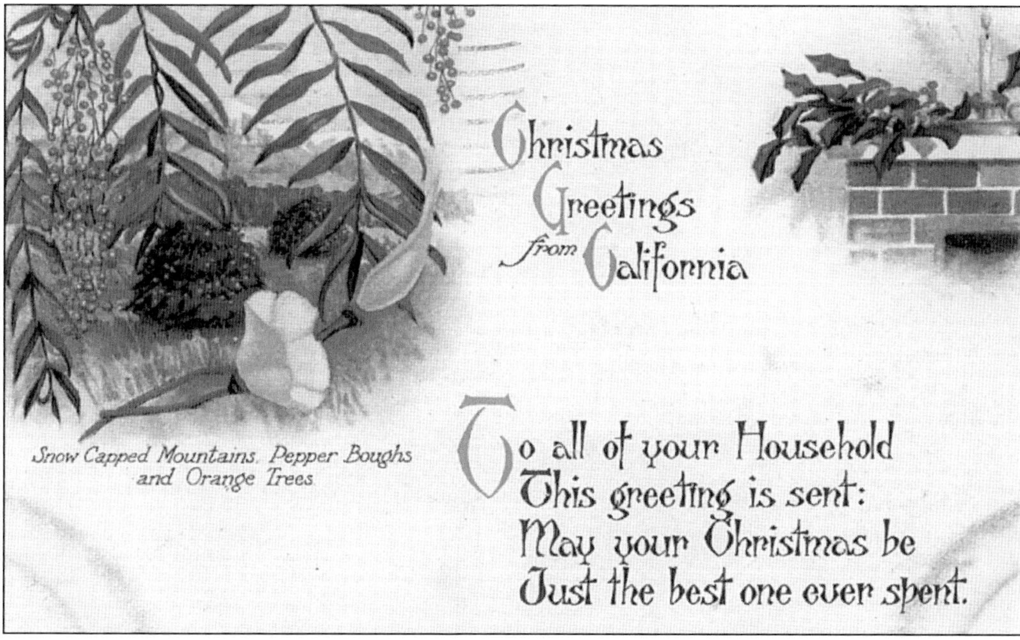

Christmas Greetings from California. Snow-capped mountains, pepper boughs, and orange trees helped Californians express Christmas greetings. (P/P: M. Kashower Co., Los Angeles; postmark: December 1919.)

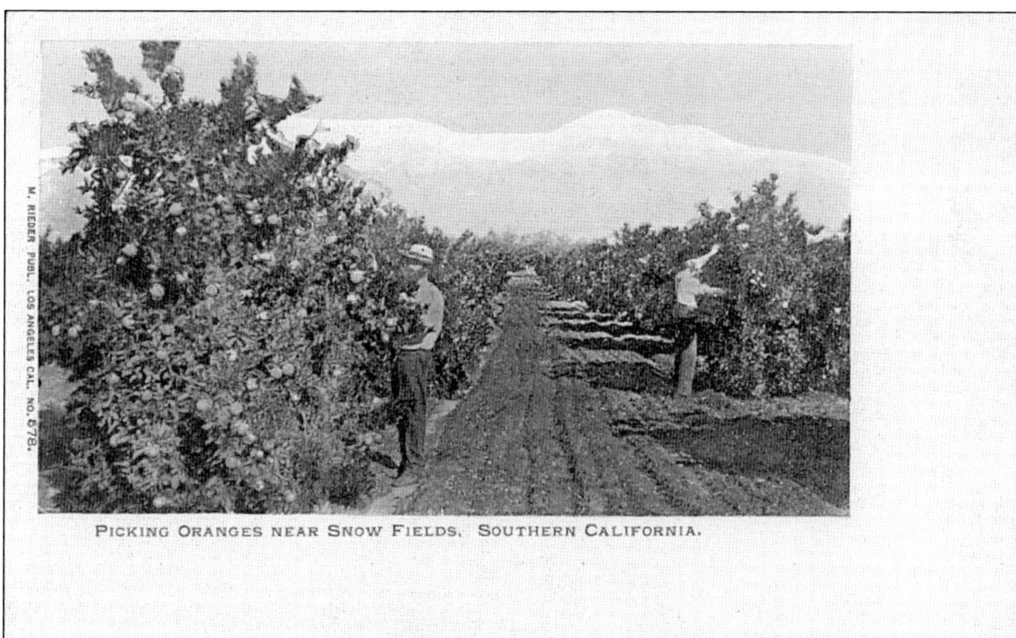

Picking Oranges near Snow Fields, Southern California. This is one of a number of cards extolling the comparison of winter in California with winter in other places. The back side was "exclusively for address." (P/P: M. Rieder, Los Angeles, No. 578.)

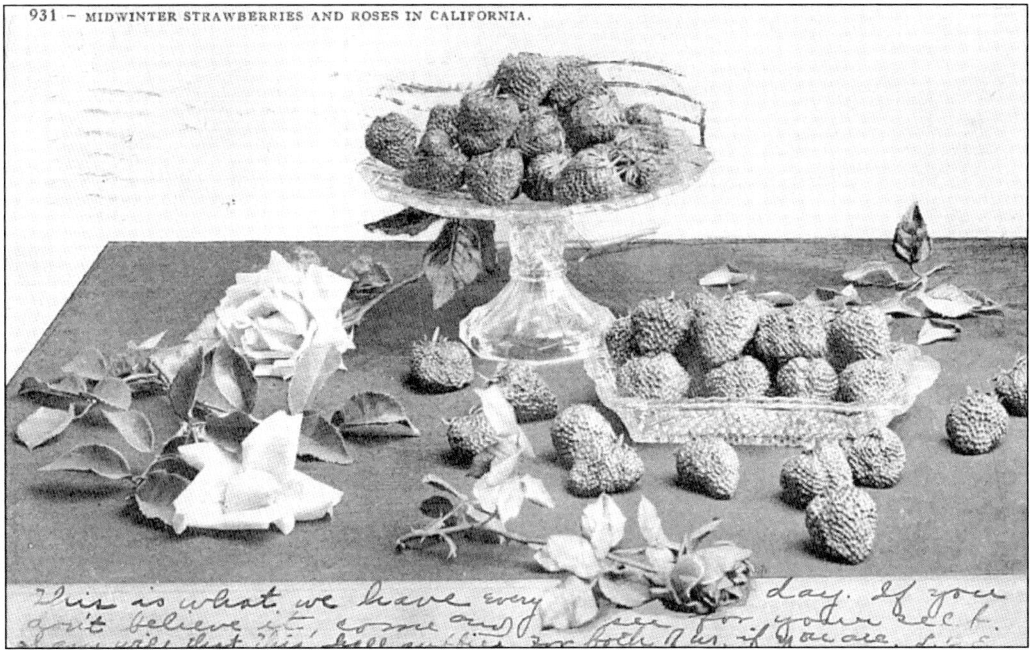

MID-WINTER STRAWBERRIES AND ROSES. Another Edward Mitchell card shows the anomaly of fruit and flowers in winter-time California. (P/P: Edward H. Mitchell, San Francisco, No. 931; postmark: January 1909.)

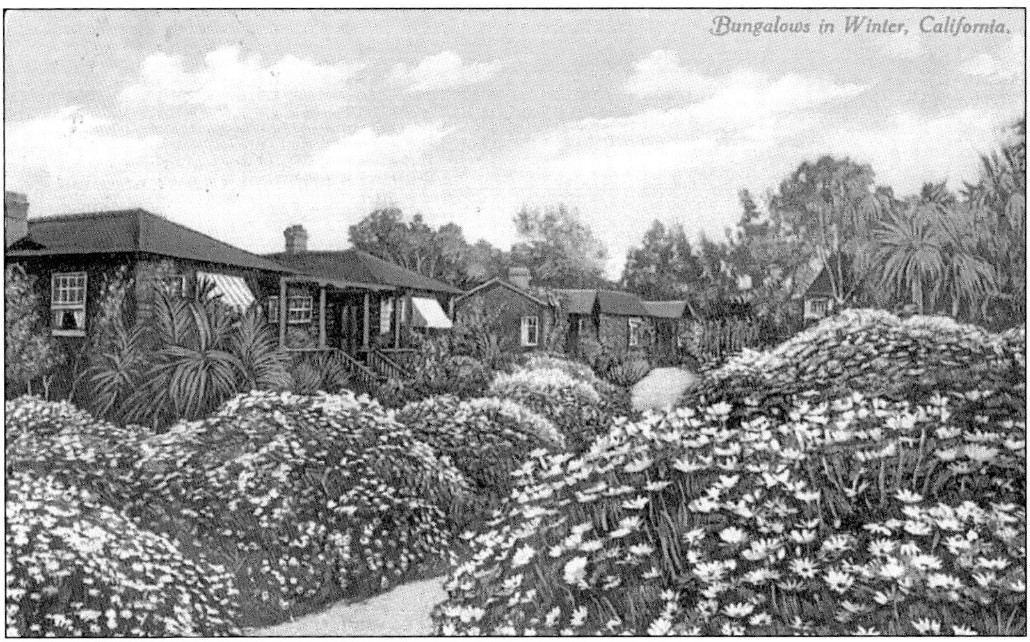

BUNGALOWS IN WINTER. Typical California bungalows are situated among the abundant flower beds. (P/P: Newman Post Card Co., Los Angeles and San Francisco; "On the Road of a Thousand Wonders," No. AB 37; postmark: December 1910.)

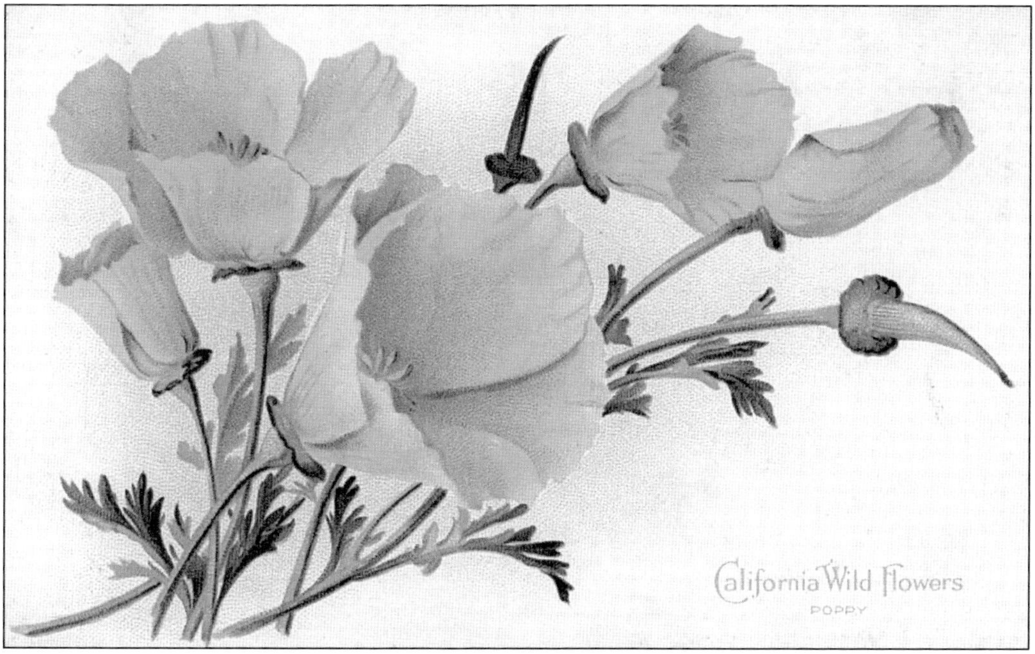

California Wild Flowers: Poppy. The poppy is the California State Flower. (P/P: California Wildflowers Series, No. 1; postmark: May 1911.)

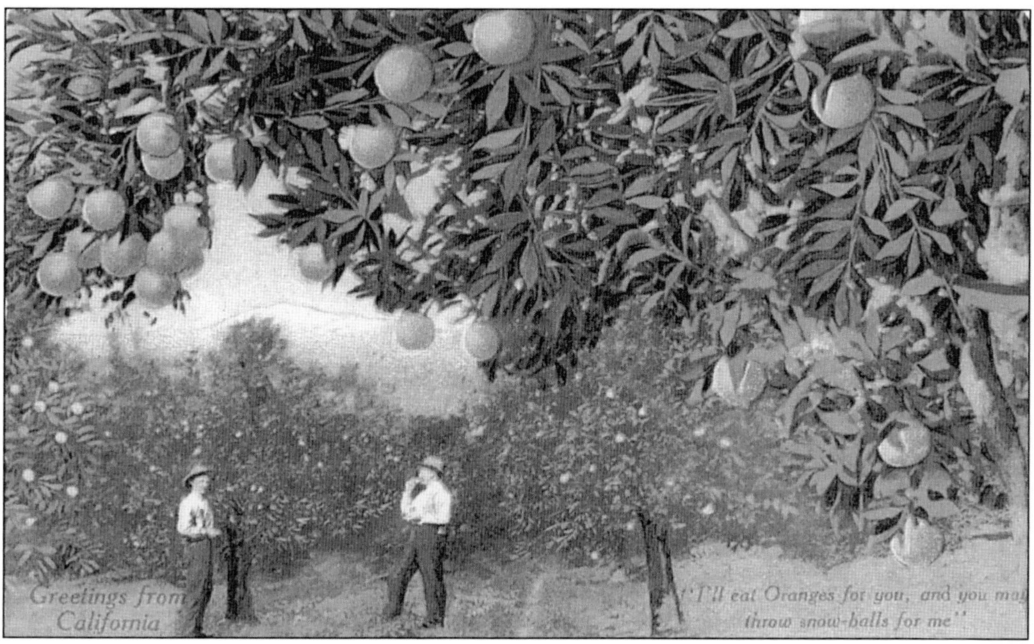

"Greetings from California. I'll Eat Oranges for You and You May Throw Snow-Balls for Me." (P/P: Newman Post Card Co., Los Angeles and San Francisco; "On the Road of a Thousand Wonders," No. AB 87; postmark: November 1912.)

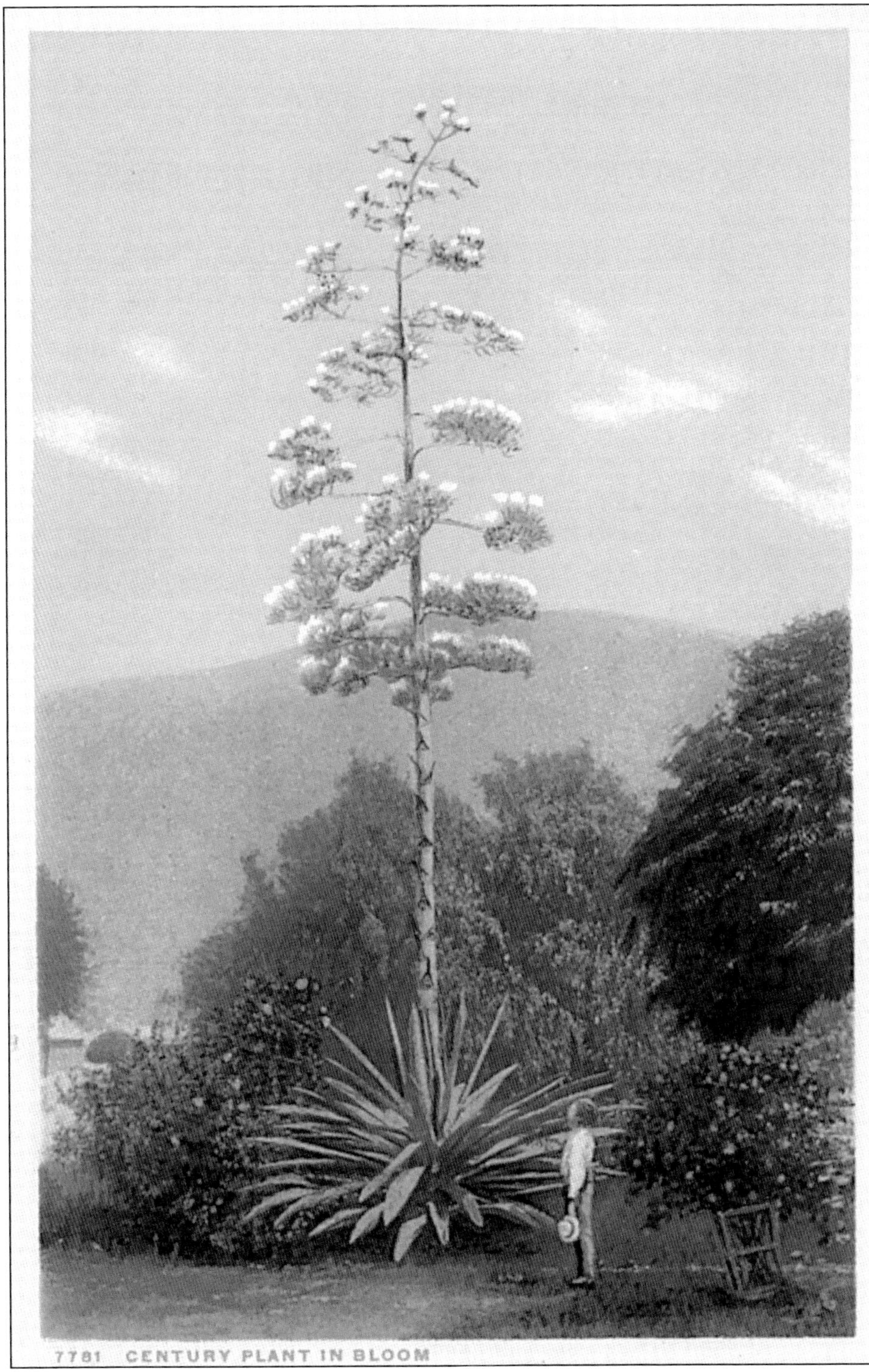

CENTURY PLANT IN BLOOM. A member of the amaryllis family, this plant attains maturity from 10 to 50 or 60 years; hence, some have thought it blooms only once in a century. (P/P: Detroit Publishing Co., No. 7781.)

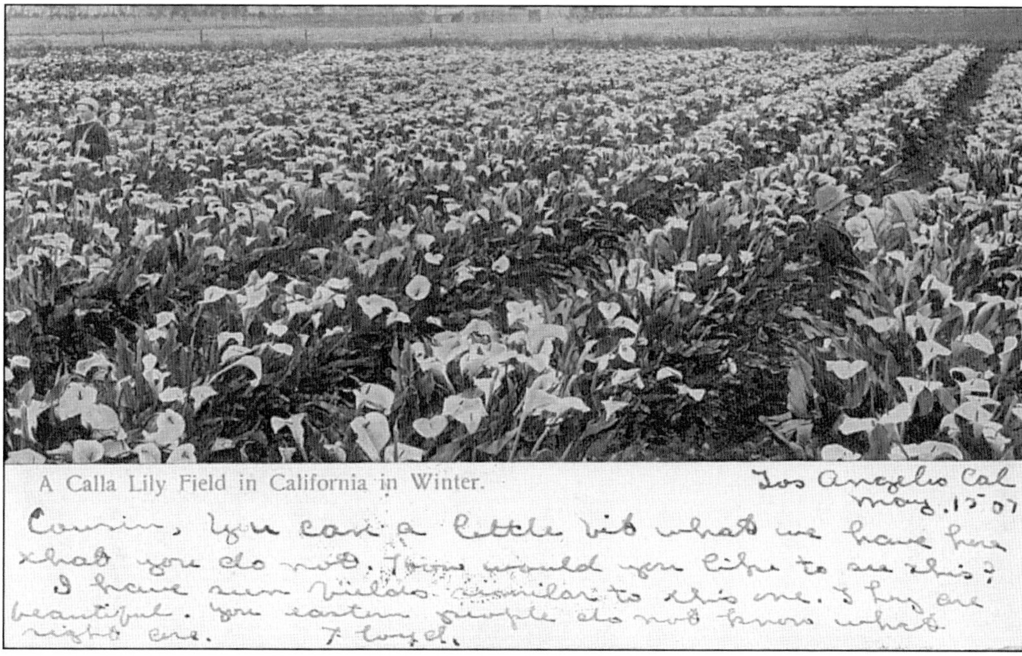

CALLA LILY FIELD IN WINTER. (P/P: M. Rieder, Los Angeles and Leipzig, No. 3025; postmark: May 1907.)

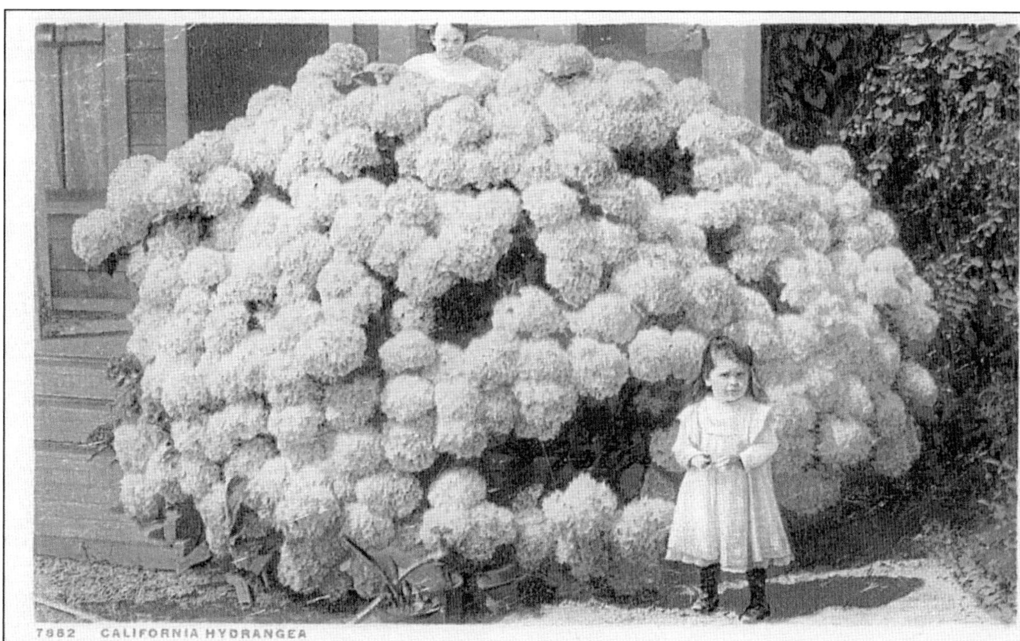

CALIFORNIA HYDRANGEA. Two little angels pose among the Hydrangea bush in full bloom. (P/P: Detroit Publishing Co., No. 7882.)

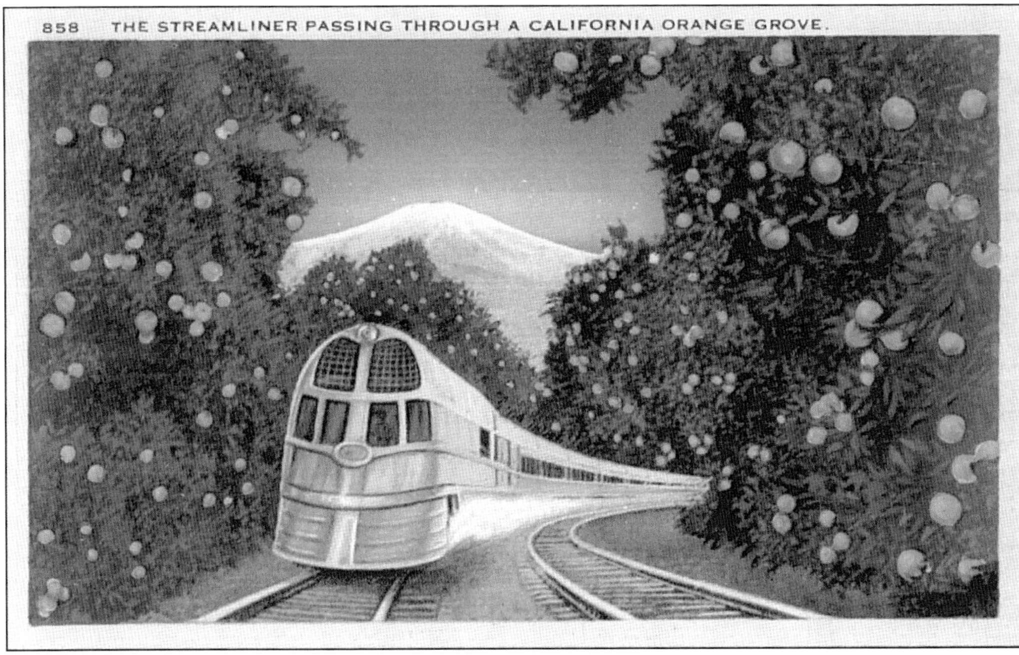

The Streamliner Passing through a California Orange Grove. (P/P: Longshaw Card Co., Los Angeles, No. 858.)

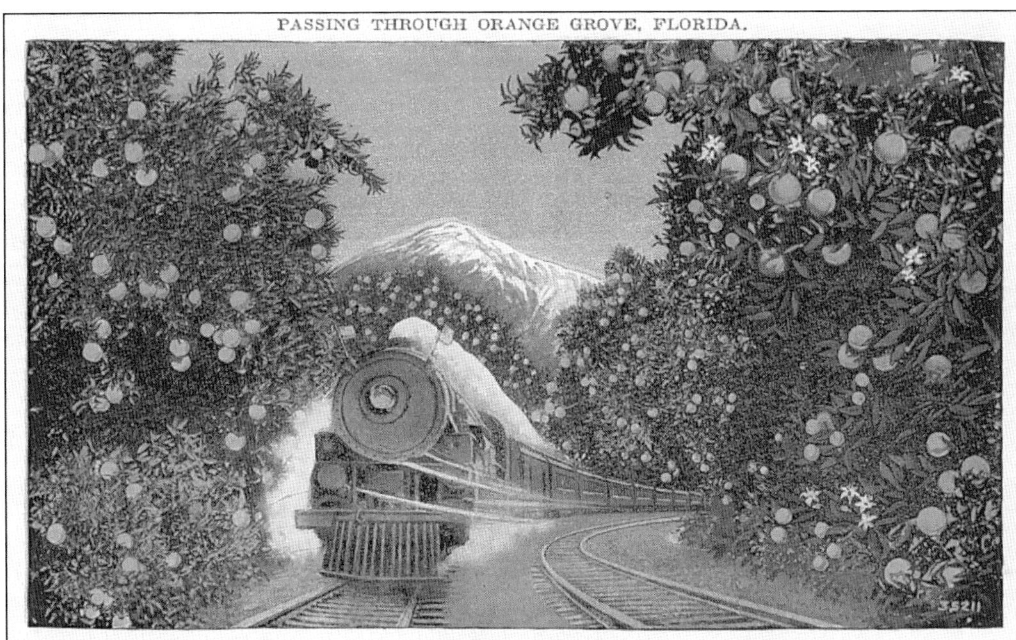

Passing through a Florida Orange Grove. Note the similarity of the background picture, complete with curving rail tracks, mountain, and similar orange branches, even though they were for different trains in different states! (P/P: Duval News Co., Jacksonville, Florida.)

Six

Modes of Transportation

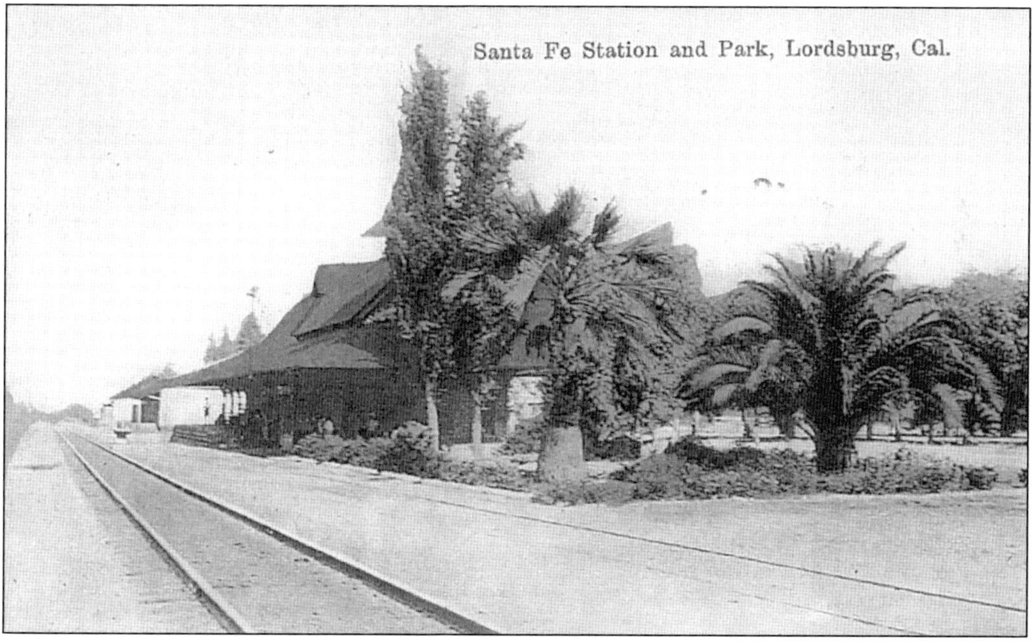

Santa Fe Station and Park, Lordsburg. With the arrival of the Santa Fe line in California in the 1880s, Lordsburg was one of several "new" towns to be founded along the railroad. (P/P: published for W.H. Posten & Co., Lordsburg, California, by "Woods," Los Angeles; postmark: February 1908; courtesy Jack McCaskill.)

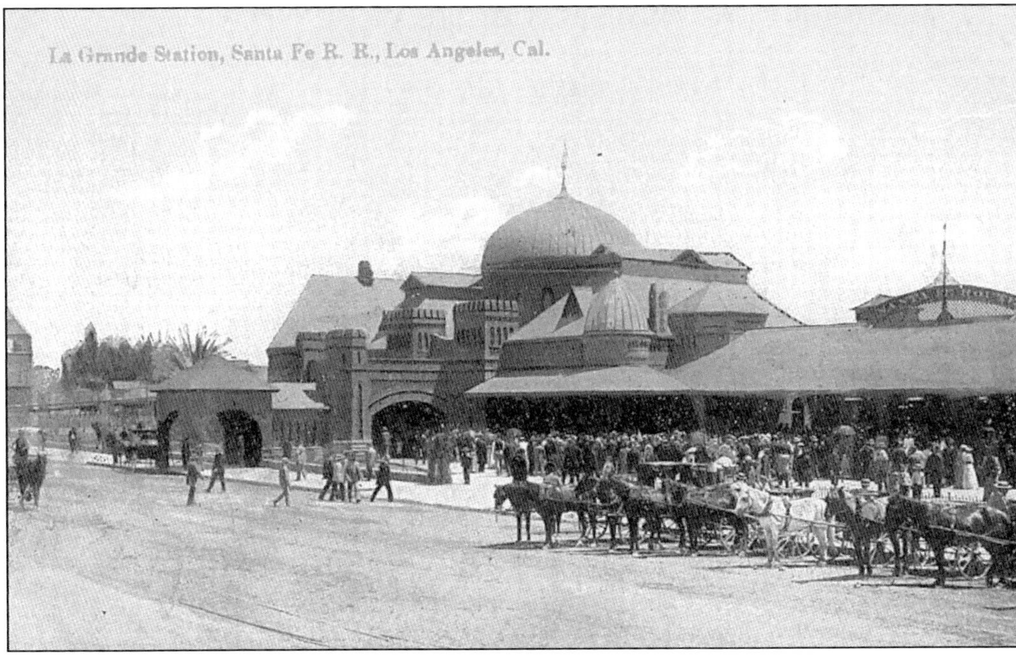

LE GRANDE STATION, SANTA FE RR, LOS ANGELES. This was the original Santa Fe station in downtown Los Angeles. The train was met by horse-drawn carriages. (P/P: Newman Post Card Co., Los Angeles and San Francisco, No. A 152; postmark: March 1901.)

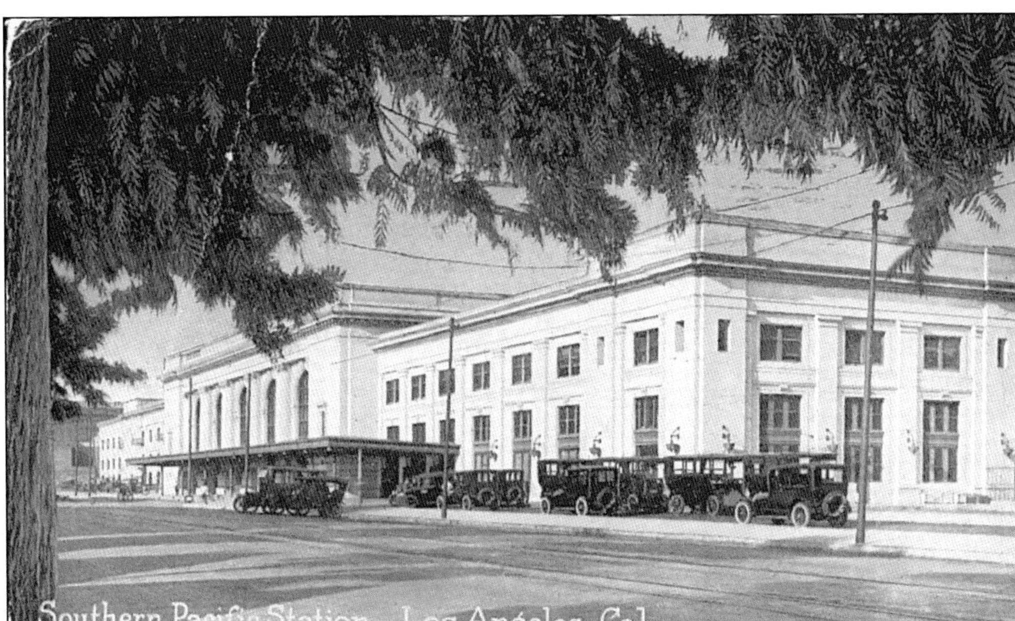

SOUTHERN PACIFIC STATION, LOS ANGELES. The Southern Pacific had its western terminus in Los Angeles. (P/P: Pacific Novelty Co., San Francisco, No. 3999; postmark: March 1911.)

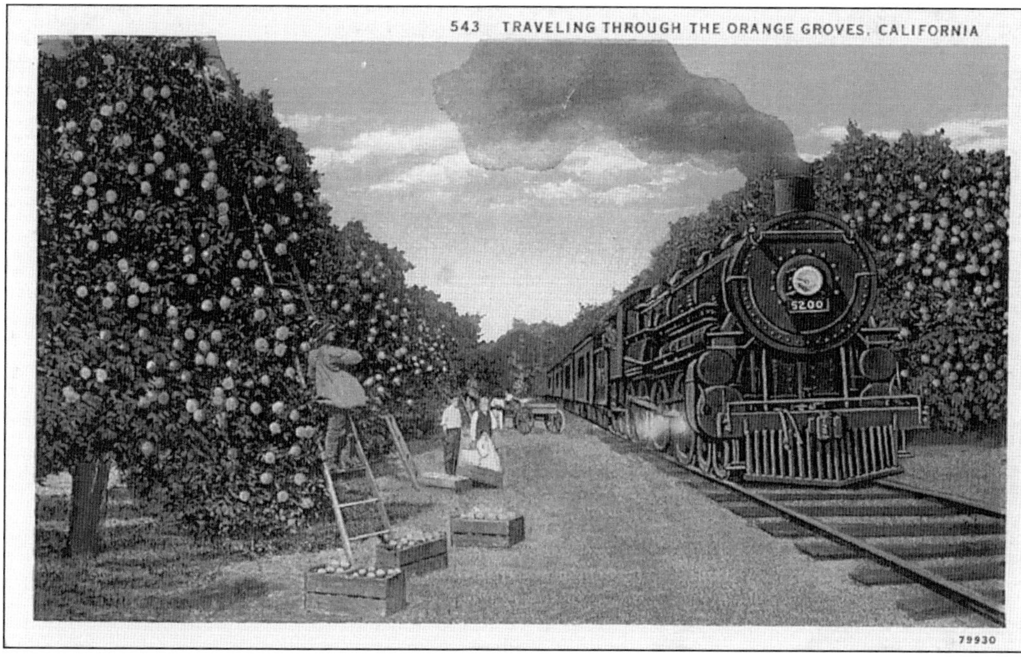

Traveling through the Orange Groves, California. The written text on the back reads, "This is truly the home of the Sunkist oranges and lemons." (P/P: Western Publishing & Novelty Co., Los Angeles.)

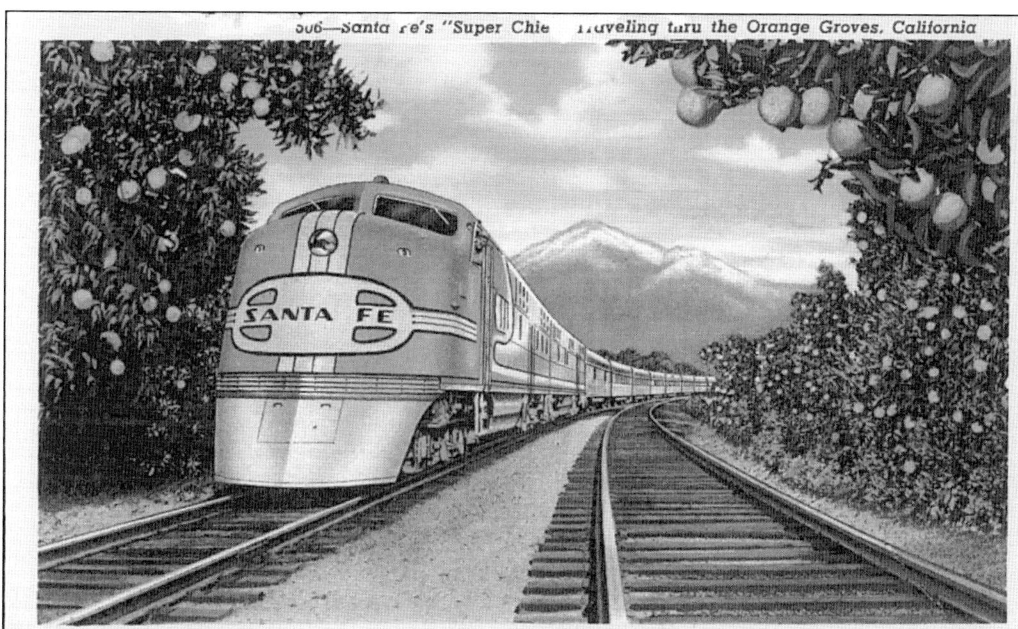

Santa Fe's "Super Chief" Traveling through the Orange Groves. "One of the Santa Fe's great fleet of streamliners. . . 39 3/4 hours from Chicago [to California]." (P/P: Western Publishing & Novelty Co., Los Angeles, No. 506.)

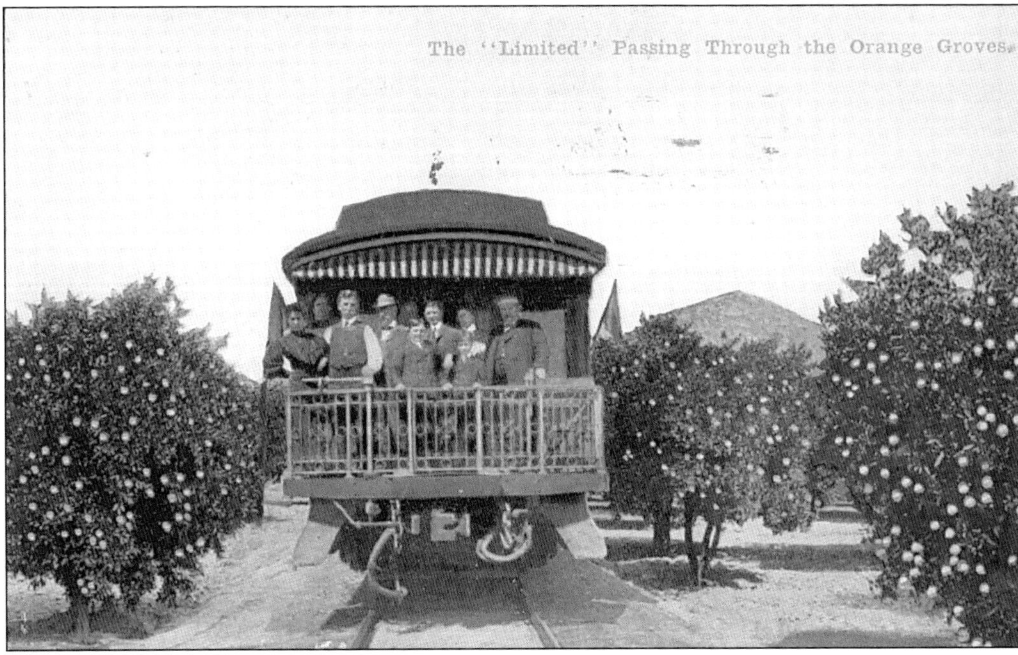

THE "LIMITED" PASSING THROUGH THE ORANGE GROVES. (P/P: Newman Post Card Co., Los Angeles and San Francisco, No. AB 181; postmark: December 1911.)

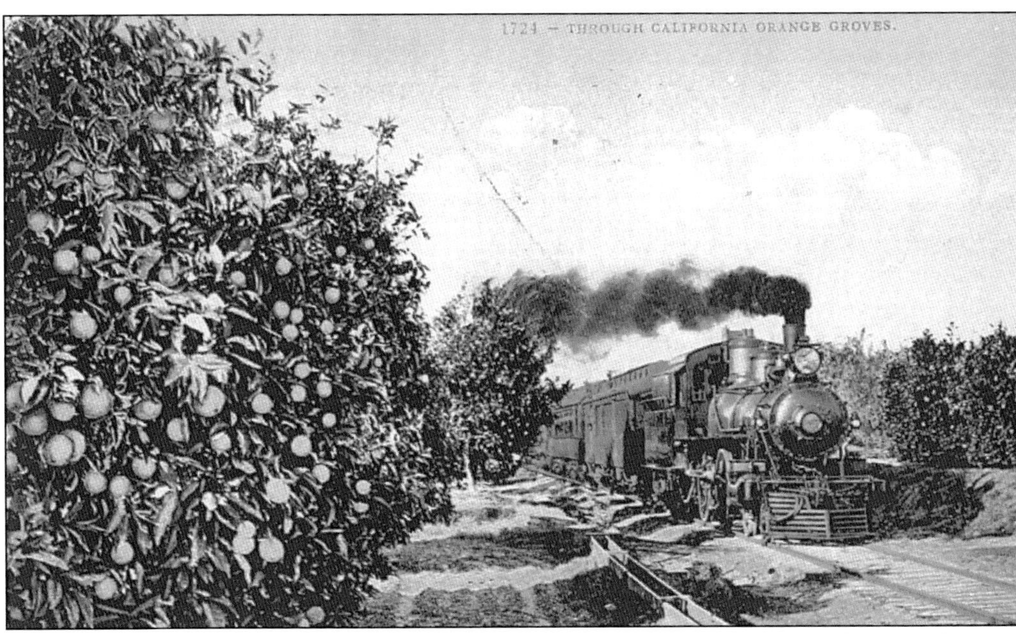

THROUGH CALIFORNIA ORANGE GROVES. The sender wrote on the back of this card, "Dear Bro., Do you think you can raise anything like this in W. Va.? Five Cents a Doz. here. Seth." (P/P: Edward H. Mitchell, San Francisco, No. 1724; postmark: June 1910.)

Pacific Electric Building, Los Angeles. From this terminal in Los Angeles, Henry E. Huntington's Pacific Electric interurban railway covered much of Southern California with some 1,200 miles of tracks. Lordsburg was one of the stations on the Pacific Electric line. (P/P: Edward H. Mitchell, San Francisco, No. 1205.)

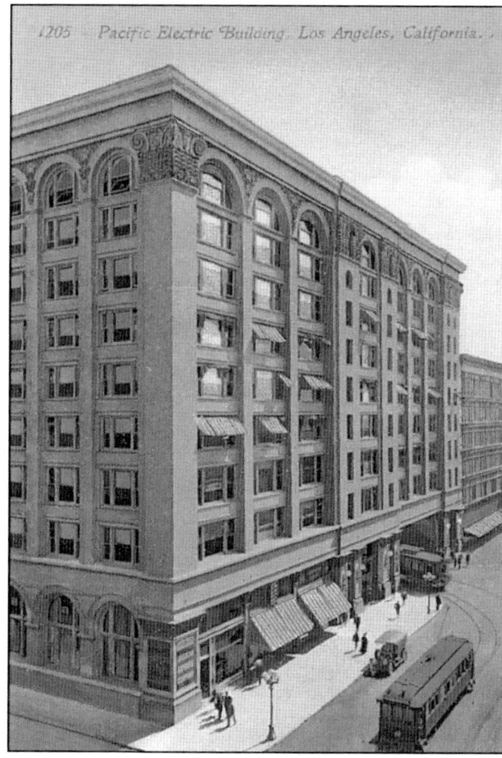

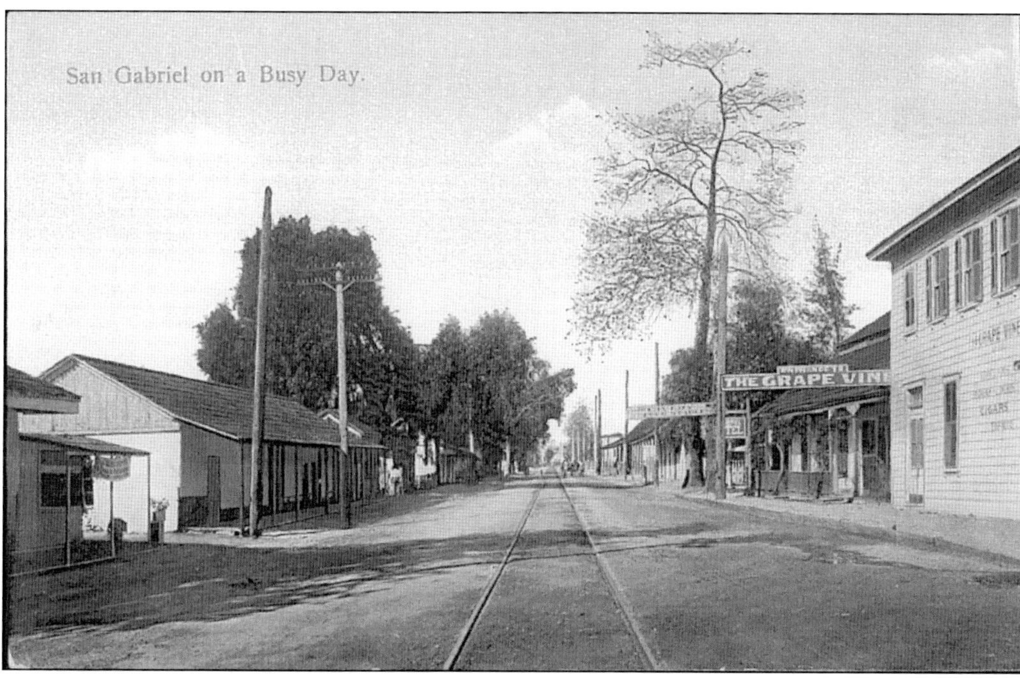

San Gabriel on a Busy Day. This is not what one would call a beehive of activity. (P/P: M. Rieder, Los Angeles, No. 4717; made in Germany.)

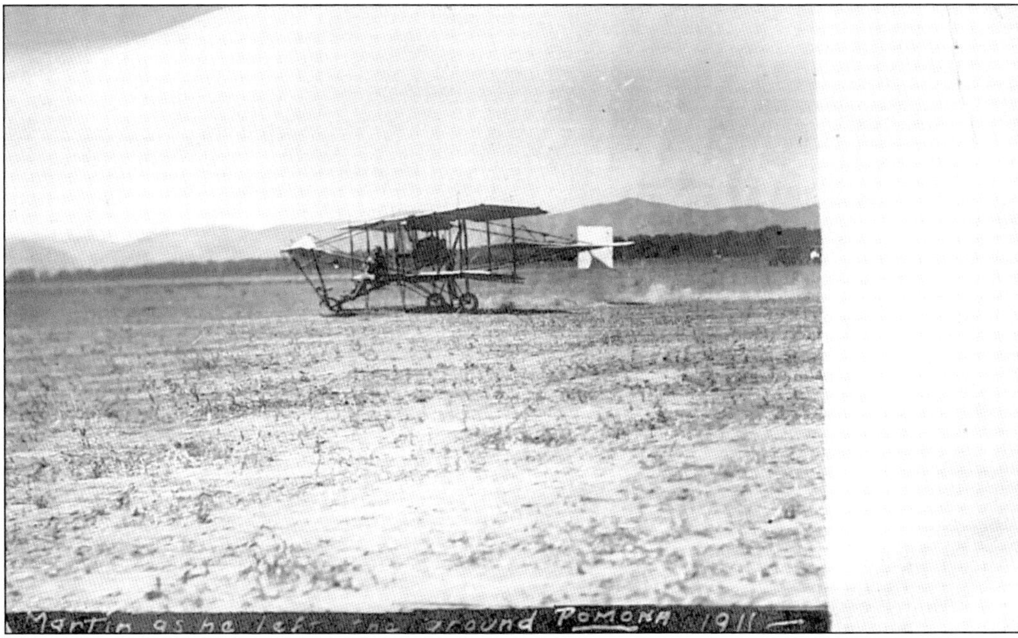

Martin Leaving the Ground in Pomona, 1911. Glenn L. Martin, aviator, stunt flyer, and later, aircraft builder, flew in and out of the Pomona Valley many times. This field, with its mountain backdrop, was located between Lordsburg and Pomona, and later became Bracket Field, La Verne. (P/P: unknown.)

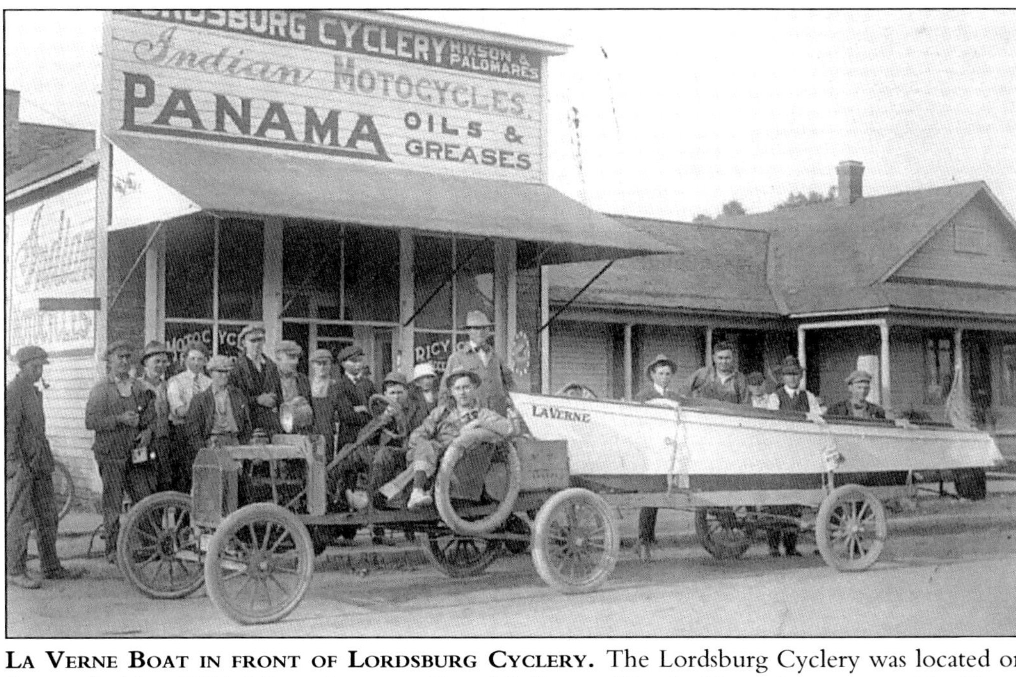

La Verne Boat in front of Lordsburg Cyclery. The Lordsburg Cyclery was located on the north side of Third Street between D and E Streets. The La Verne boat pictured had been rebuilt and was being taken to Big Bear Lake behind this car. (P/P: Frasher, Pomona, No. A 20; courtesy City of La Verne Planning Department.)

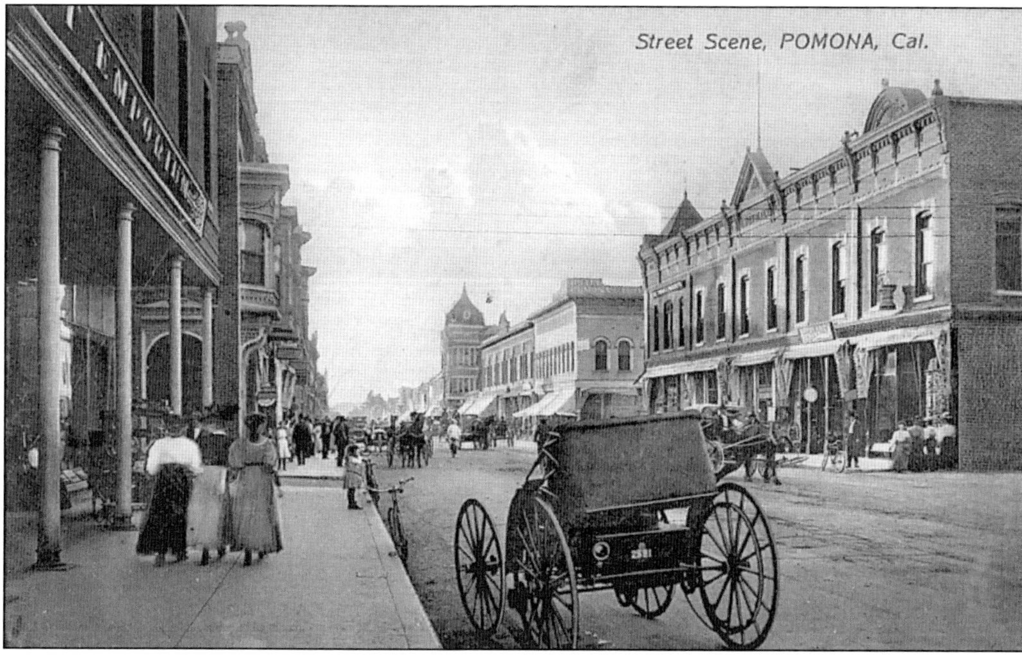

Buggies along Second Street in nearby Pomona. Buggies appear to be the main means of transportation on Pomona's business street. The Orange Belt Emporium Department Store is pictured on the left of the photo. (P/P: Published for T.S. Newby, Pomona, by "Woods," Los Angeles, No. H-C-95; printed in Germany.)

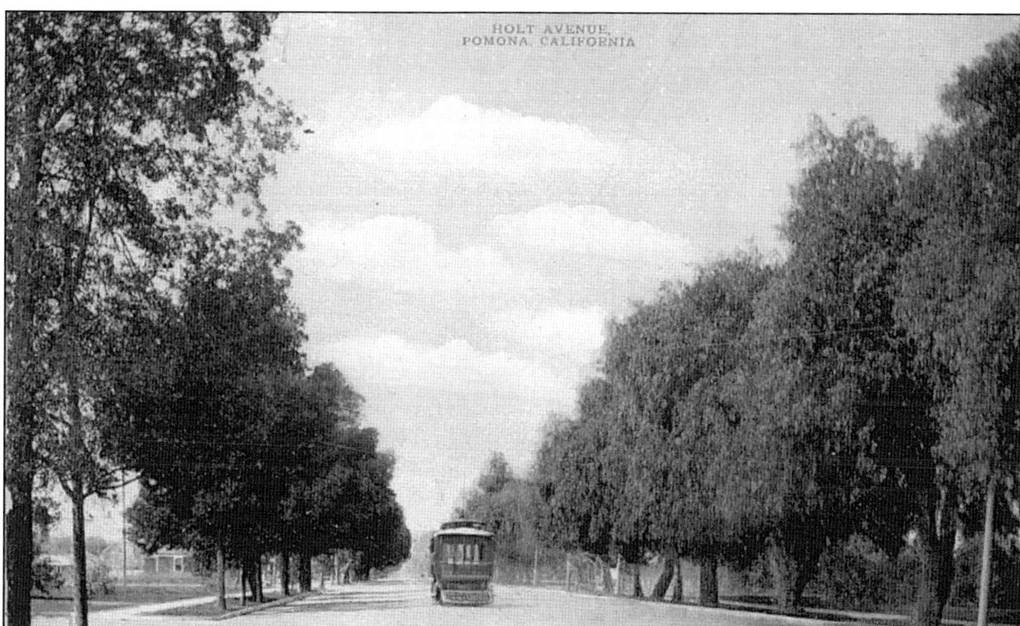

Street Car Line on Holt Avenue, Pomona. This scene was taken just south of Lordsburg. (P/P: Benham Co., Los Angeles, No. 1566; made in California.)

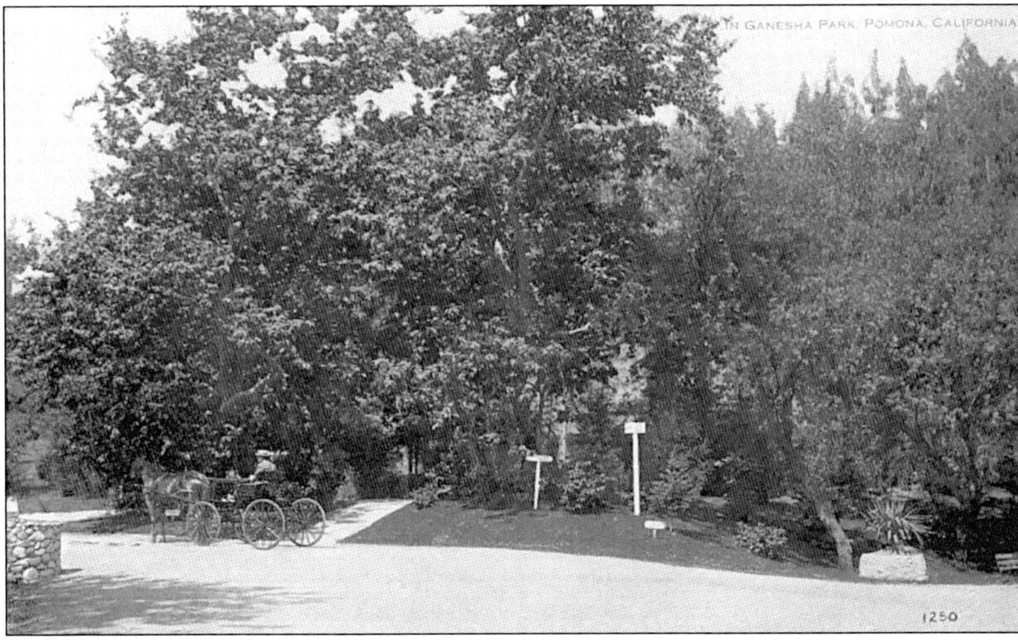

Buggy in Ganesha Park, Pomona. When this park was purchased by the city in 1890, it was a beautiful wooded area with a stream through it, located just south of Lordsburg on the northern edge of Pomona. (P/P: Benham Indian Trading Co., Los Angeles, No. 1230; postmark: June 1911.)

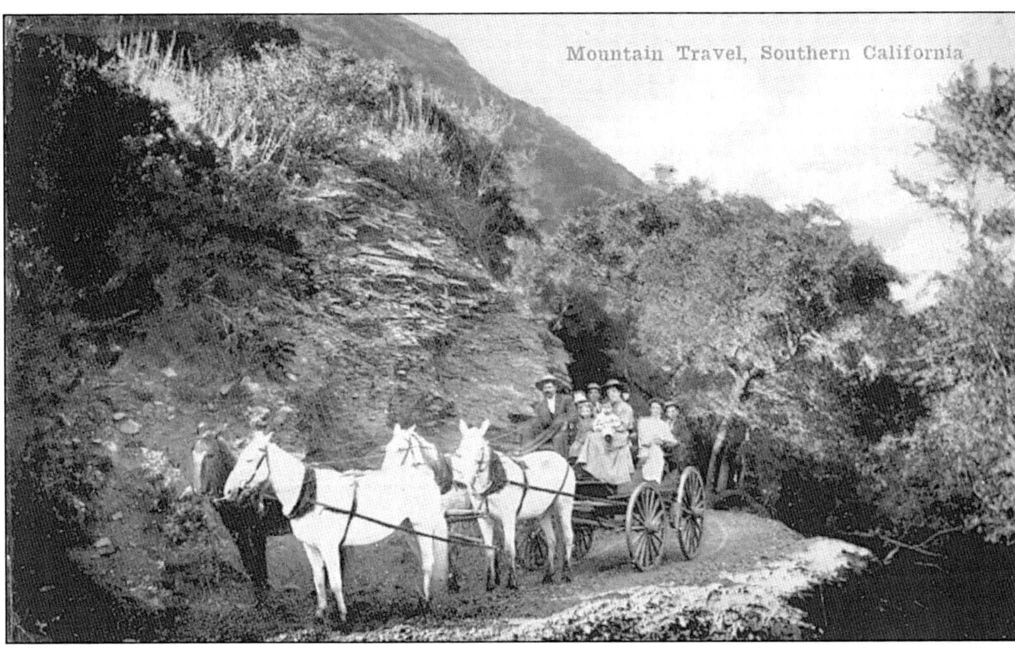

Mountain Travel, Southern California. This is another example of Californians' love of the mountains. (P/P: Van Ornum Colorprint Co., Los Angeles, No. 577.)

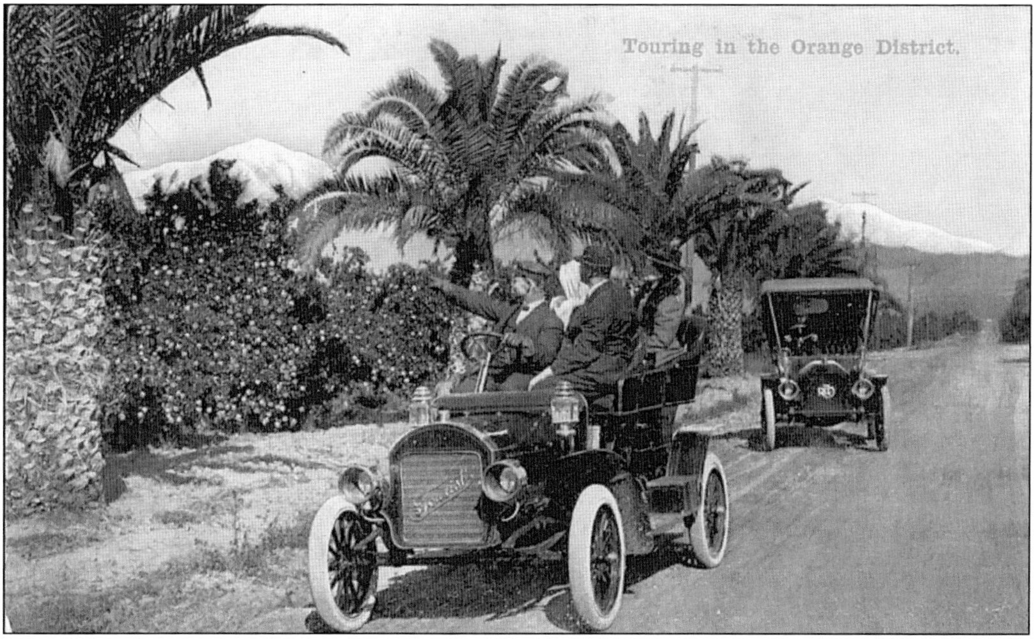

TOURING THE ORANGE DISTRICT BY AUTO. Where else would you take guests, but to view the orange groves? (P/P: Newman Post Card Co., Los Angeles and San Francisco; "On the Road of a Thousand Wonders," No. AB 140.)

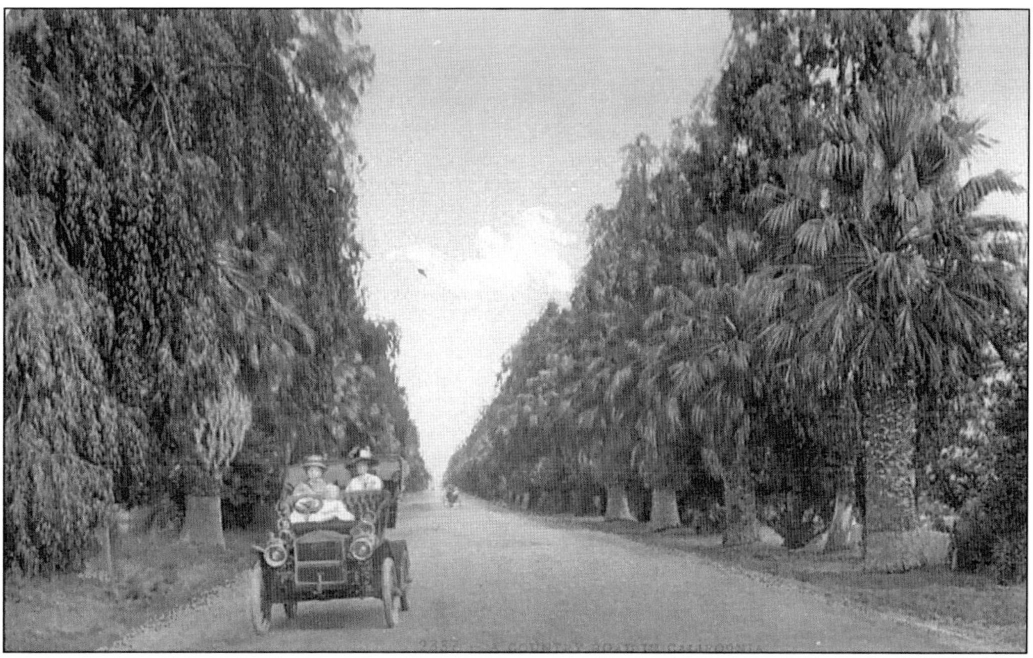

A COUNTRY ROAD IN CALIFORNIA. Two different modes of transportation are seen on this country road. (P/P: Edward H. Mitchell, San Francisco, No. 2337.)

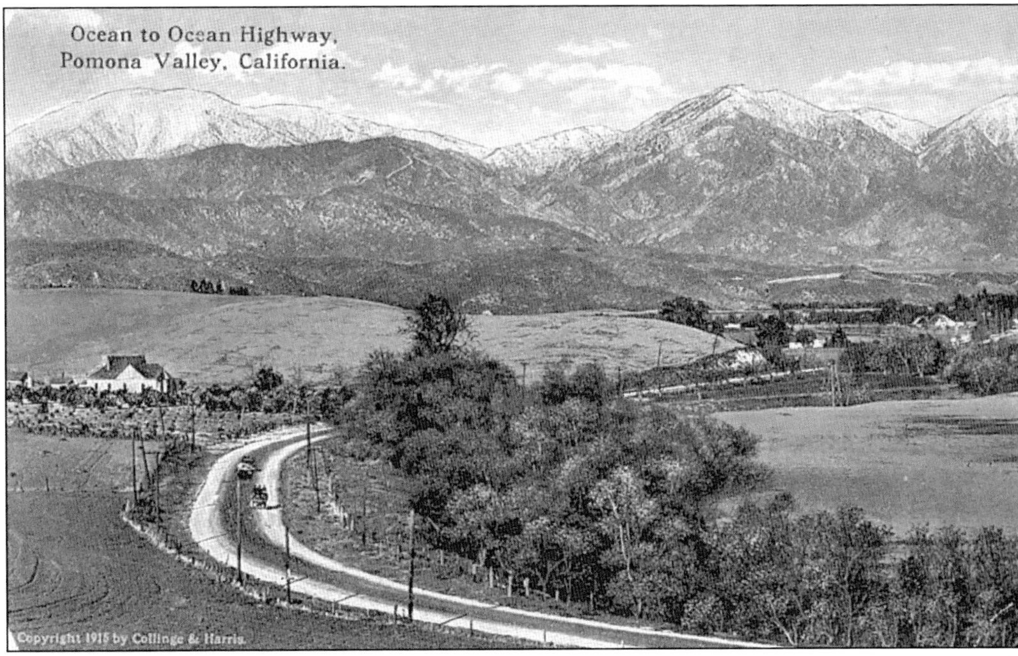

Ocean to Ocean Highway, Pomona Valley. A postcard from an unknown location in the Pomona Valley area shows the ever present mountain backdrop. (P/P: Julius Hecht, Los Angeles, No. A64408; made in the U.S.A; photo copyright 1915 by Collinge & Harris.)

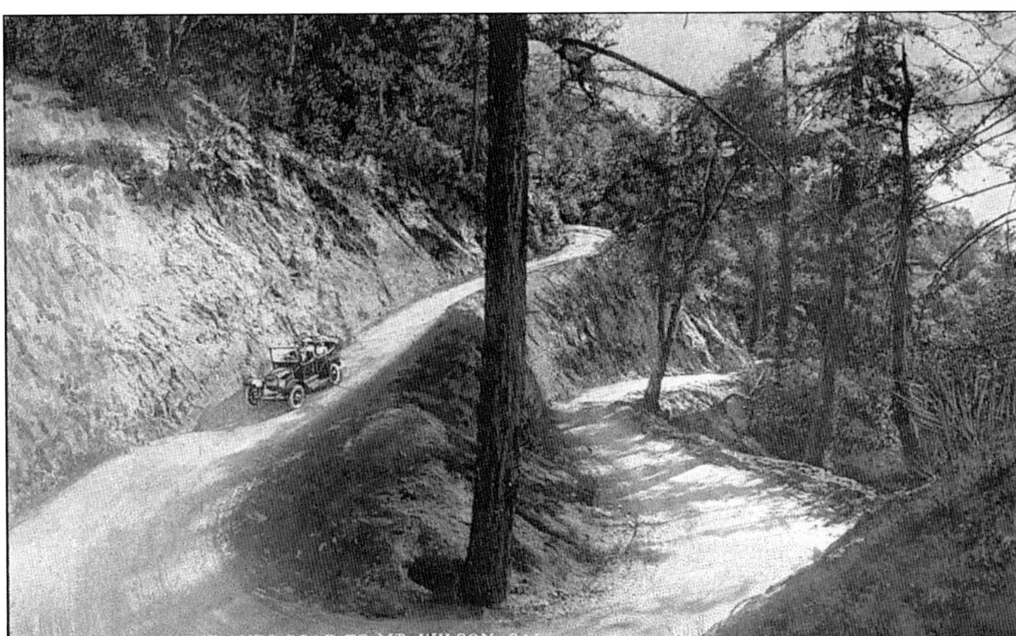

Turnout on the Road to Mt. Wilson. A good place to master one's driving skills? (P/P: Western Publishing & Novelty Co., No. 754; made in the U.S.A.)

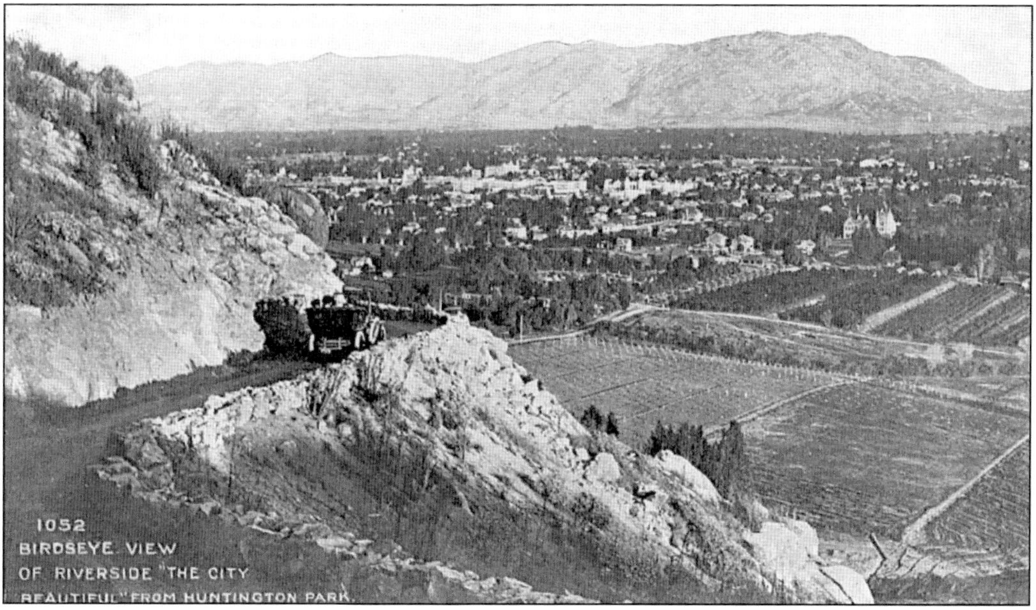

Bird's-Eye View of Riverside, "The City Beautiful," from Huntington Park. A quote by John Muir is printed on the back of this card: "Climb the mountains and get their good tidings. Nature's peace will flow into you as sunshine flows into the trees. The winds will blow their freshness into you, and the storms their energy, while cares will drop off like autumn leaves." (P/P: Benham Indian Trading Co., Los Angeles, No. 1052.)

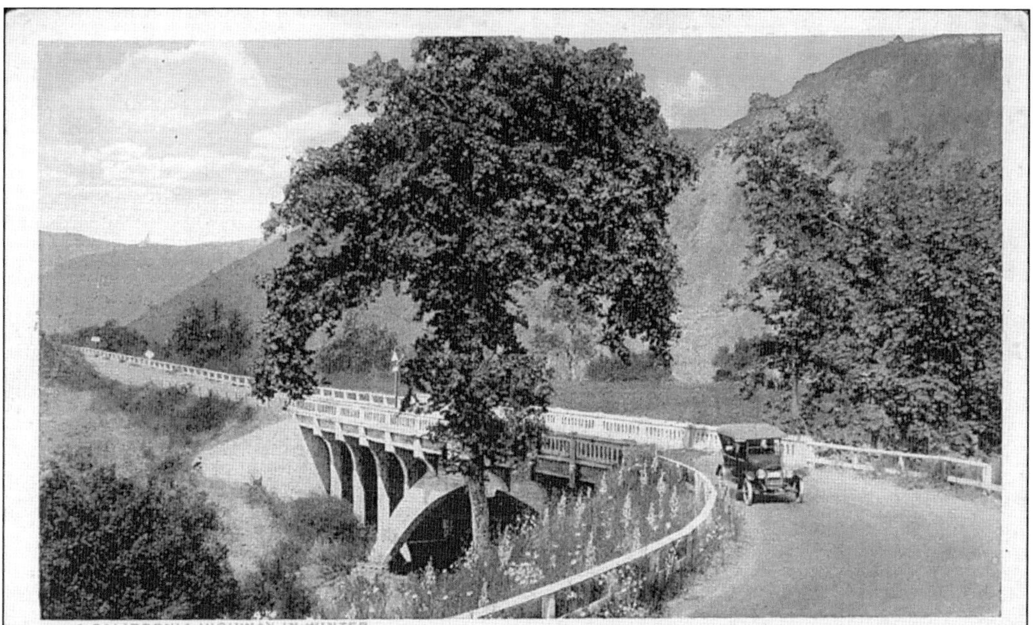

A California Highway in Winter. This card is yet another tease for eastern friends and relatives. Look, no snow! (P/P: Western Publishing & Novelty Co., Los Angeles; made in the U.S.A.)

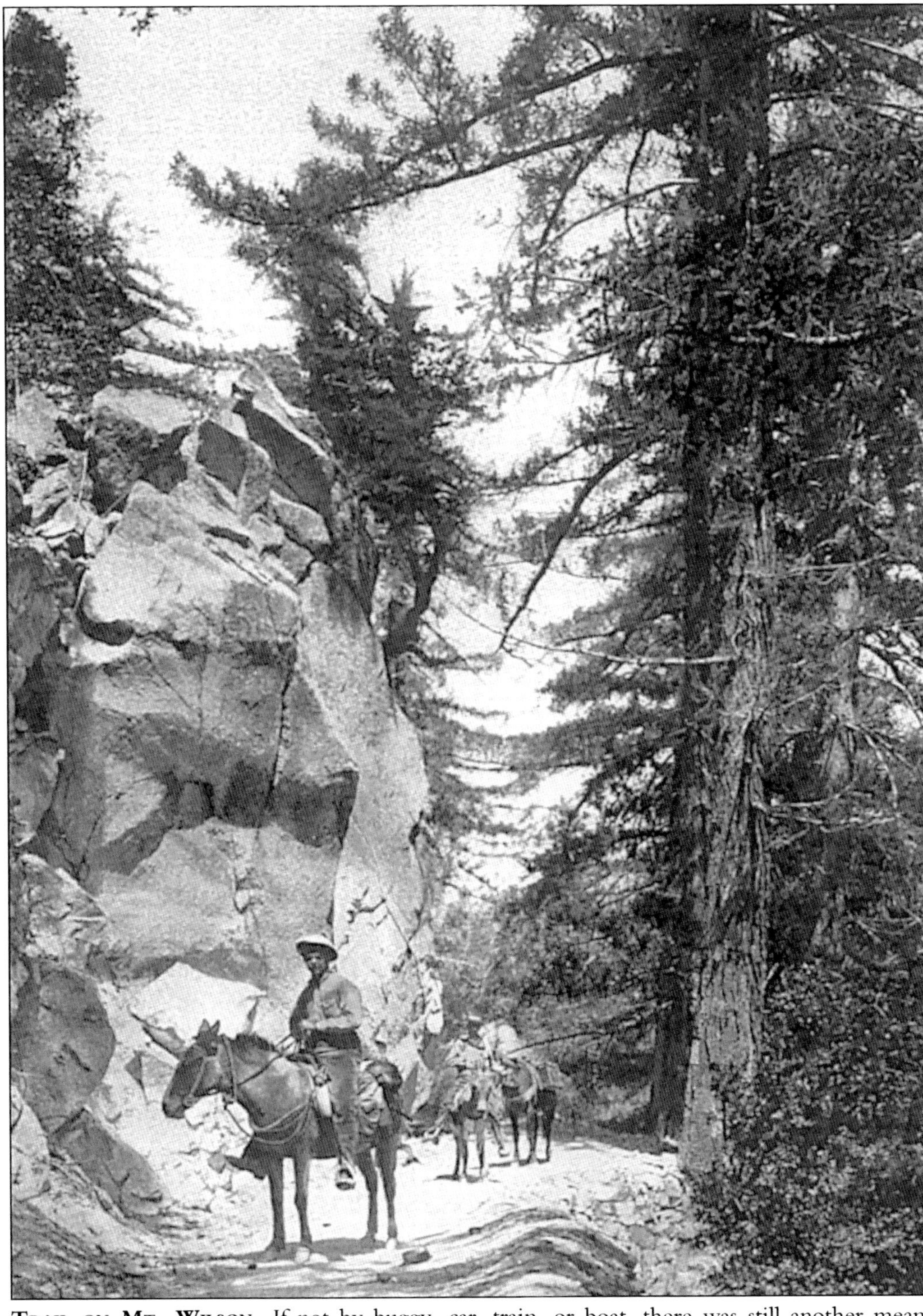

TRAIL ON MT. WILSON. If not by buggy, car, train, or boat, there was still another means of transportation. (P/P: Newman Post Card Co., Los Angeles, No. C106; made in Germany; postmark: June 1910.)

Seven

Neighboring Towns and Communities

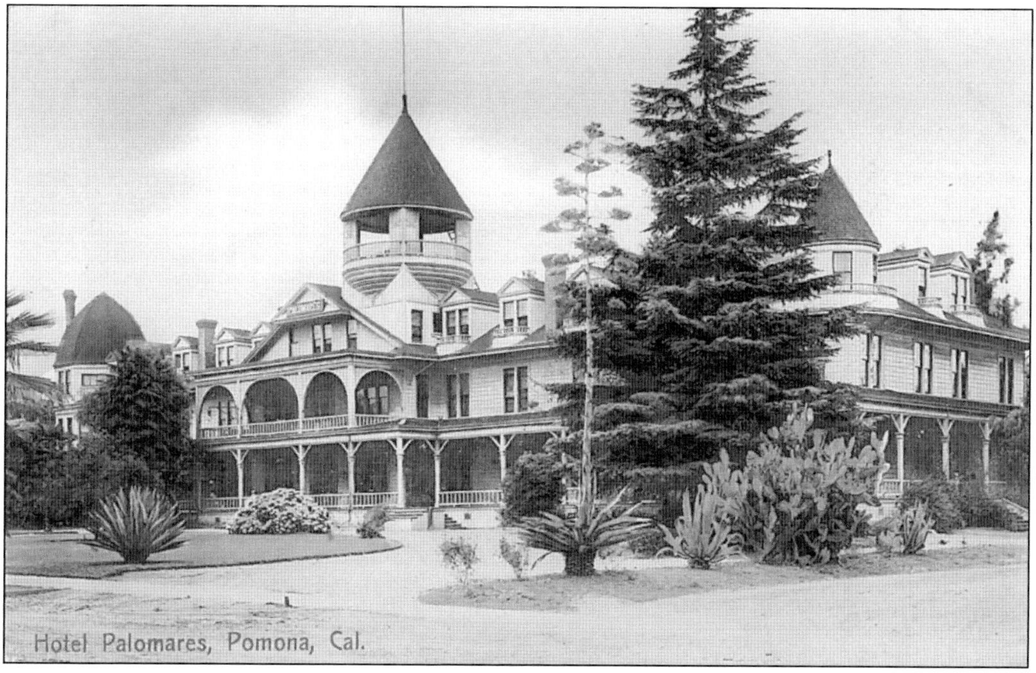

Hotel Palomares, Pomona. This popular hotel, described as "a social hub of the valley," was destroyed by fire in June 1914. (P/P: M. Rieder, Los Angeles, No. 20184; made in Germany.)

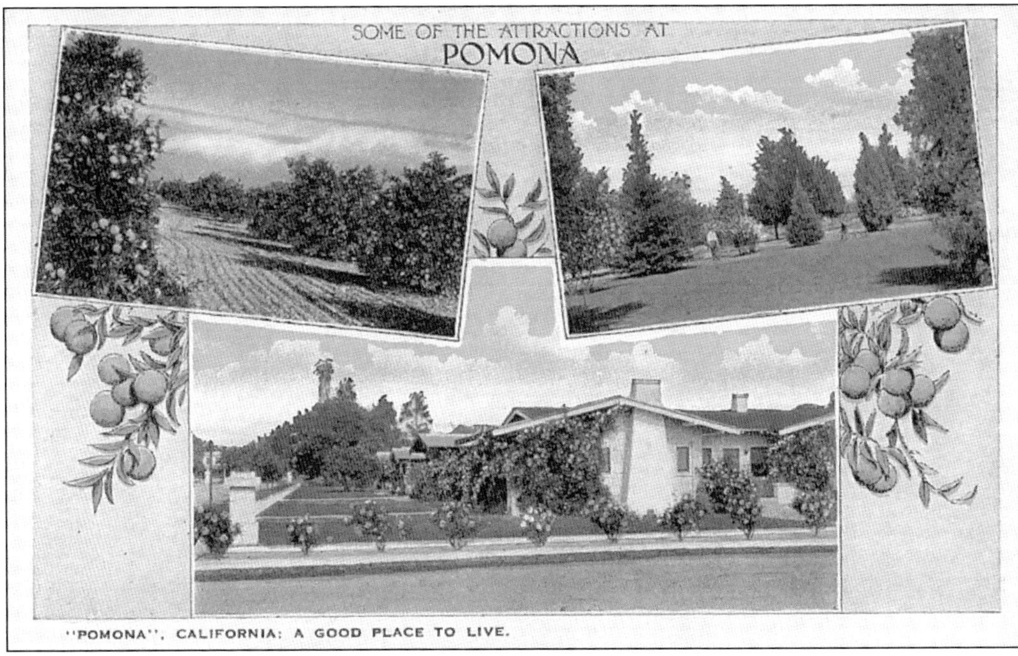

Various Attractions at Pomona. "Pomona," California, was a good place to live. (P/P: B.R. Montgomery, Riverside, Cal., No. 118203.)

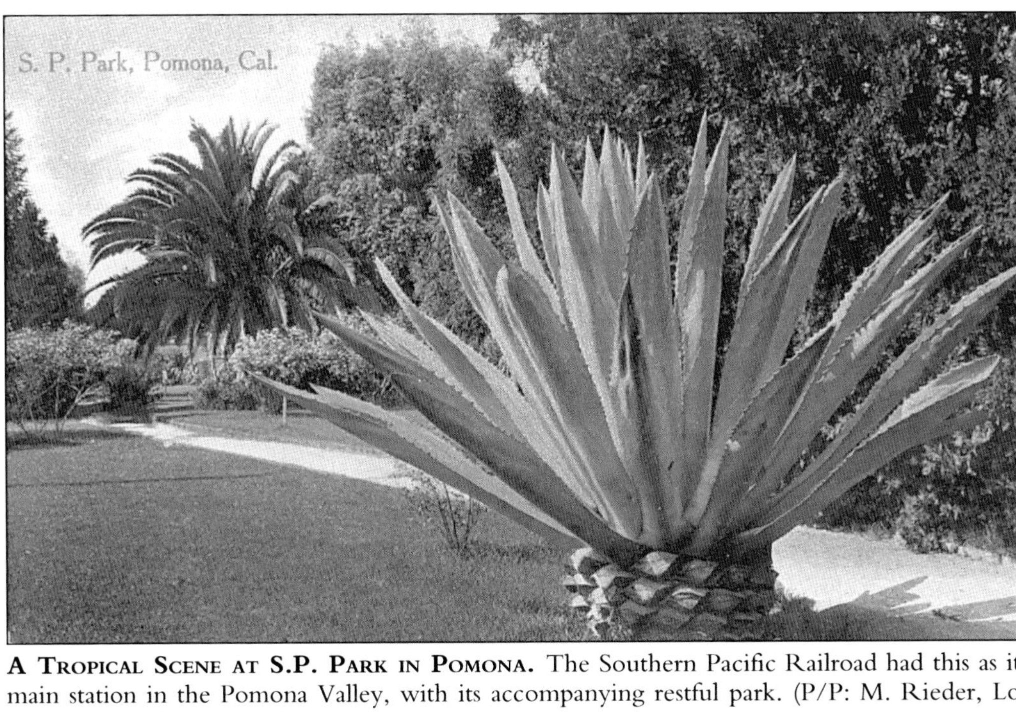

A Tropical Scene at S.P. Park in Pomona. The Southern Pacific Railroad had this as its main station in the Pomona Valley, with its accompanying restful park. (P/P: M. Rieder, Los Angeles, No. 4594; made in Germany.)

A Typical California Scene: Oranges, Roses, and Century Plant in Bloom. This image was taken near Pomona. (P/P: Newman Post Card Co., Los Angeles, No. 5358; made in Germany; postmark: October 1909.)

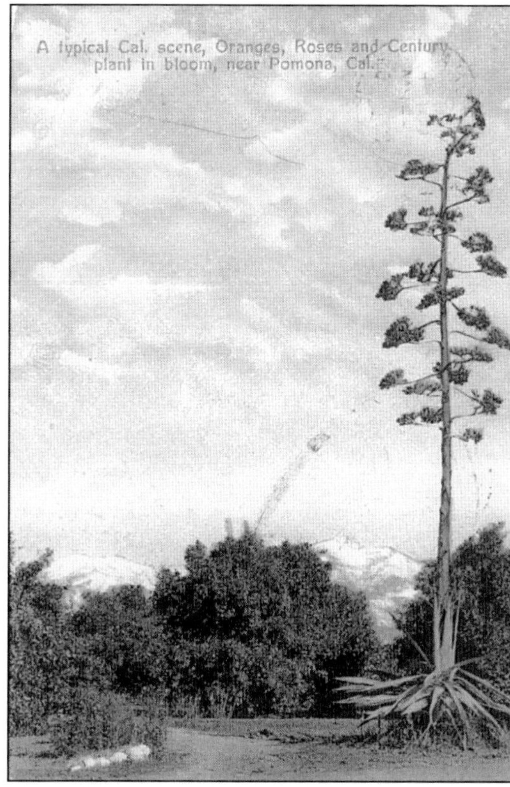

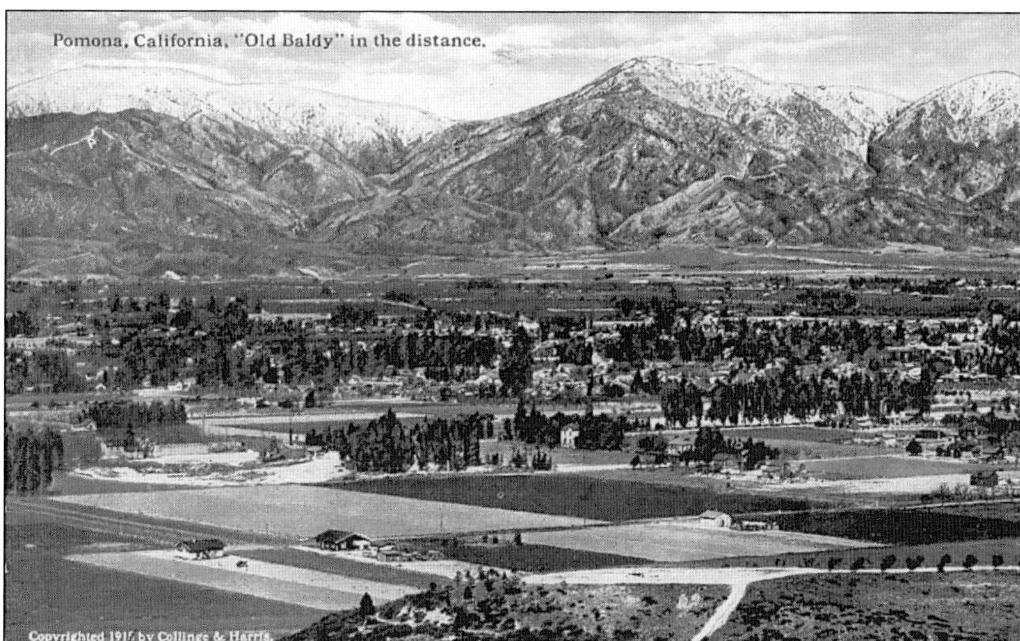

Pomona, with "Old Baldy" in the Distance. (P/P:Julius Hecht, Los Angeles, No. P-116; copyright 1915 by Collinge & Harris; made in the U.S.A.; postmark: October 1917.)

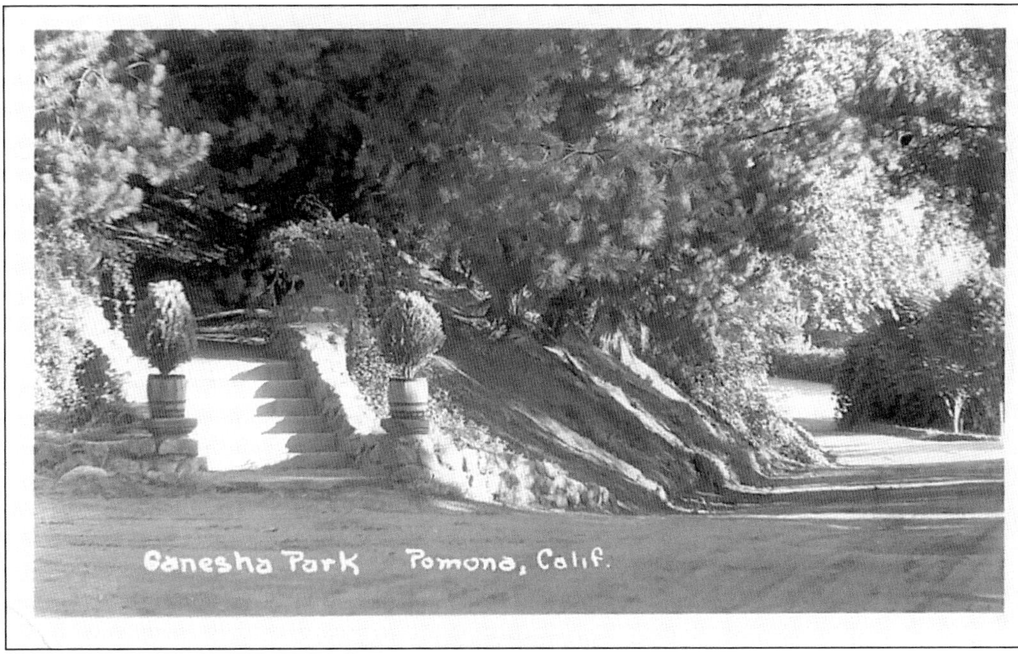

Ganesha Park, Pomona. This park was named for one of the first gods of Hindu mythology. (P/P: unknown.)

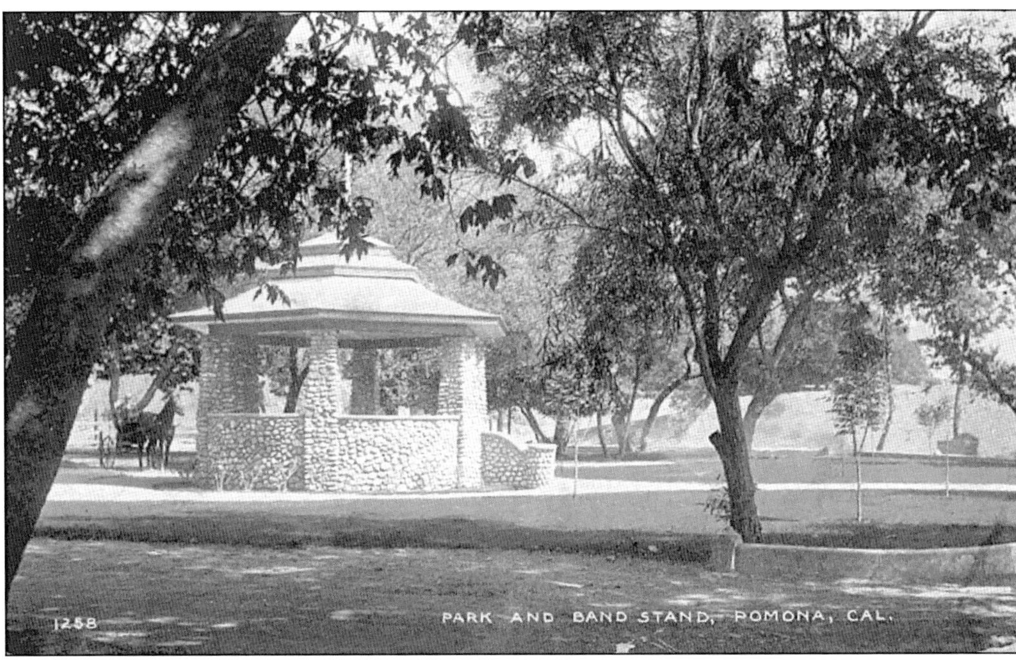

Park and Bandstand, Pomona. This bandstand was part of the early Ganesha Park. In 1999, weekly summer concerts still drew crowds to enjoy music from a newer band shell. (P/P:Benham Co., Los Angeles, No. 1258; made in California; postmark: September 1911.)

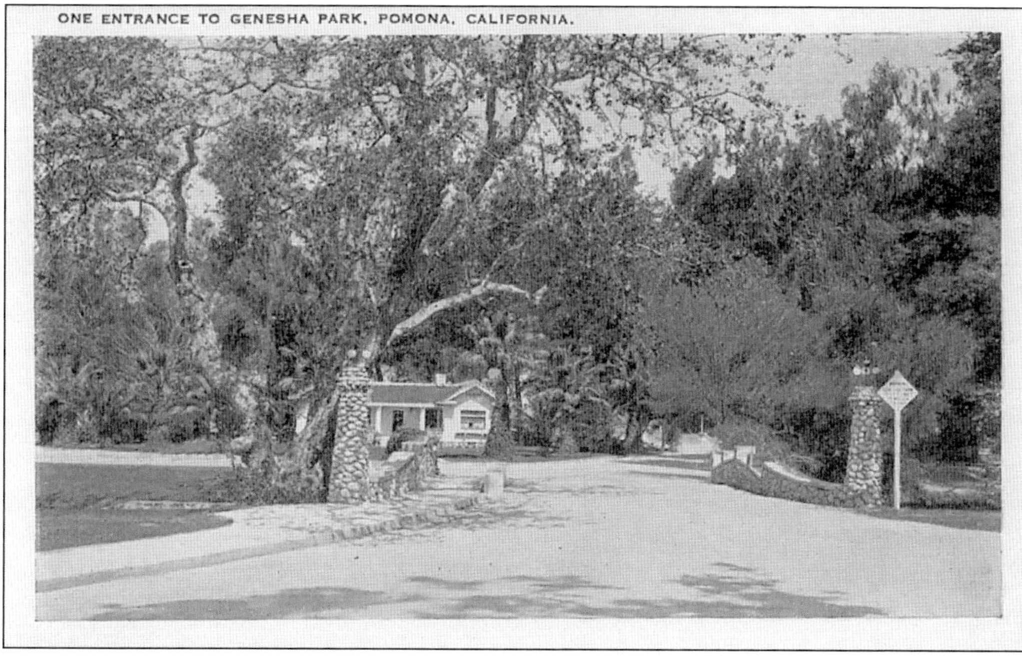

One Entrance to Ganesha Park. Before the arrival of the freeway in the 1960s through the northern edge of Pomona, Ganesha Park was easily accessible from the south. (P/P: Tichnor Quality Views, No. 12240.)

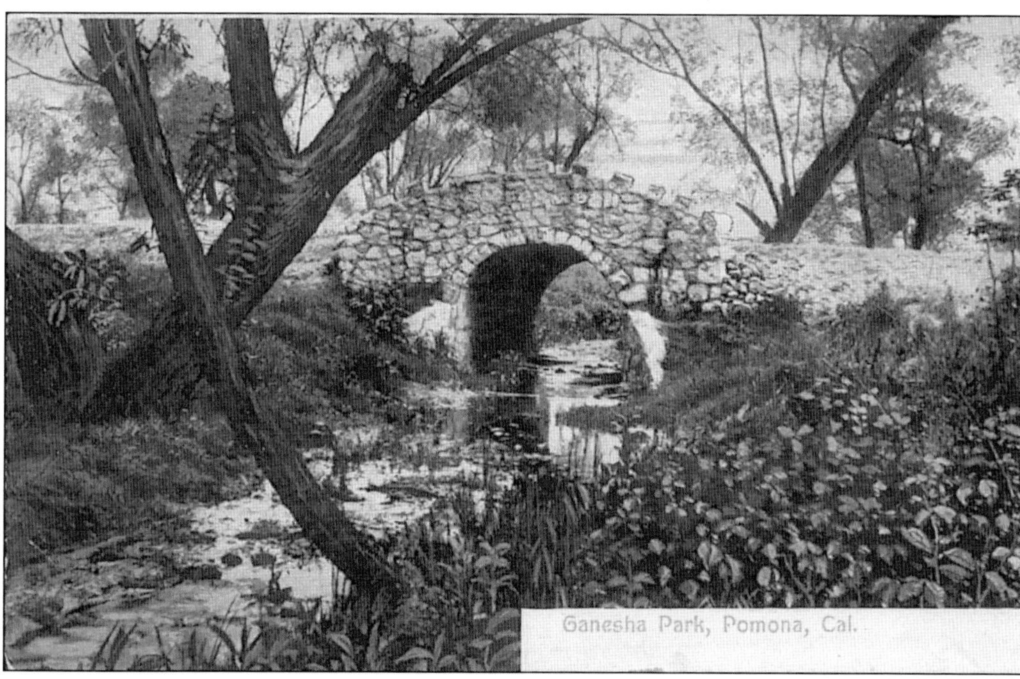

Another View of Ganesha Park. A quiet stream flowed under the stone bridge, enhancing the peaceful setting of the park. (P/P:Newman Post Card Co., Los Angeles, No. J 308; made in Germany; postmark: November 1908.)

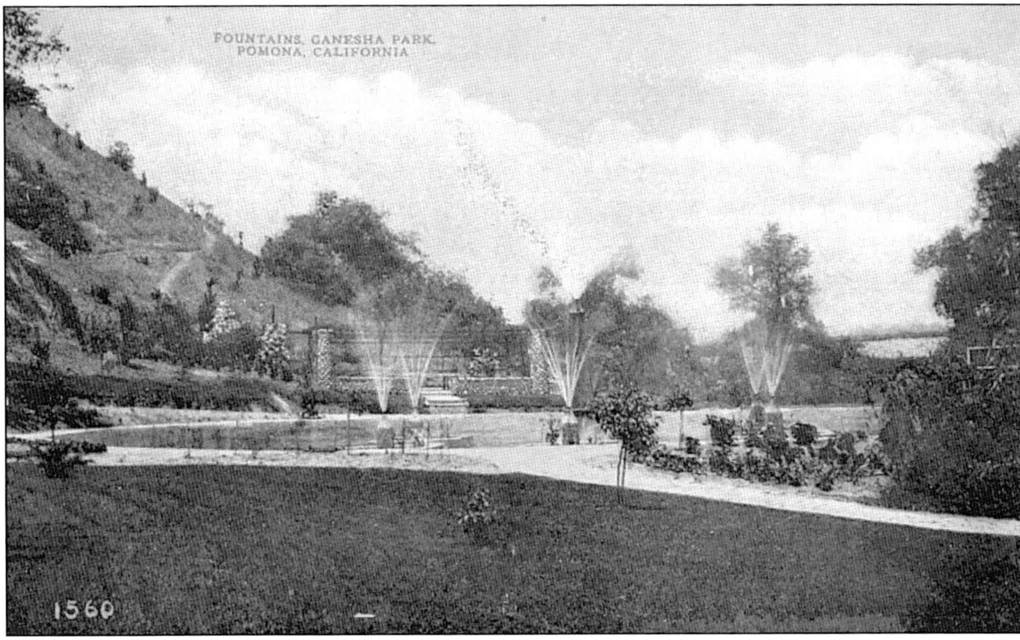

FOUNTAINS AT GANESHA PARK. The sender wrote on the back, "I am sending you a picture of the park where we spent one afternoon. It is a beautiful park for a town of this size." (P/P: Benham Co., Los Angeles, No. 1560; made in California; postmark: February 1911.)

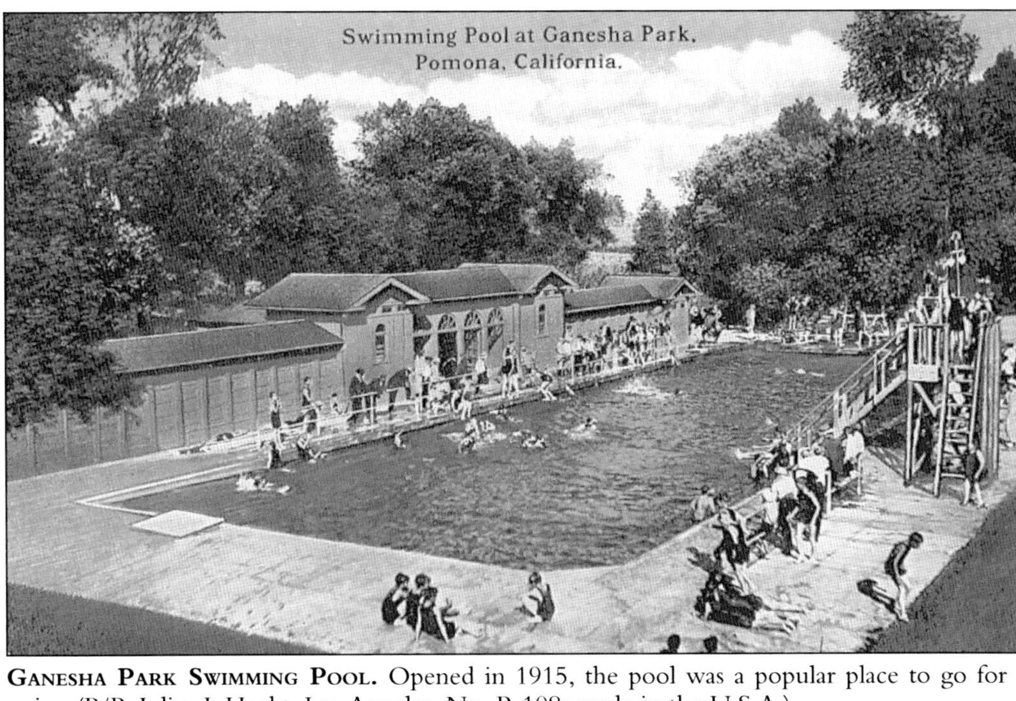

GANESHA PARK SWIMMING POOL. Opened in 1915, the pool was a popular place to go for a swim. (P/P: Julius J. Hecht, Los Angeles, No. P-108; made in the U.S.A.)

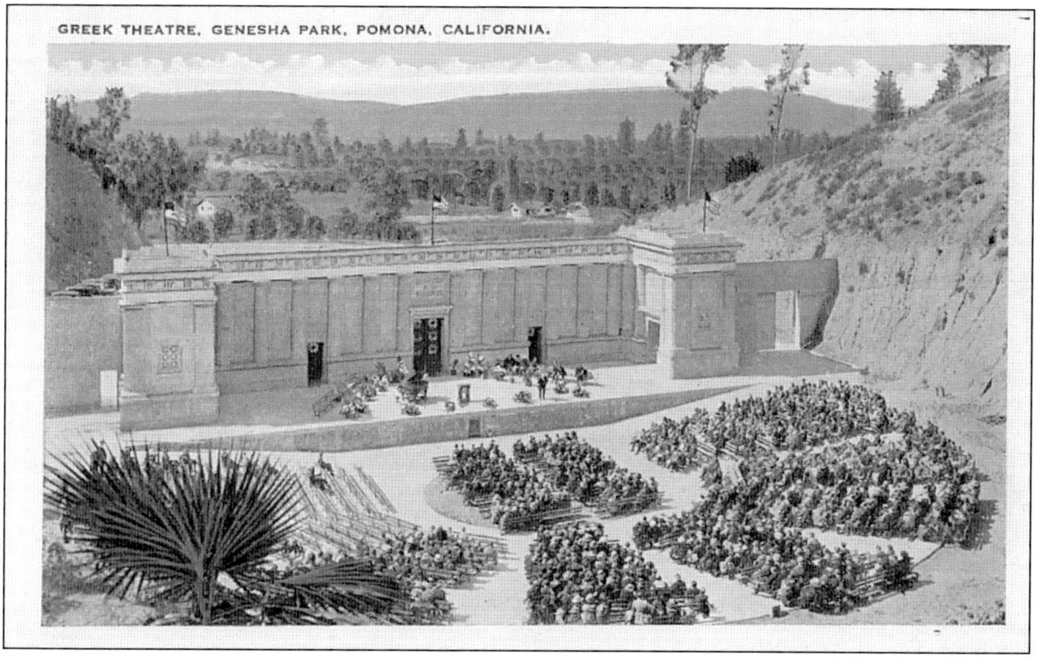

GREEK THEATRE IN GANESHA PARK. The Greek Theatre, constructed in 1916, was used some for productions and musical presentations, but especially for high school commencements. In the early 1960s, it was torn down. (P/P: Tichnor Quality Views, No. 122241.)

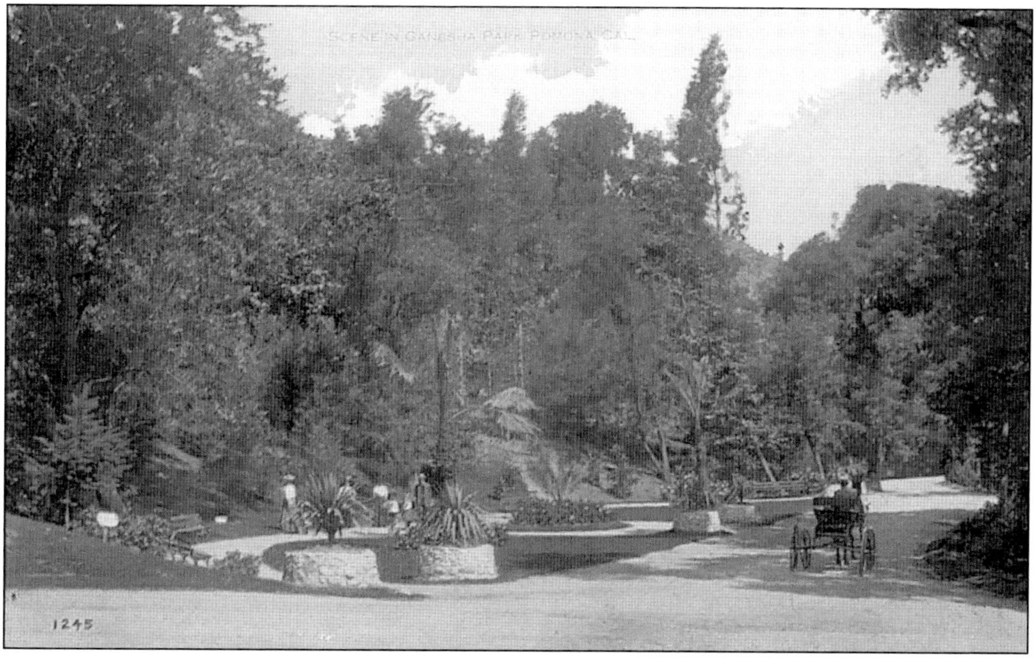

GANESHA PARK SCENE. Casual strollers enjoy the park as a buggy passes by. (P/P: Benham Indian Trading Co., Los Angeles, No. 1245; made in California.)

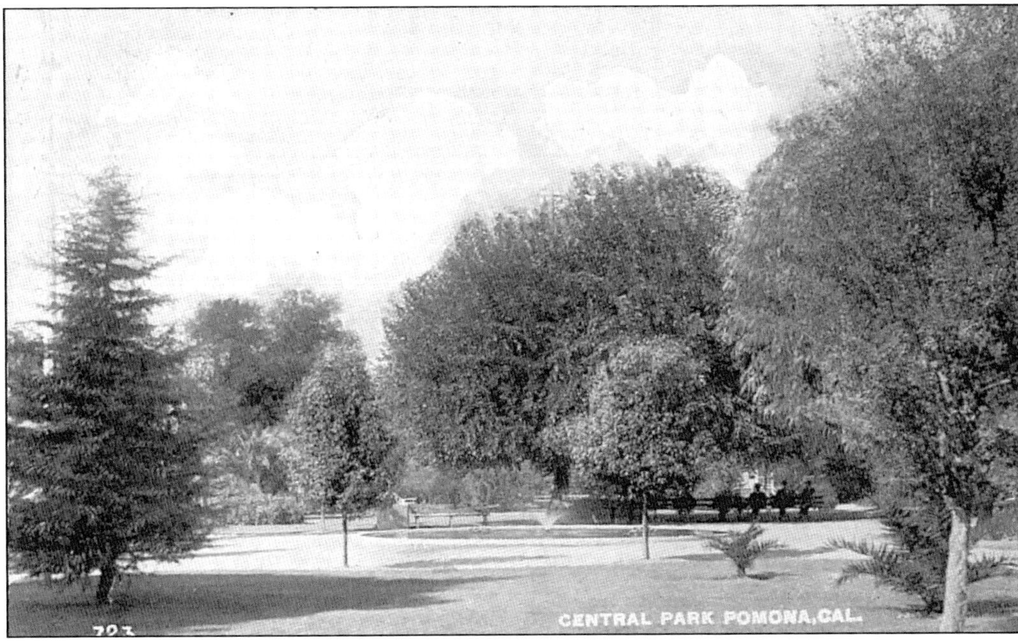

Central Park, Pomona. (P/P: Edward H. Mitchell, San Francisco, No. 723.)

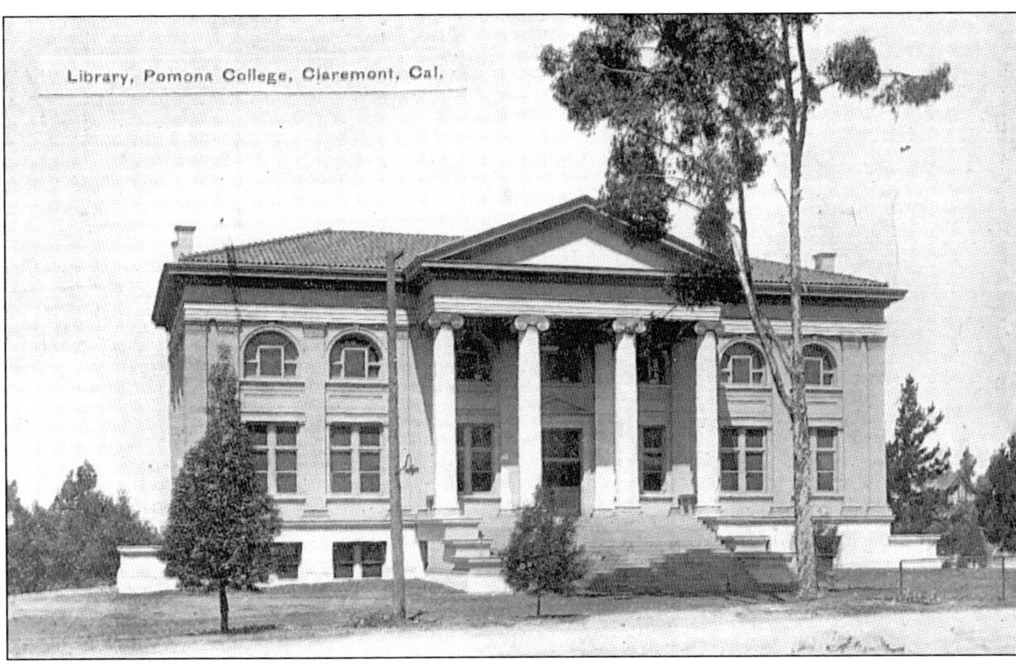

The Library at Pomona College, Claremont. Pomona College was founded in a land boom hotel in Claremont, about 3 miles east of Lordsburg/La Verne. The Carnegie Library, which served both the city and the college, was built in 1908. (P/P: Published for the College Book and Drug Store, Claremont.)

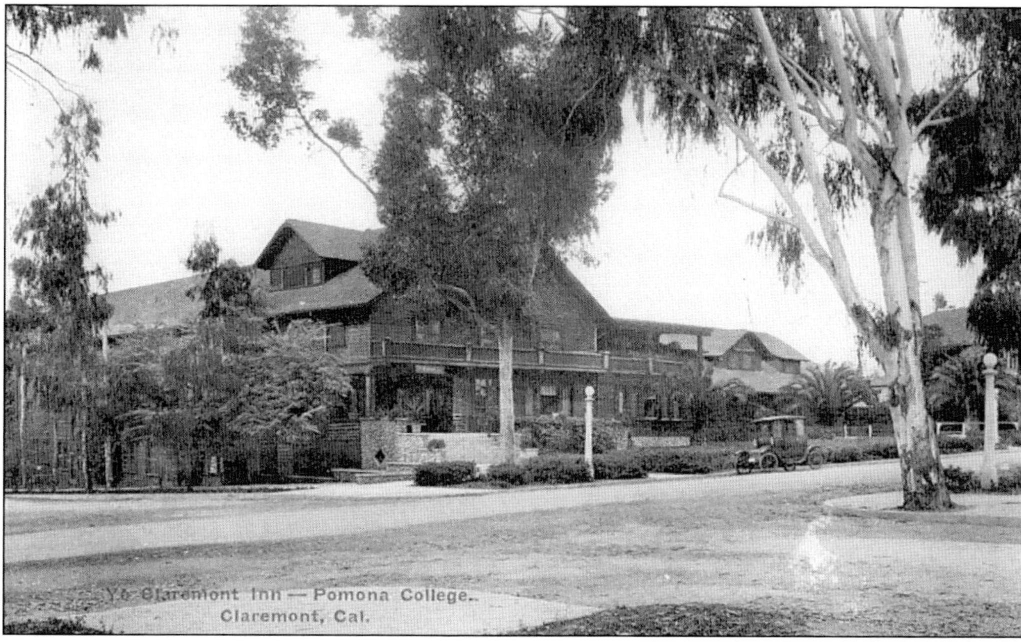

Ye Claremont Inn—Pomona College, Claremont. The inn opened in 1907 and was razed in 1968. (P/P: Pomona College, Cooperative Store, Claremont; Postcards of Quality, The Albertype Co., Brooklyn, New York.)

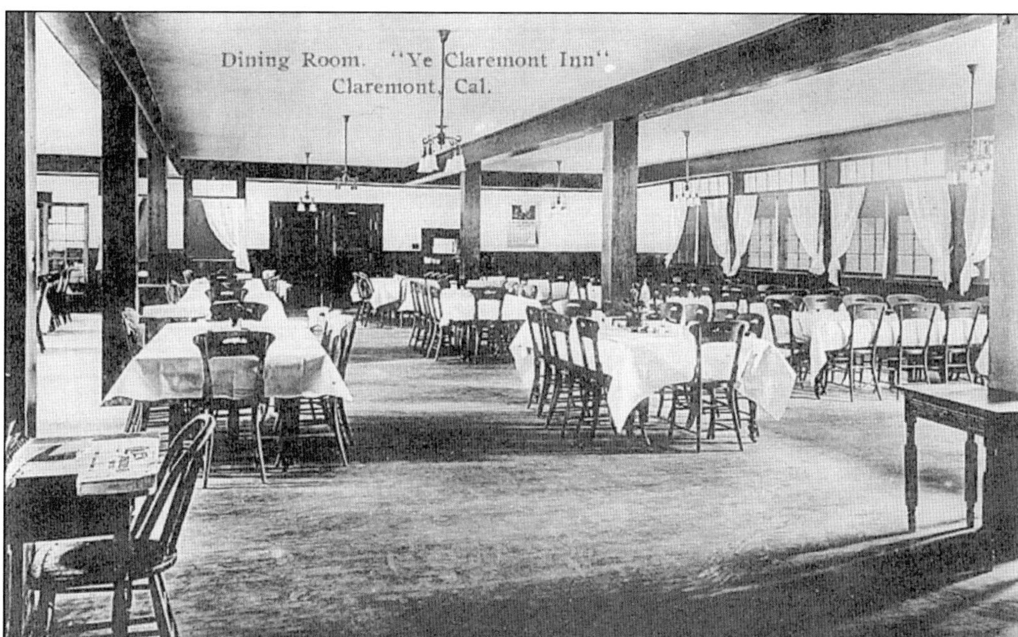

Dining Room, "Ye Claremont Inn," Claremont. Many meals were served for both campus and non-campus events in this dining room. (P/P: Published for College Book and Drug Store, Claremont.)

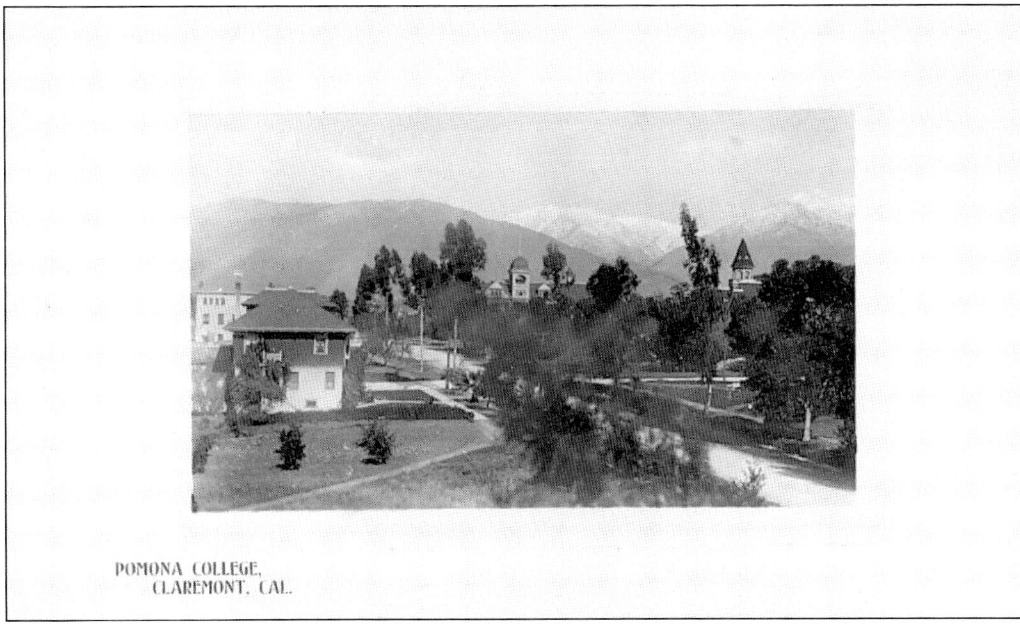

Pomona College, Claremont. (P/P: Newman Post Card Co., Los Angeles.)

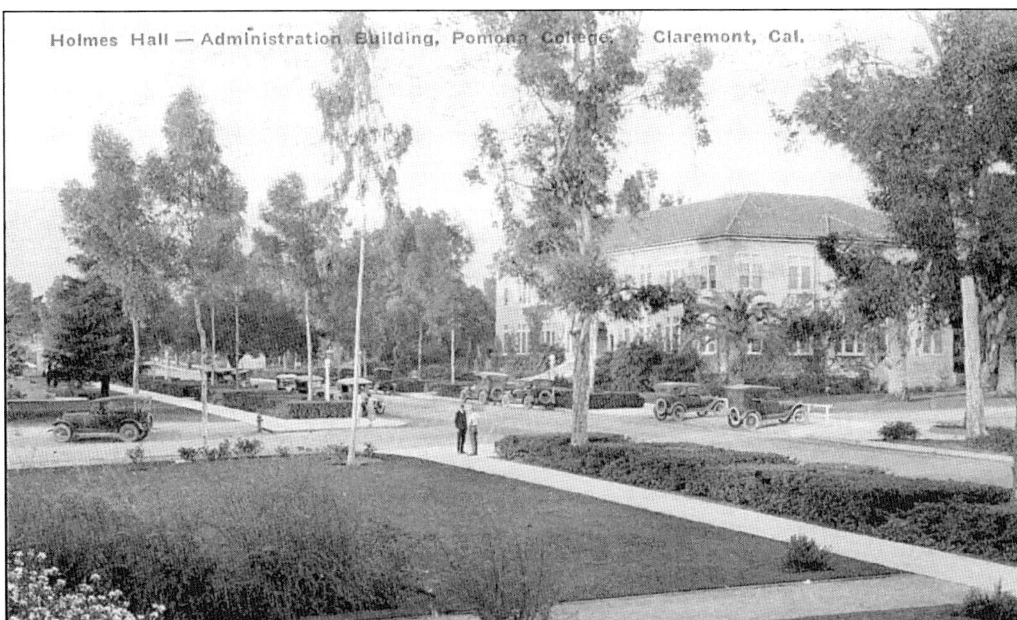

Holmes Hall-Administration Building. This building was constructed on the Pomona College campus in 1892. (P/P: Pomona College, Cooperative Bookstore, Claremont; Postcards of Quality, The Albertype Co., Brooklyn, New York.)

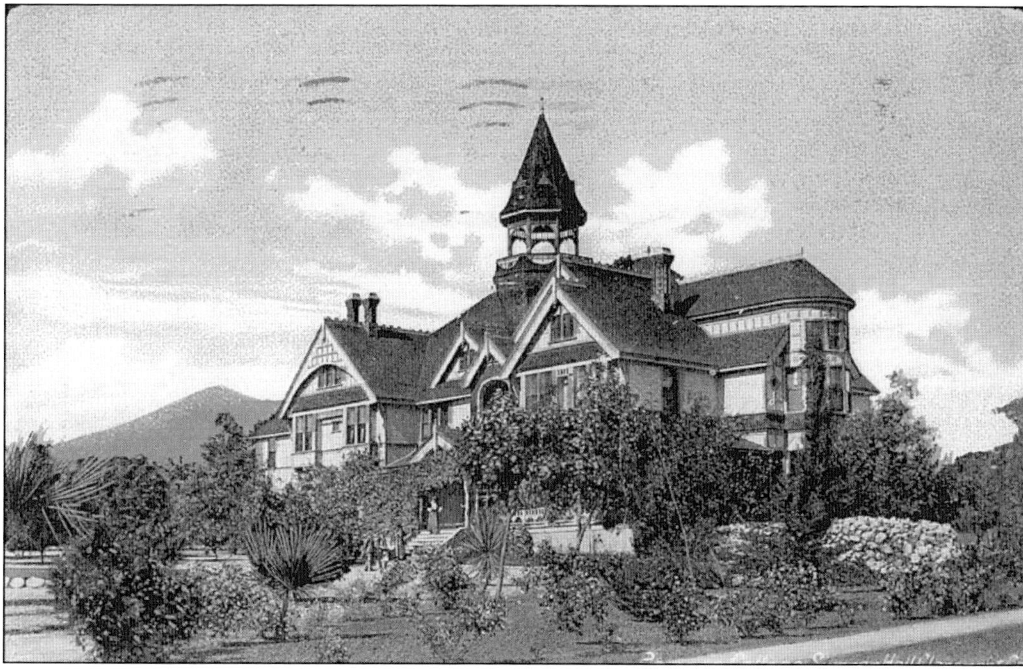

SUMNER HALL, POMONA COLLEGE, CLAREMONT. This building was originally a land boom hotel. (P/P: Newman Post Card Co., Los Angeles and Leipzig, No. 6001; made in Germany; postmark: May 1911.)

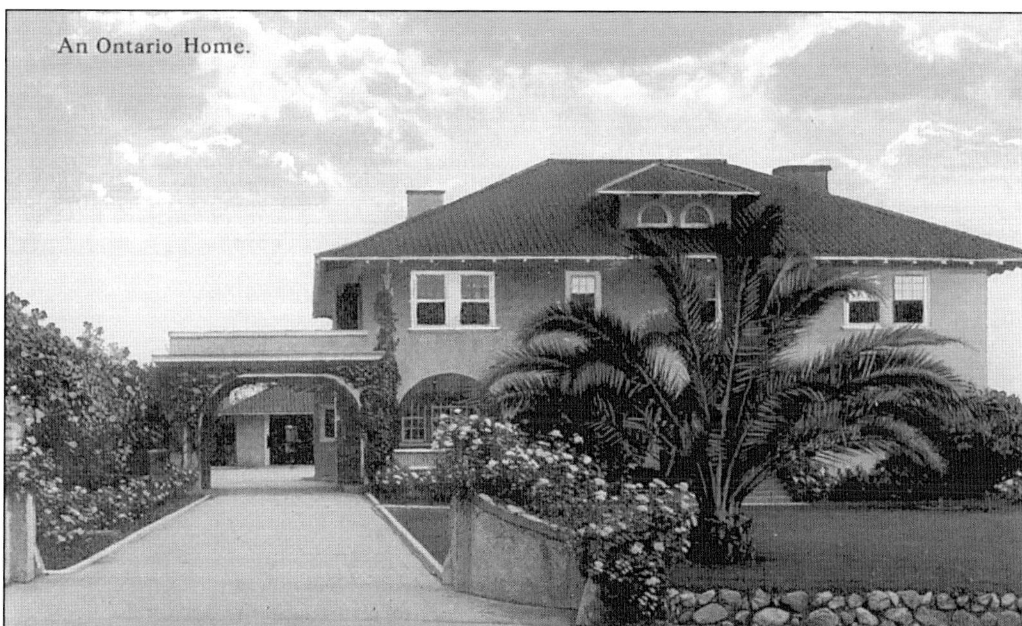

AN ONTARIO HOME. The printed text on the back reads, "I am writing from Ontario, Cal., a hustling city of commerce that is surrounded by the most beautiful California scenery. As far as you can see are great orange and lemon orchards." (P/P: C.T. Photochrome, No. A49810.)

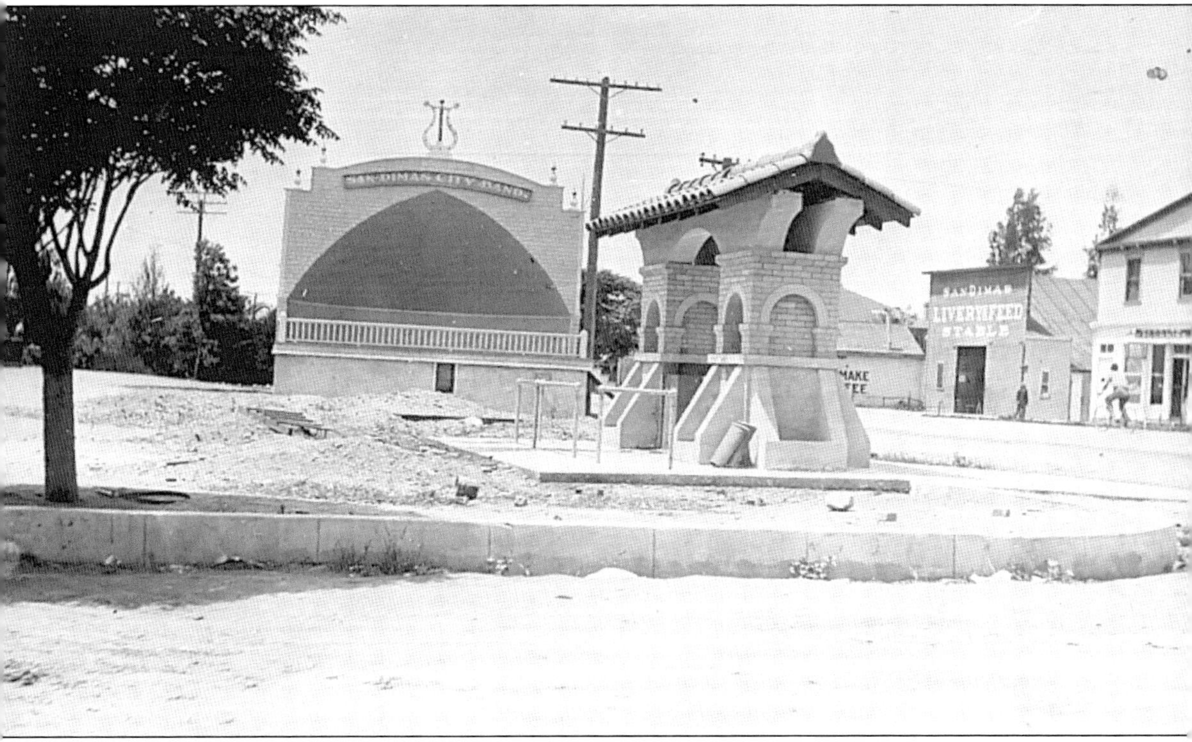

SAN DIMAS CITY BANDSTAND. The bandstand was built in 1911 between Bonita Avenue and the Santa Fe station. Once a band was organized, the community enjoyed Sunday evening concerts. (P/P: unknown; postmark: October 1913; card purchased in October 1998 in South Bend, Indiana.)

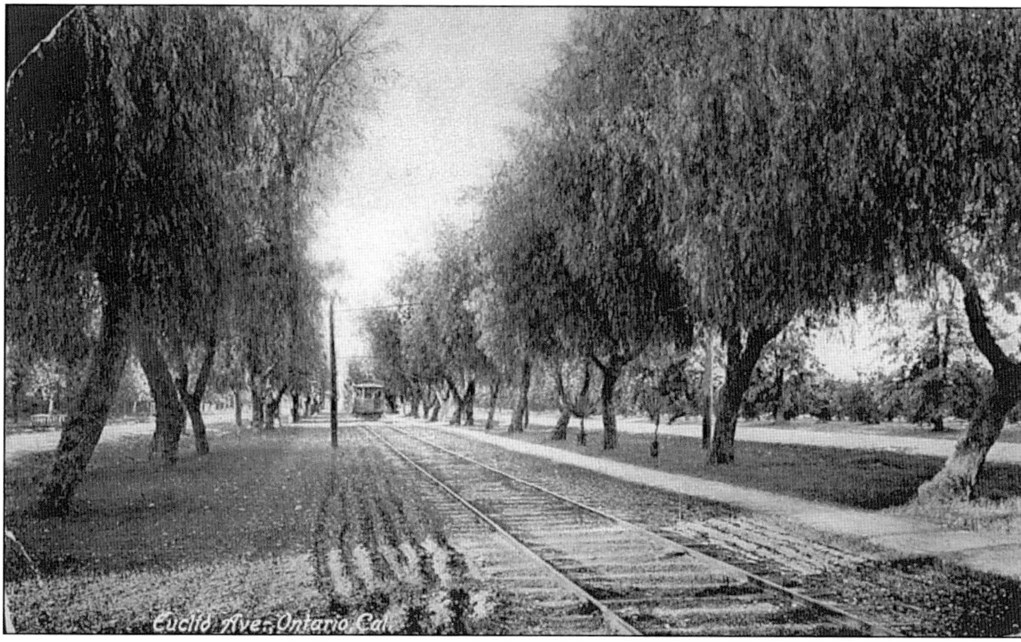

EUCLID AVENUE, ONTARIO. The printed text on the back reads, "Ontario is a thriving town. . . the main industry is raising oranges and almost $1,250,000 are shipped yearly. . ." (P/P: M. Rieder, Los Angeles, No. 4989; made in Germany.)

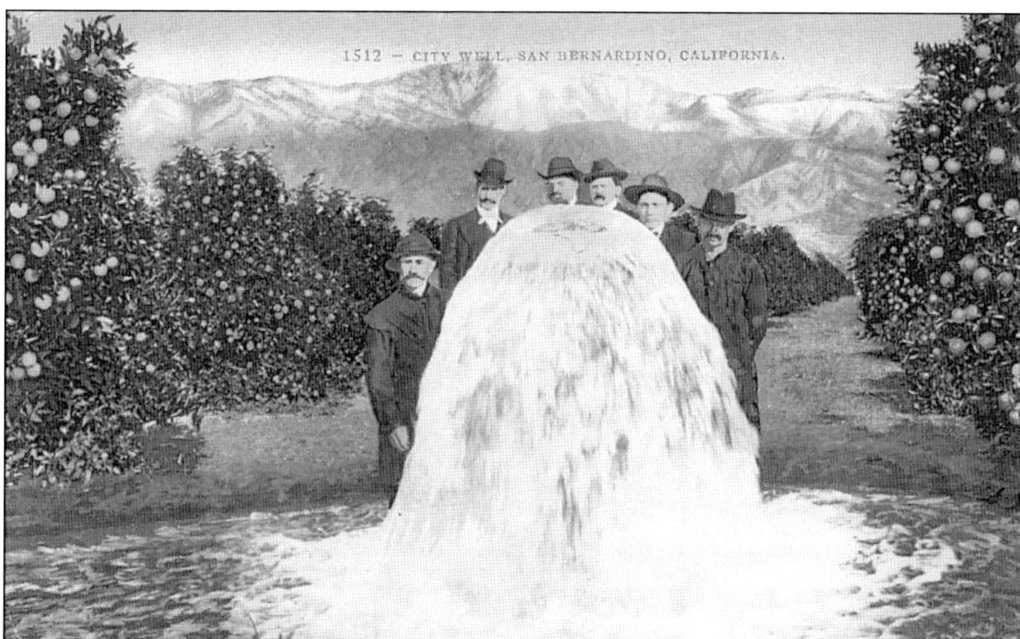

CITY WELL IN SAN BERNARDINO, CALIFORNIA. Sources of water were plentiful before the days of increased population. (P/P: Edward H. Mitchell, San Francisco, No. 1512; postmark: January 1911.)

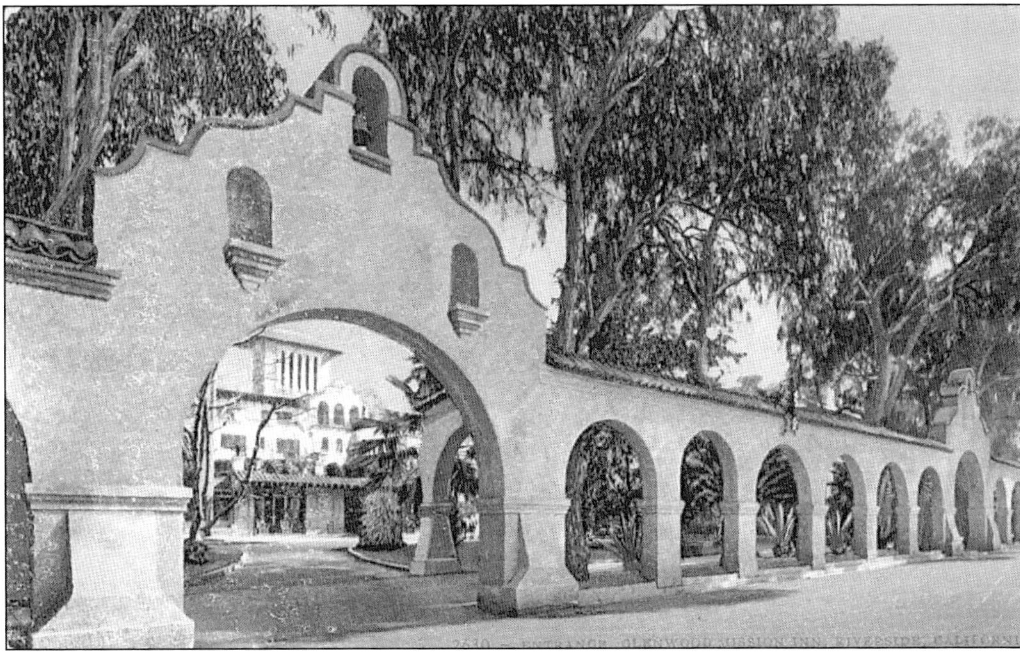

The Entrance to Glenwood, Mission Inn, Riverside, California. The Mission Inn is a showplace hotel in Southern California, following yet another renovation. (P/P: Edward H. Mitchell, San Francisco, No. 2630.)

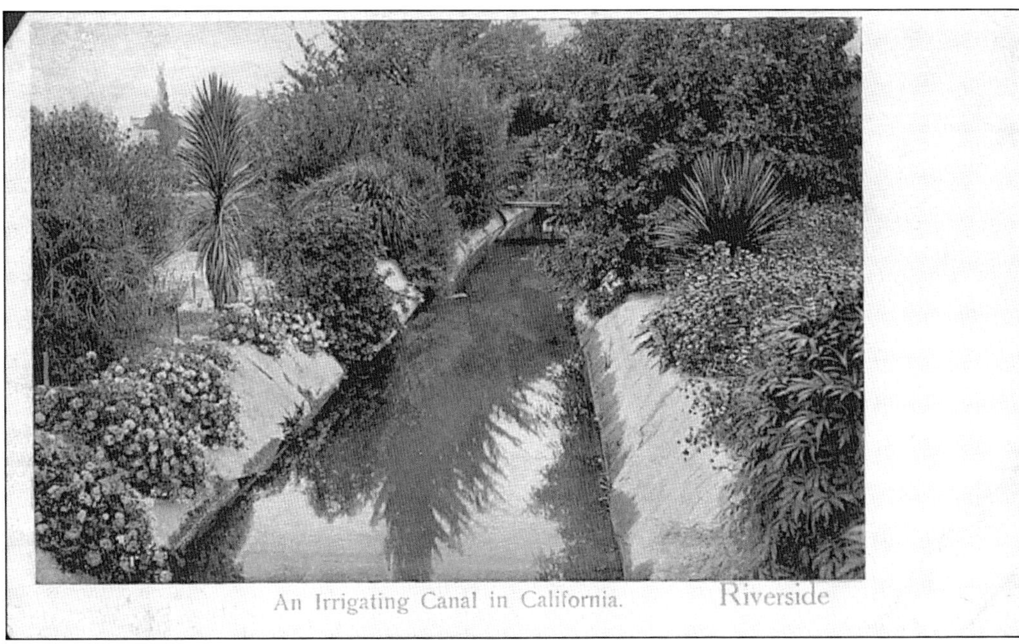

An Irrigating Canal in Riverside. California has always used multiple means of transporting water, due to low rainfall in most areas. The back side of this card was designated as exclusively for address. (P/P: M. Rieder, Los Angeles, No. 2; made in Germany.)

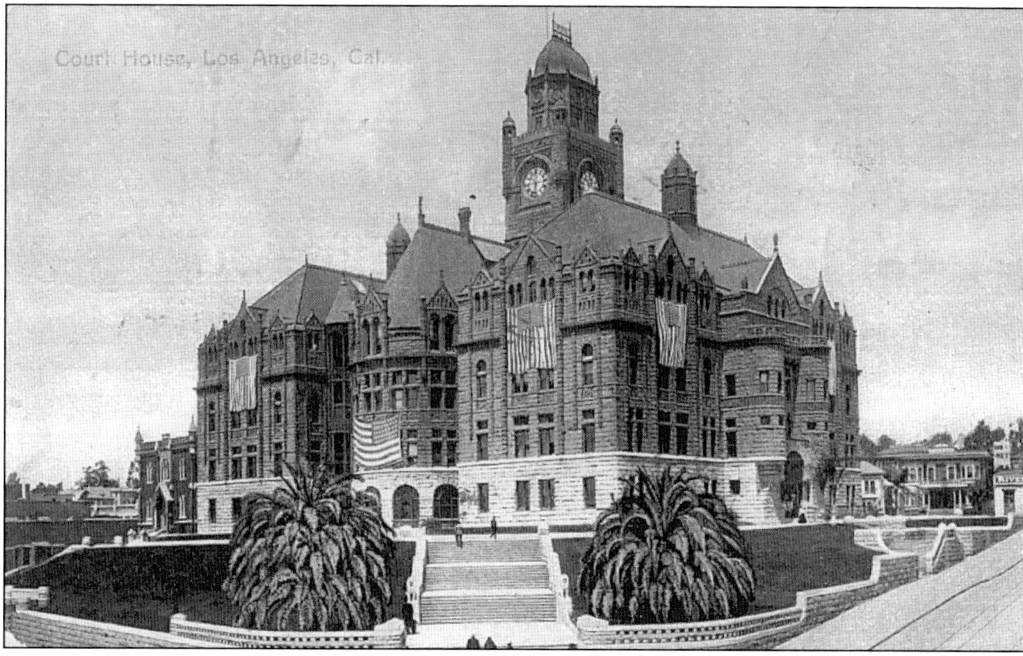

Los Angeles Courthouse. This example of early Los Angeles architecture has long since been lost to new development. (P/P: Newman Post Card Co., Los Angeles, No. 5269; made in Germany; postmark: August 1907.)

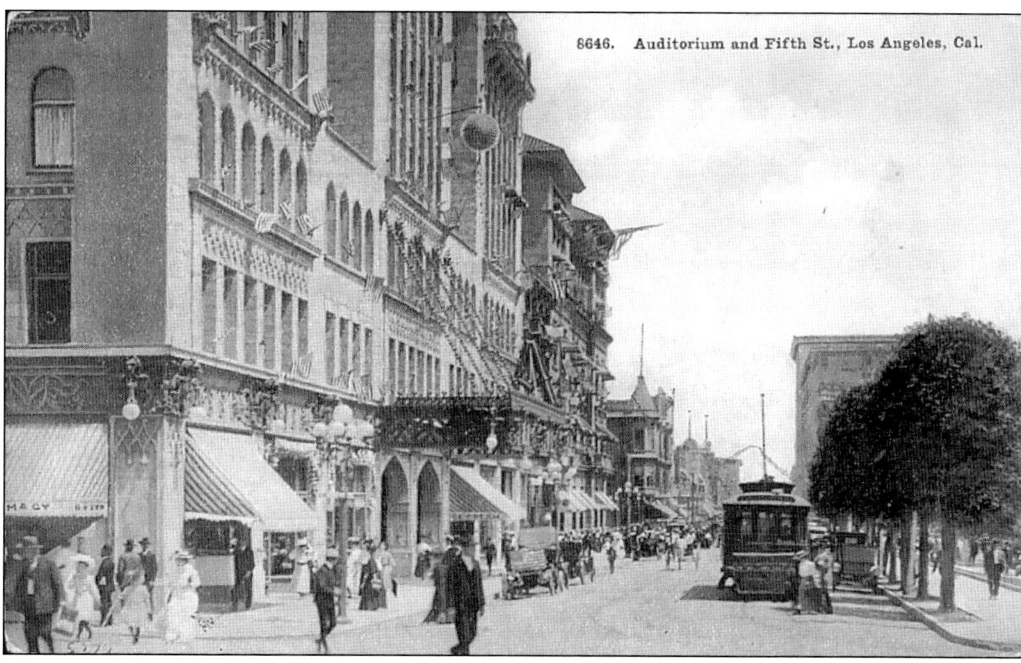

Auditorium and Fifth Street, Los Angeles. The Auditorium, home of Temple Baptist Church, was called, at one time, the world's largest congregation. "The services are unique and of special interest to tourists. The church itself is a great department store of Christian activities." (P/P: unknown.)

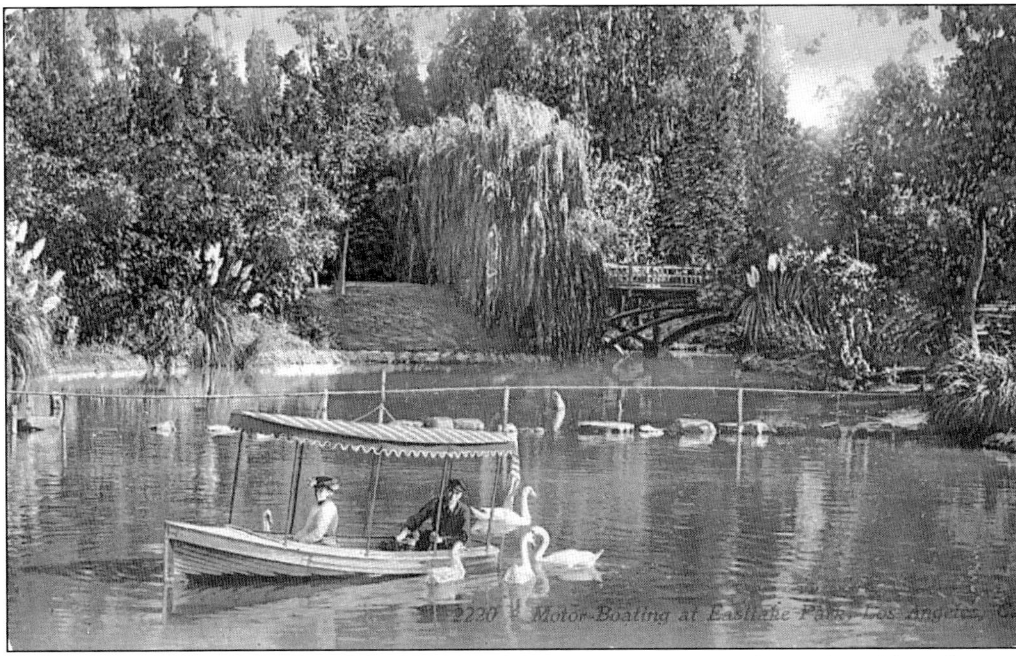

Motor-Boating at Eastlake Park, Los Angeles. Los Angeles parks, although some distance from Lordsburg/La Verne, provided opportunities for various types of entertainment to residents of towns to the east. (P/P: Edward H. Mitchell, San Francisco, No. 2220; postmark: December 1913.)

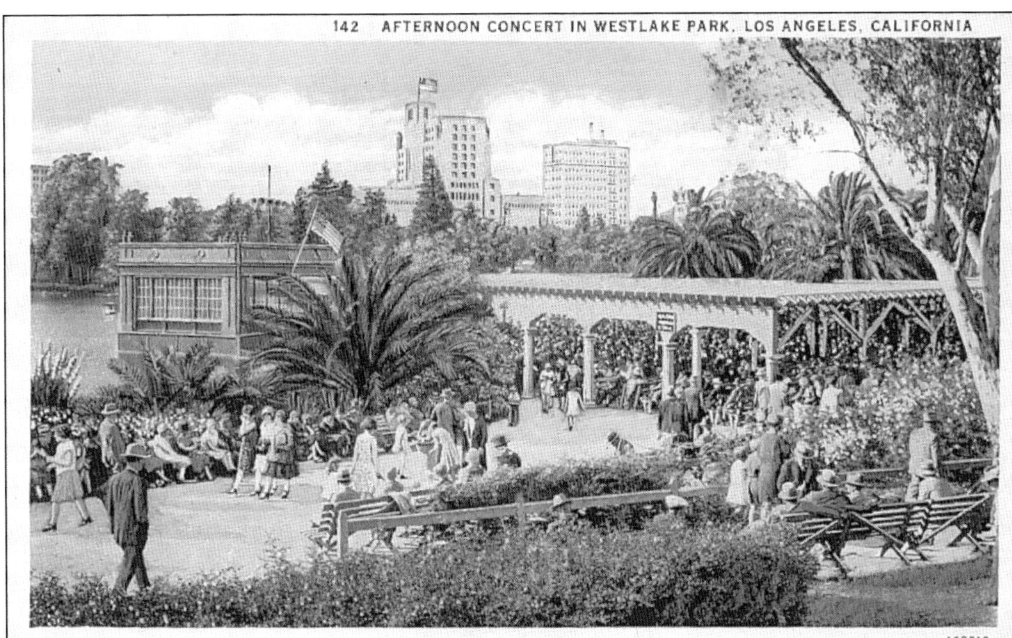

Afternoon Concert in Westlake Park, Los Angeles. (P/P: Western Publishing & Novelty Co., Los Angeles, No. 142.)

Eight

Venues of Entertainment

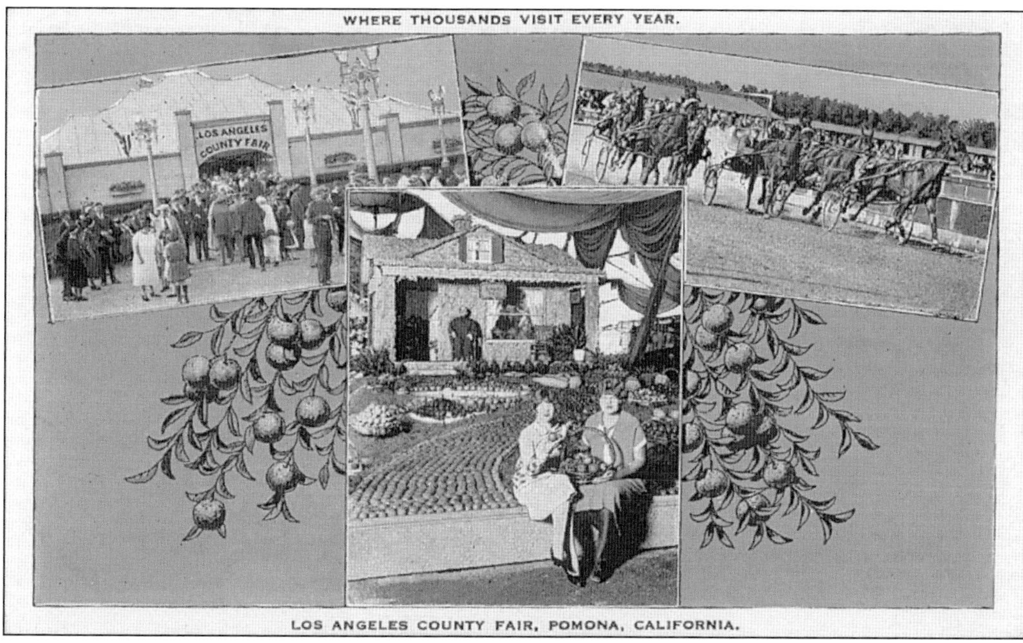

Los Angeles County Fair, Pomona. Thousands visit this fair every year. It is described as "the largest county fair in the west, situated in the heart of the richest agricultural section in the United States." (P/P: B.R. Montgomery, Riverside, No. 12057.)

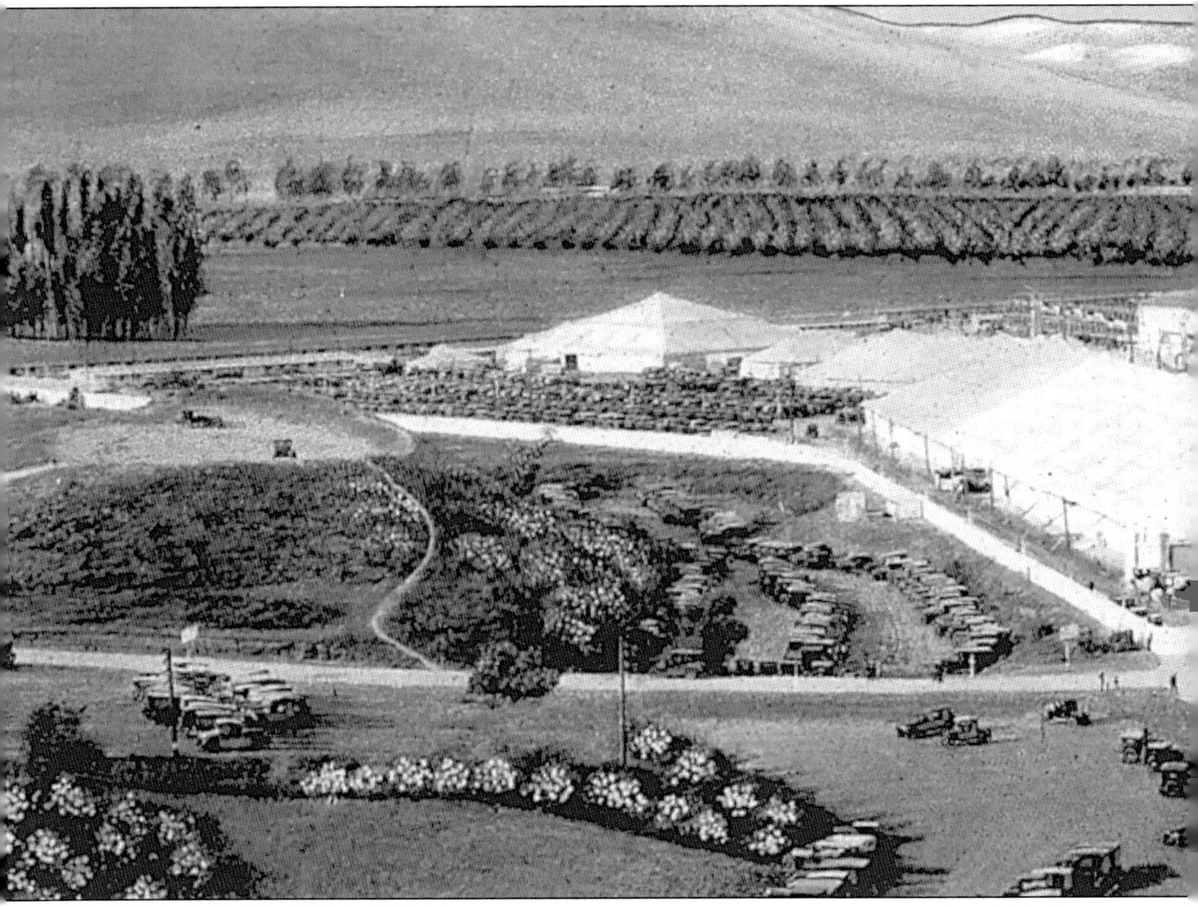

Los Angeles County Fair, Pomona, Cal., September 28–October 2, 1926, Fourth Year. According to the text on this card, "The Los Angeles County Fair, held every Fall at Pomona, California, is one of the best attended fairs in the West, visitors averaging over one hundred thousand. There are wonderful exhibits of live stock, poultry, rabbits, pigeons, agricultural and horticultural goods, affording pleasure and valuable suggestions. The fastest half-mile track on the Pacific Coast assures splendid racing and the night horse show is unexcelled. Women visitors say that the Art and Women's Work exhibit is the best in the land. Clean entertainment affords keen delight. To miss the Fair is to miss the Best Fair in the West." (P/P: B.R. Montgomery, Riverside; photo by Frasher, No. 12216.)

Opposite, Below: **Bird's-Eye View of L.A. County Fair, Pomona.** The city of La Verne is visible in the distance, immediately north of the Los Angeles County Fair grounds. Known today as the Fairplex, the fairgrounds are home to multiple interest activities throughout the year. (P/P: Frashers, Pomona.)

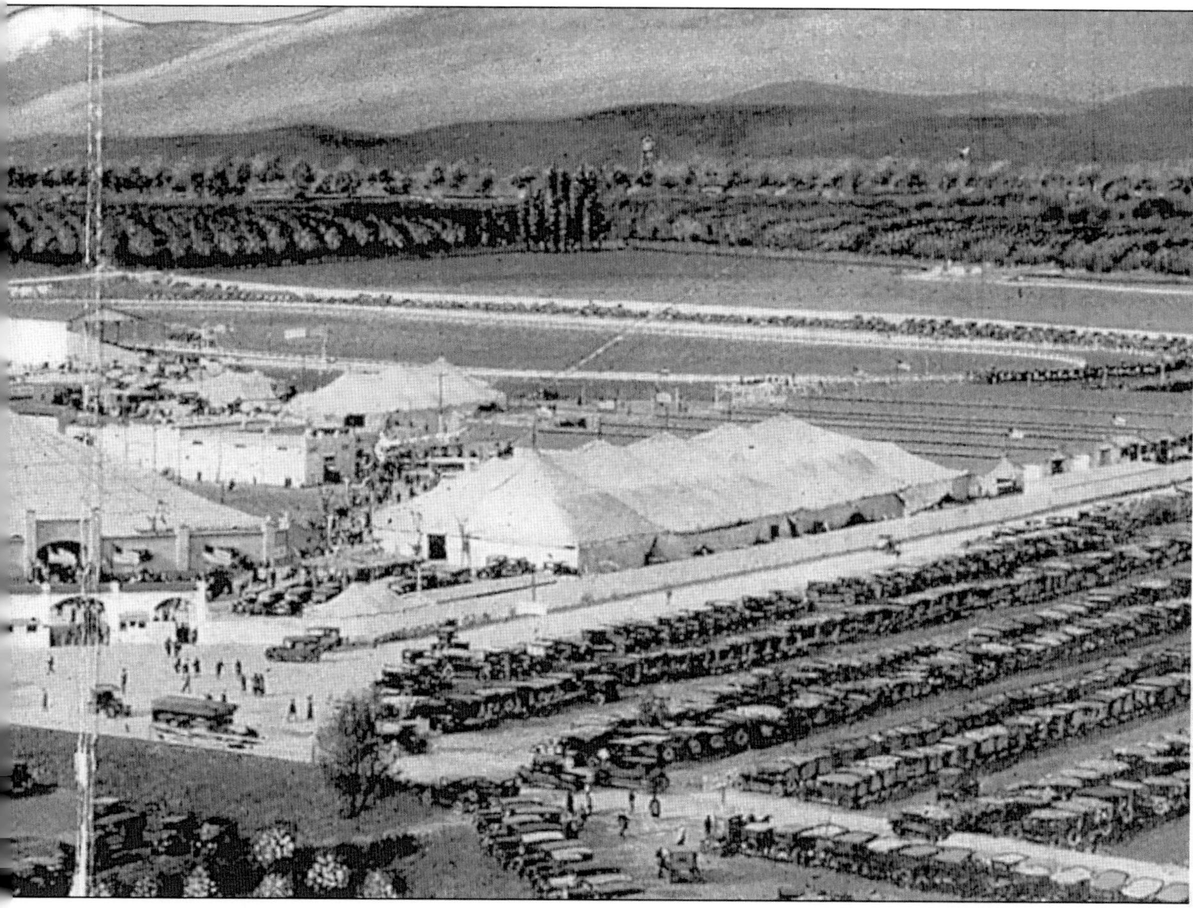

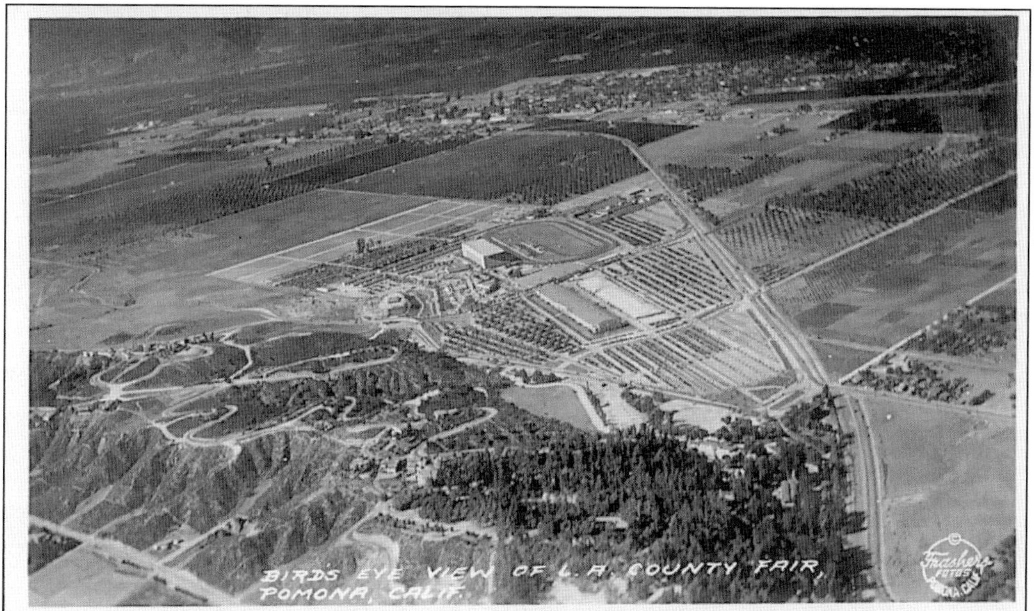
BIRD'S EYE VIEW OF L.A. COUNTY FAIR,
POMONA, CALIF.
Frasher Fotos

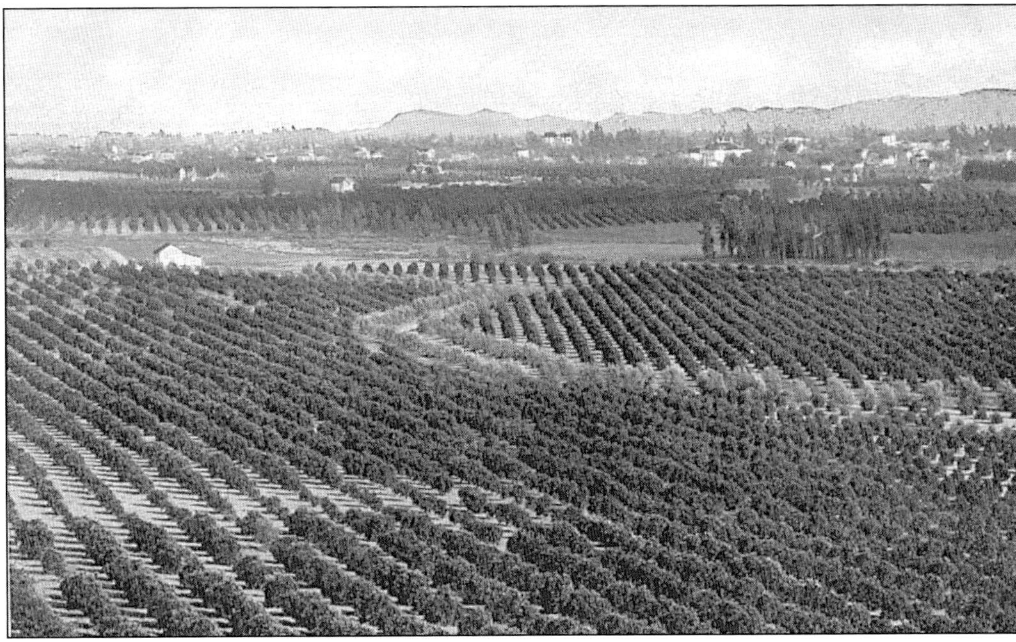

VIEW OF POMONA FROM THE ORANGE ORCHARDS. (P/P: M Rieder, Los Angeles, No. 4589; made in Germany.)

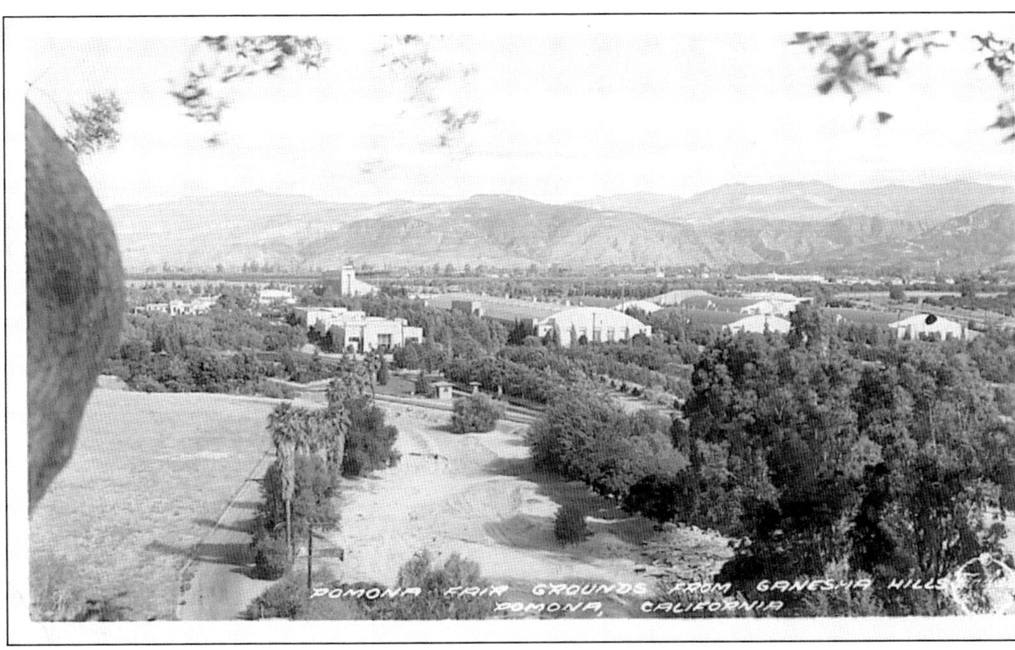

POMONA FAIR GROUNDS, FROM GANESHA HILLS IN POMONA. The sender wrote this message: "We stay in the one with the ink spot on and work in the one with the X on. The largest building in the picture burnt down the 28th of November." (P/P: Frashers, Pomona.)

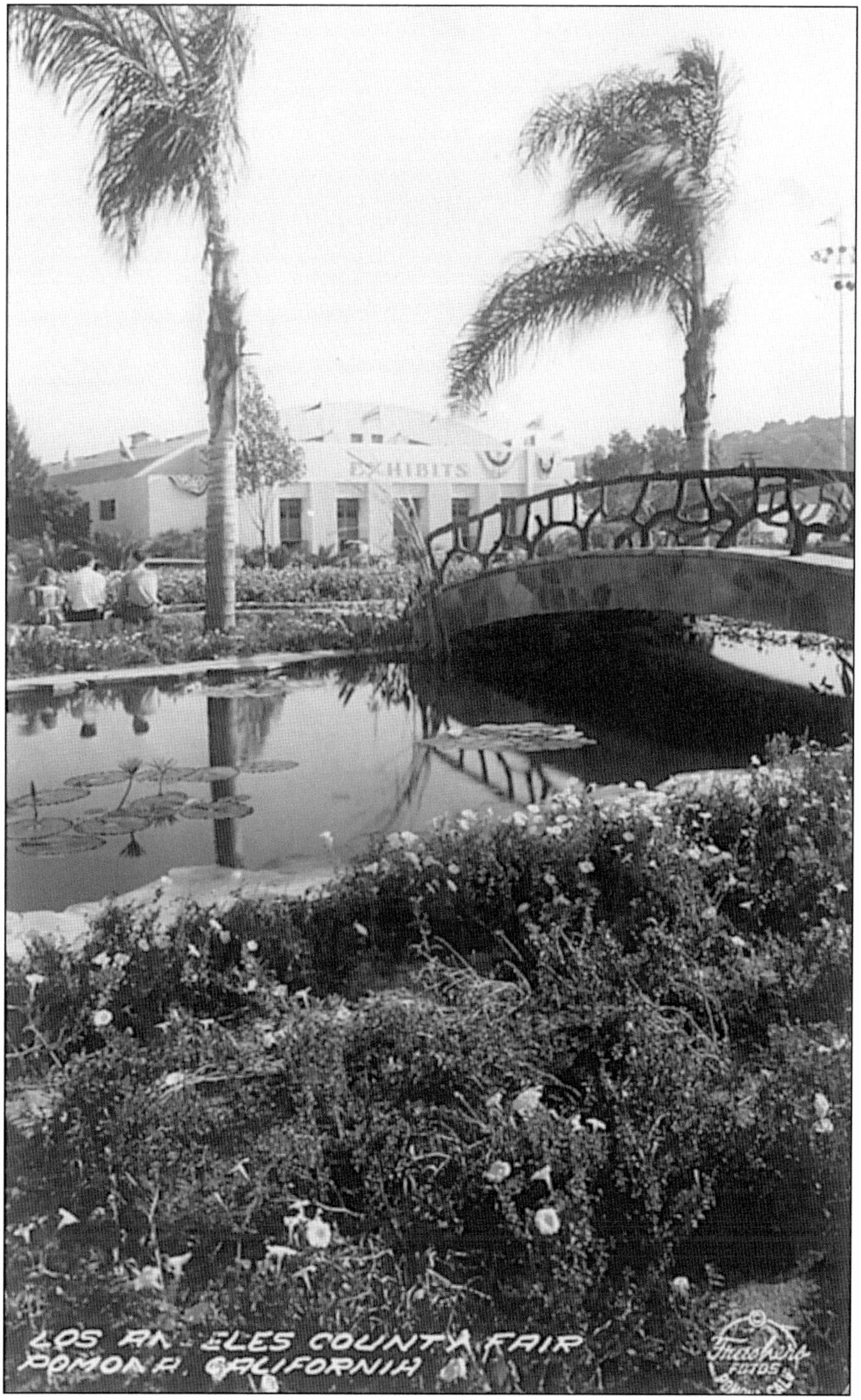

Los Angeles County Fair, Pomona. The back of the card reads, "This is the large building where the beautiful flowers were on exhibition, also, the large variety of fruits and vegetables." Six permanent buildings were constructed by Works Progress Administration in 1940. (P/P: Frashers, Pomona.)

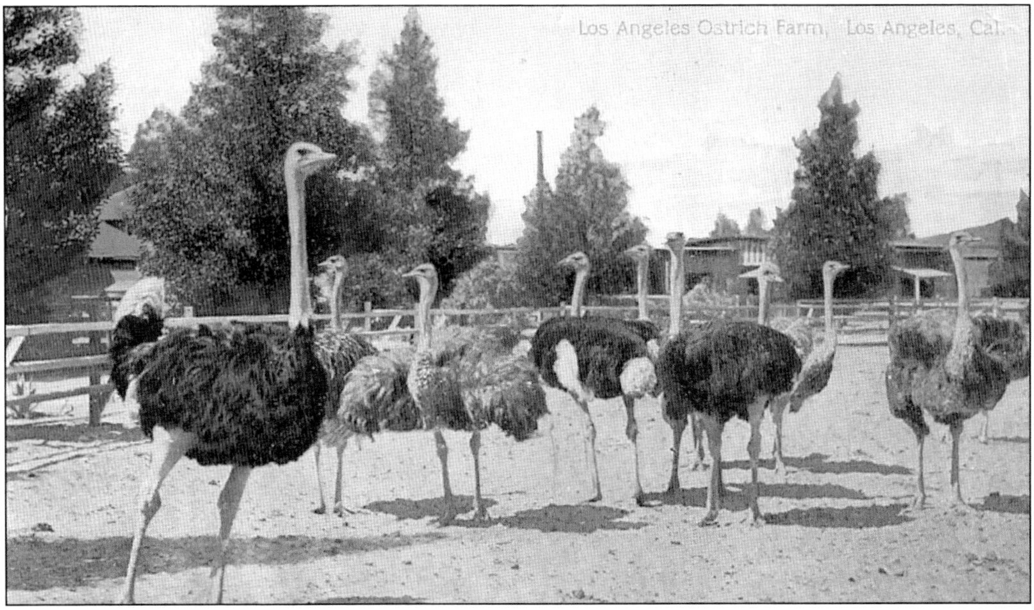

Los Angeles Ostrich Farm. This farm was one of a variety of entertainment venues where families enjoyed outings. Established *c.* 1887, Cawston's Ostrich Farm was in business for the feathers, and visits were an important additional source of income. (P/P: Newman Post Card Co., Los Angeles and San Francisco; "On the Road of a Thousand Wonders," No. A 21; postmark: October 1911.)

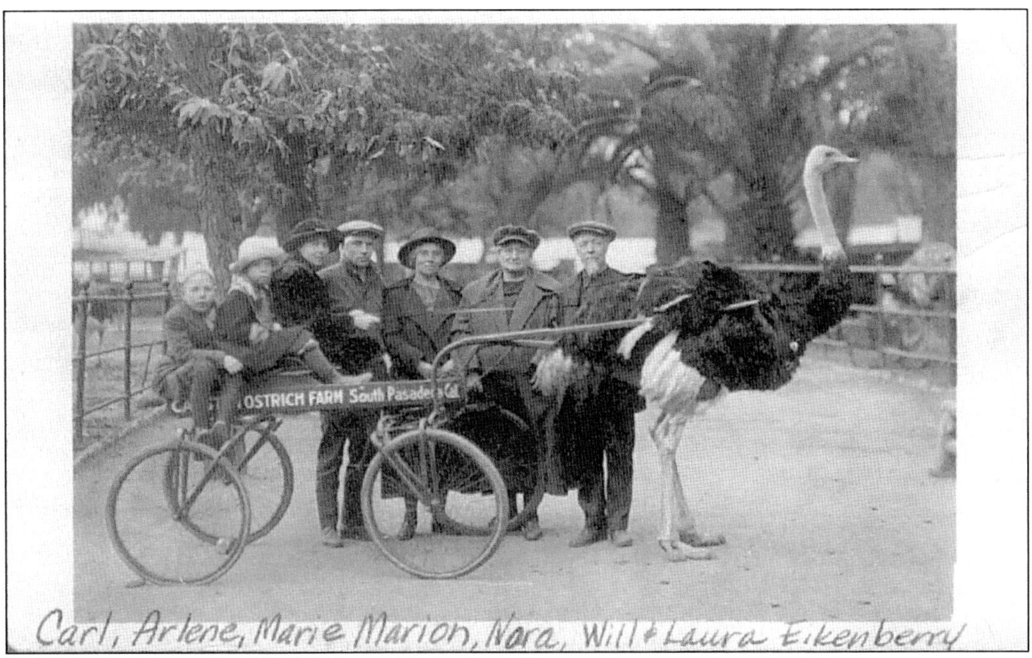

Cawston's Ostrich Farm, South Pasadena. A family visiting the ostrich farm is pictured. From left to right are Carl, Arlene, Marie, Marion, and Nora Roynon, with Will and Laura Eikenberry. (P/P: unknown; courtesy Roynon family album.)

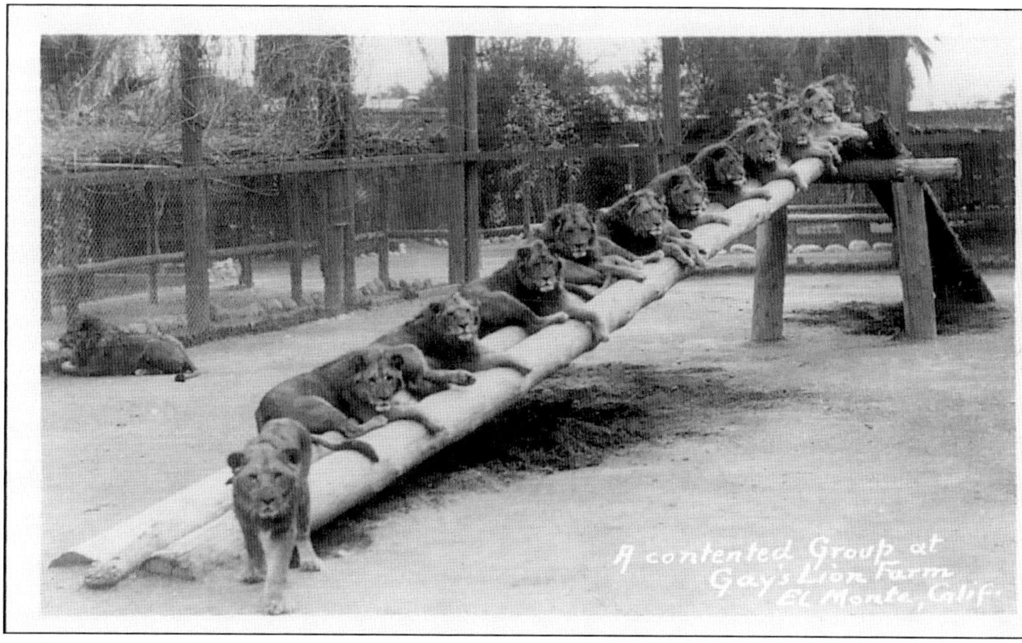

A Contented Group at Gay's Lion Farm, El Monte. In 1999, a small sign along the Metrolink track in El Monte identifies the former location of Gay's Lion Farm. (P/P: unknown.)

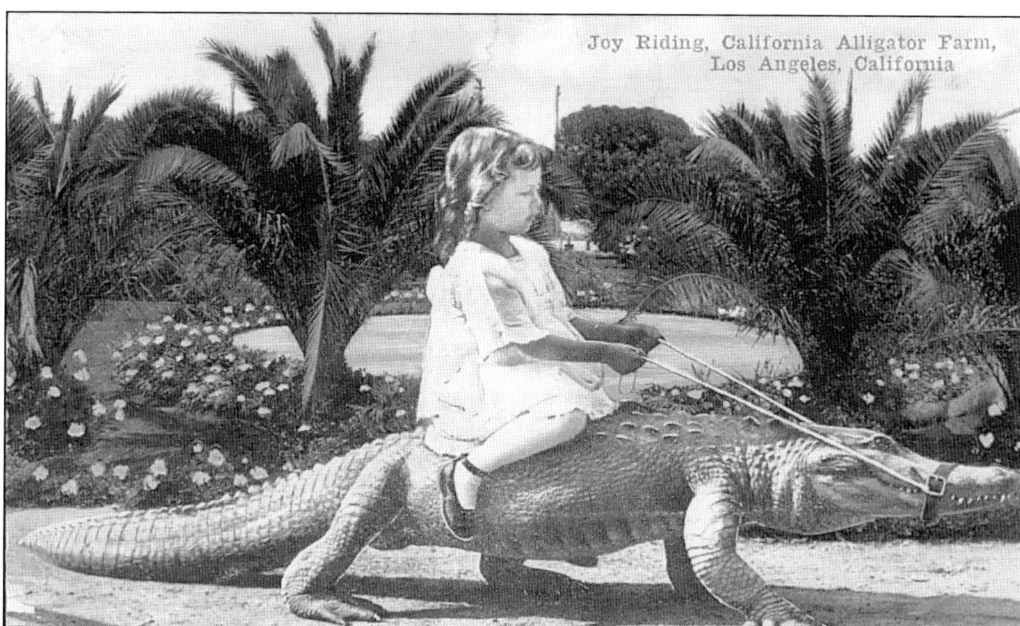

Joy Riding, Alligator Farm, Los Angeles. This card depicts another favorite family activity in nearby Buena Park. (P/P: Van Ornum Colorprint Co., Los Angeles, No. 558; postmark: April 1915.)

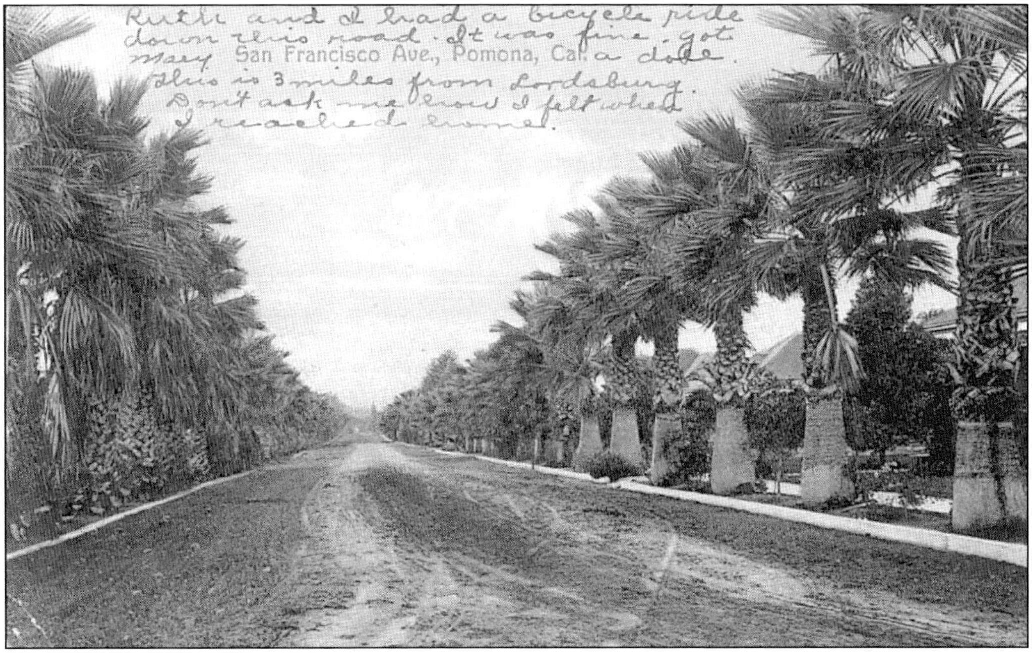

San Francisco Avenue, Pomona. The sender wrote, "Ruth & I had a bicycle ride down this road. It was fine. . . This is 3 miles from Lordsburg. Don't ask me how I felt when I reached home." (P/P: Newman Post Card Co., Los Angeles, No. 5434; made in Germany; postmark: May 1907.)

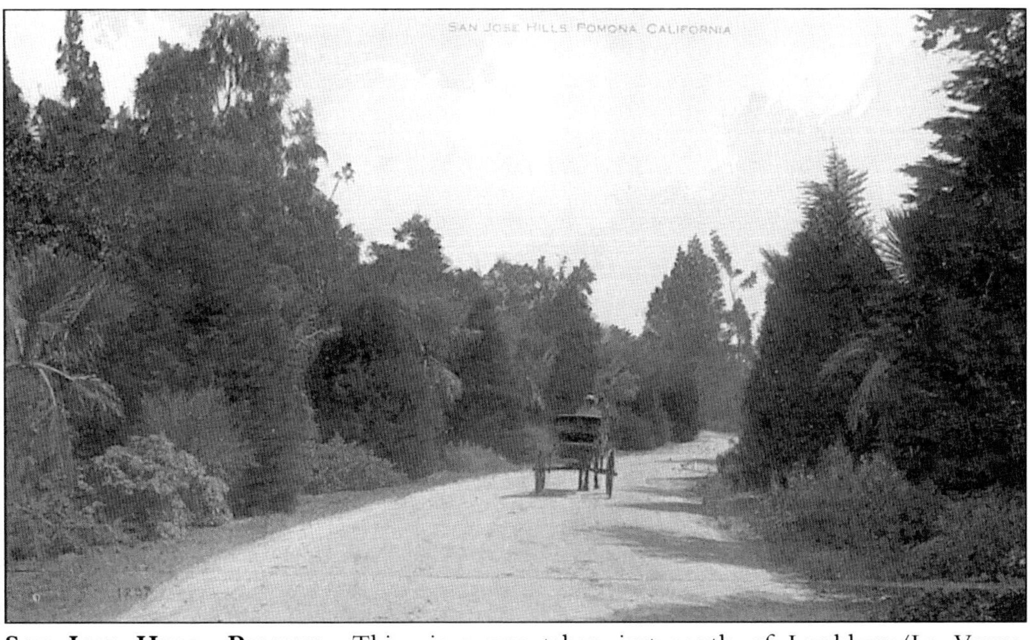

San Jose Hills, Pomona. This view was taken just south of Lordsburg/La Verne. The Los Angeles County Fairgrounds and Ganesha Park are both situated against the north and northeast sides of the San Jose Hills. (P/P: Benham Indian Trading Co., Los Angeles, No. 1257.)

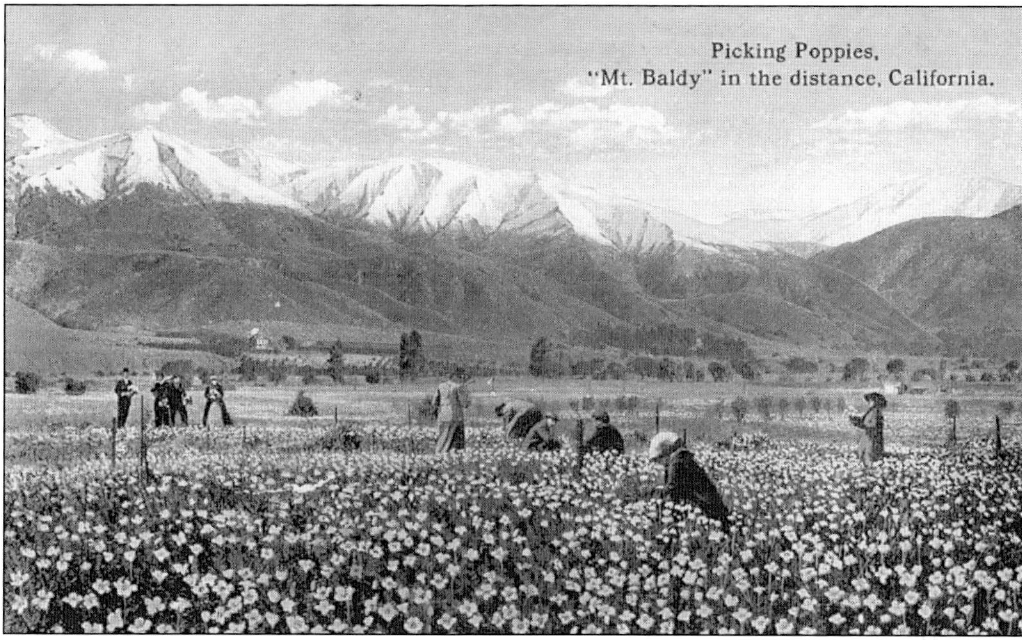

PICKING POPPIES, "MT. BALDY" IN THE DISTANCE. The printed text reads, "An interesting and beautiful sight, when the poppies are in bloom. Acres and acres will be a mass of golden yellow." The sender wrote, "Dear Lawrence, Your aunt Mary is having a great old time drinking water that tastes like bad eggs and bathing in hot water that cooked her." (P/P: Western Publishing & Novelty Co., Los Angeles, No. 508; made in Germany; postmark: November 1917.)

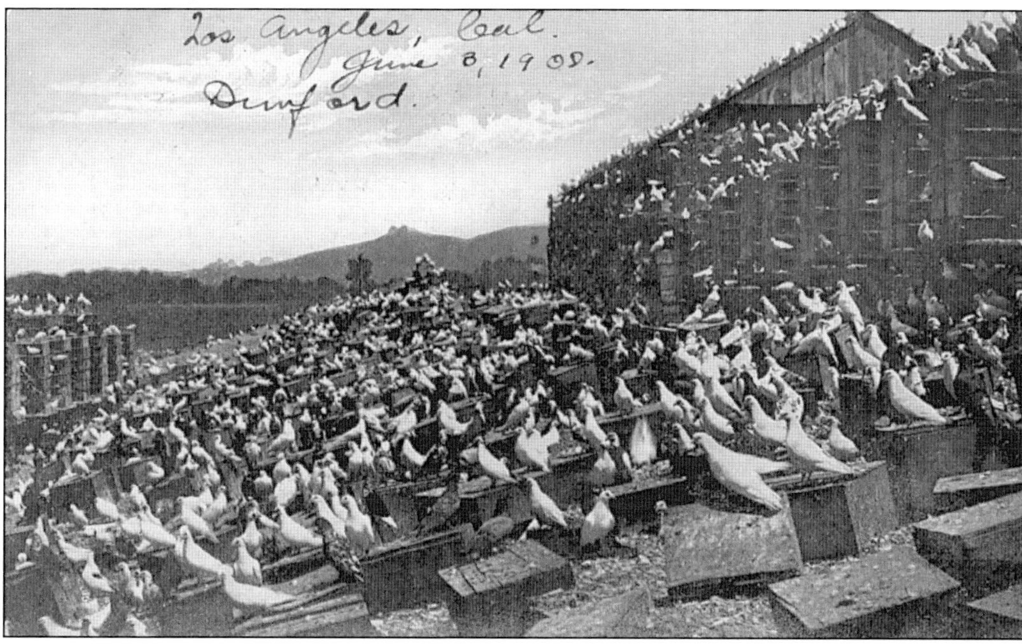

PIGEON FARM, LOS ANGELES. This farm is described as "one of the unique industries of California. It has over 100,000 birds. They consume three tons of wheat daily." (P/P: Benham Indian Trading Co, Los Angeles, No. 1004; postmark: June 1908.)

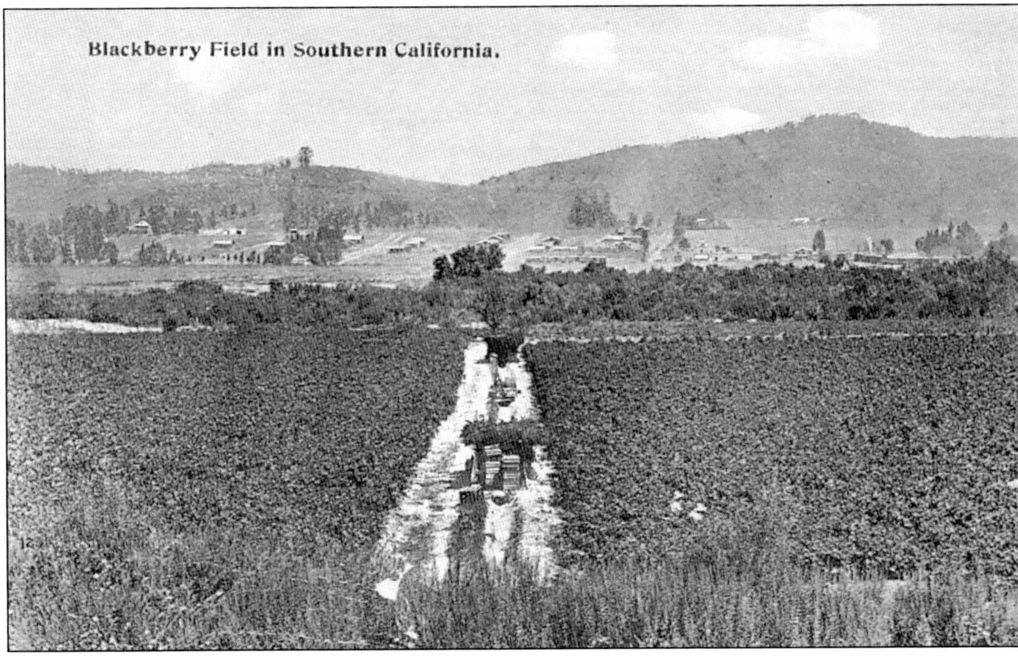

Blackberry Field in Southern California. According to longtime resident Stuart Wheeler, Dr. E. Henderson and Son operated the Park View Rancho, growing berries north of the San Jose Hills, south of Lordsburg. (P/P: Western Publishing & Novelty Co., Los Angeles.)

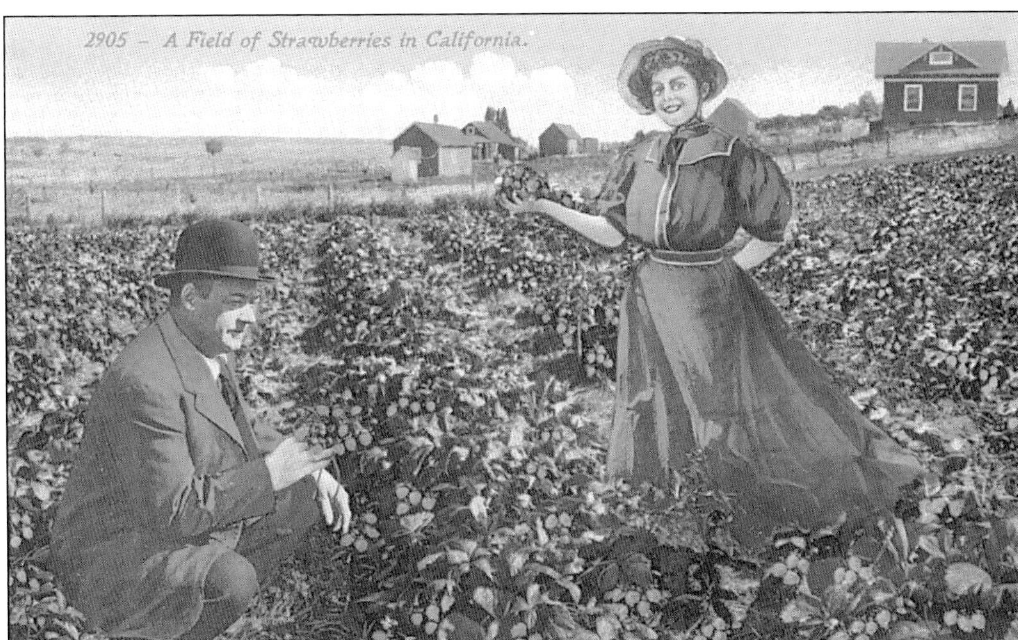

A Field of Strawberries. Strawberries are still grown in the area, but many of the fields have given way to development just like the citrus groves before them. (P/P: Edward H. Mitchell, San Francisco, No. 2905.)

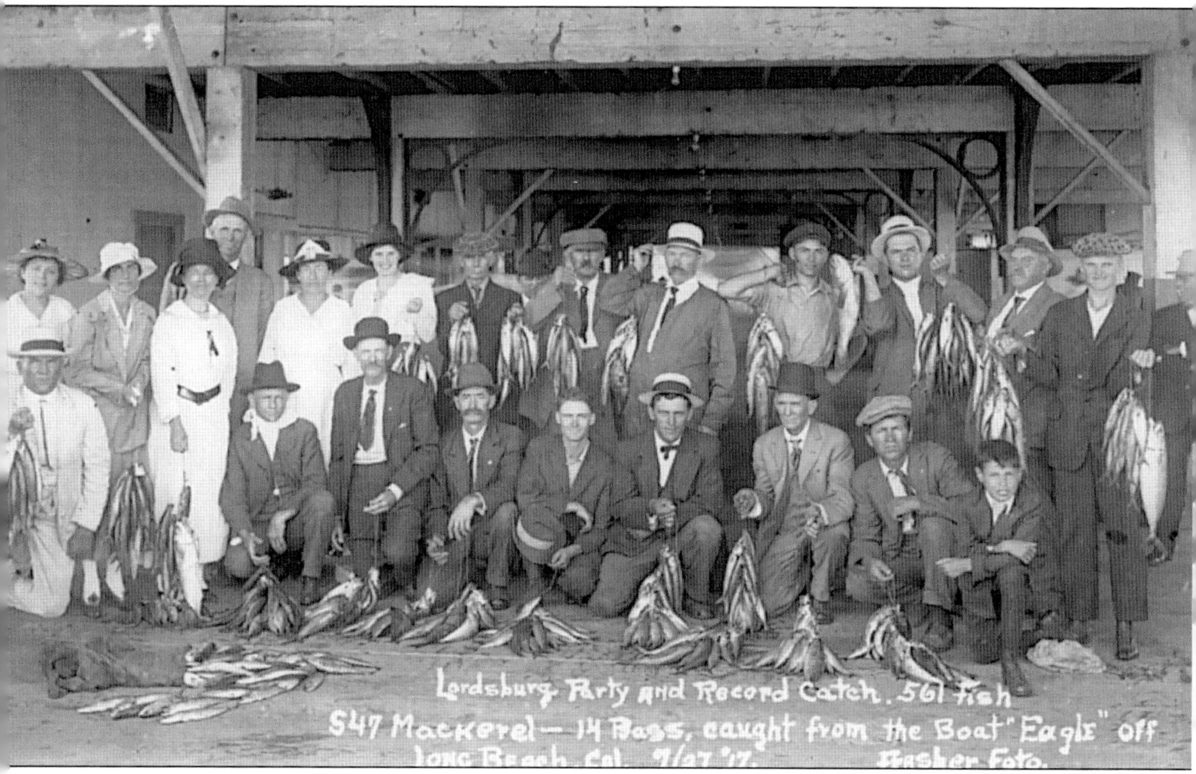

A RECORD CATCH ON THE *EAGLE* OUT OF LONG BEACH, 1917. Twenty-three Lordsburg residents and friends caught a record of 561 fish—547 mackerel and 14 bass—on July 27, 1917. The party was composed of Henry Hall, Mr. and Mrs. Burton Frasher, J.S. Bunch, C.A. Arnold, O.E. Haines, George Silvey, Clifford Moore, Lloyd Moore, Wellington Green, Mr. and Mrs. W.S. Romick, Lois Straight, Geo. Cross, J.S. Mills, J.W. Romick, O.S. Jewett, E.E. Clark and son (from Claremont), Mr. and Mrs. J.S. Fairfield (from Guthrie, OK), and J.E. Douglass and his daughter, Miss Ethel (also from Guthrie). (P/P: Frasher; courtesy University of La Verne, Wilson Library Archives.)

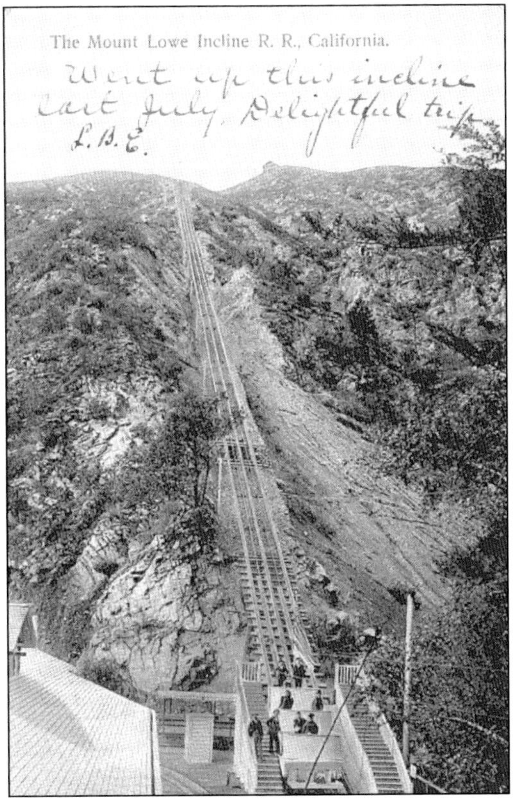

The Mount Lowe Incline RR, California. One railroad advertisement called this "a trolley trip to cloudland." (P/P: M. Rieder, Los Angeles, No. 3028; made in Germany; undivided back.)

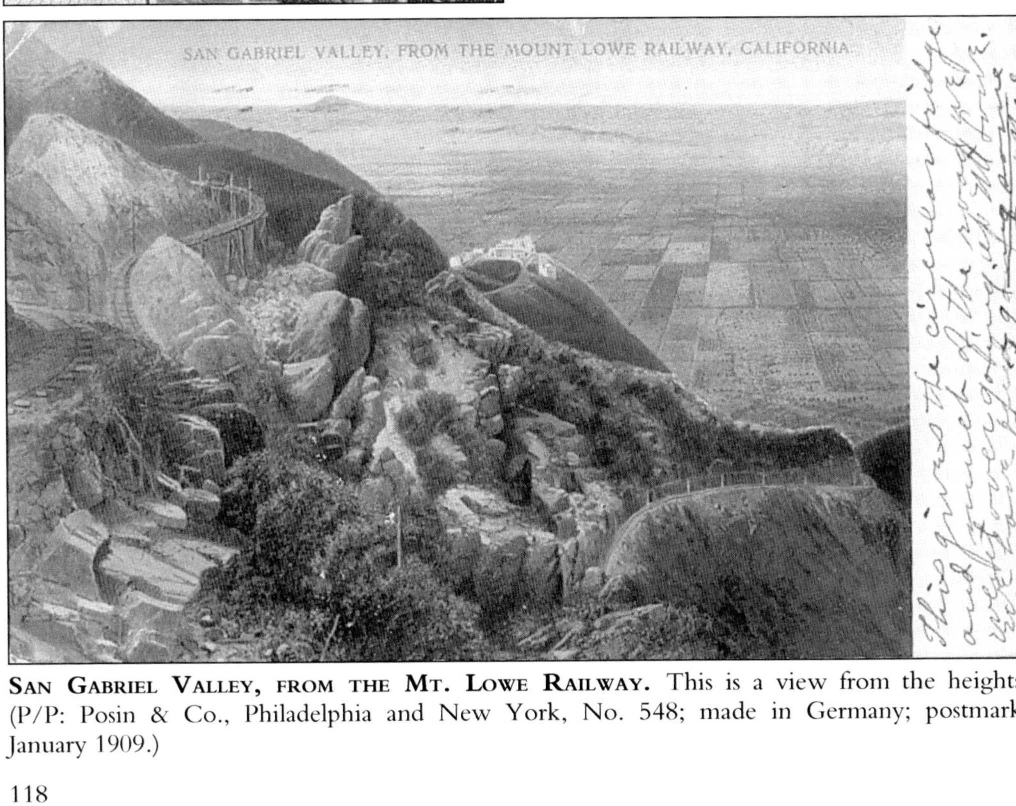

San Gabriel Valley, from the Mt. Lowe Railway. This is a view from the heights. (P/P: Posin & Co., Philadelphia and New York, No. 548; made in Germany; postmark: January 1909.)

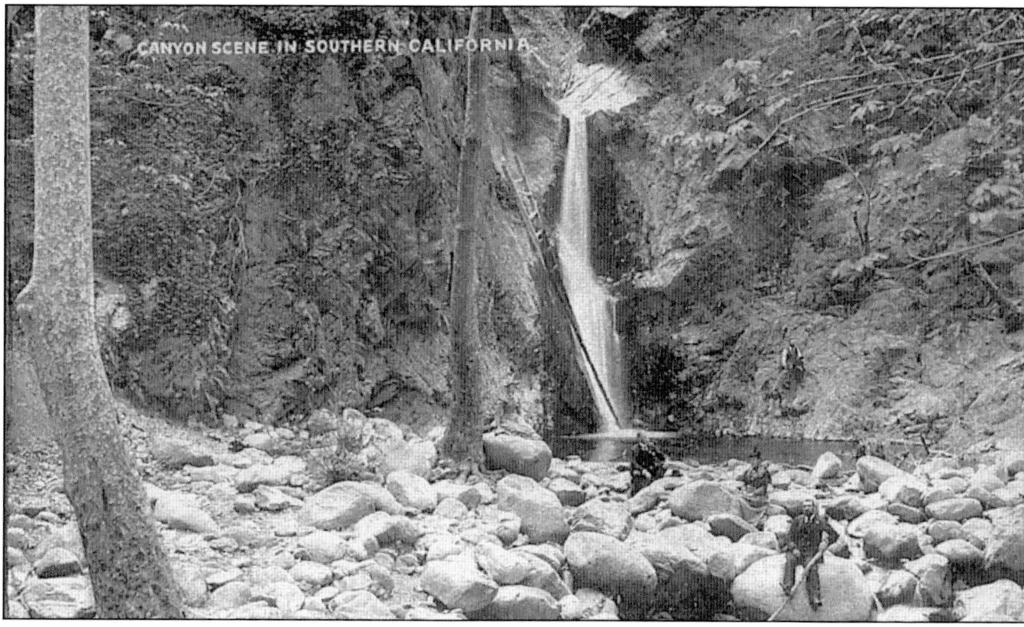

CANYON SCENE IN SOUTHERN CALIFORNIA. (P/P: M. Rieder, Los Angeles; "On the Road of a Thousand Wonders," No. B 25.)

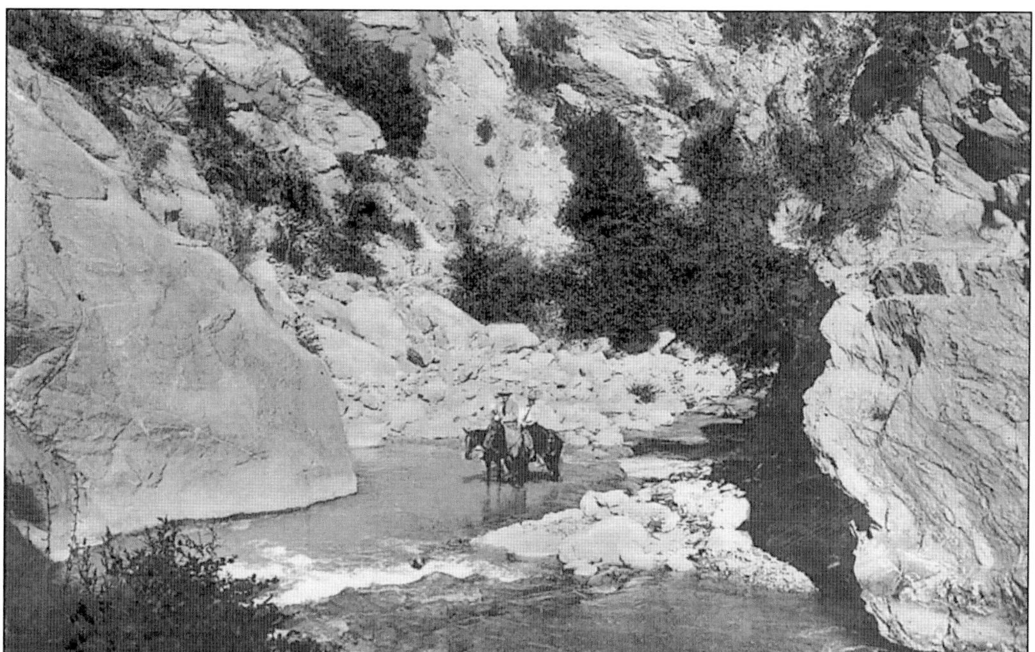

SAN GABRIEL CANYON. Nearby mountains and canyons have provided an easy access to the beautiful out of doors for many Southern Californians over the years. (P/P: M. Rieder, Los Angeles, No. 20130; made in Germany.)

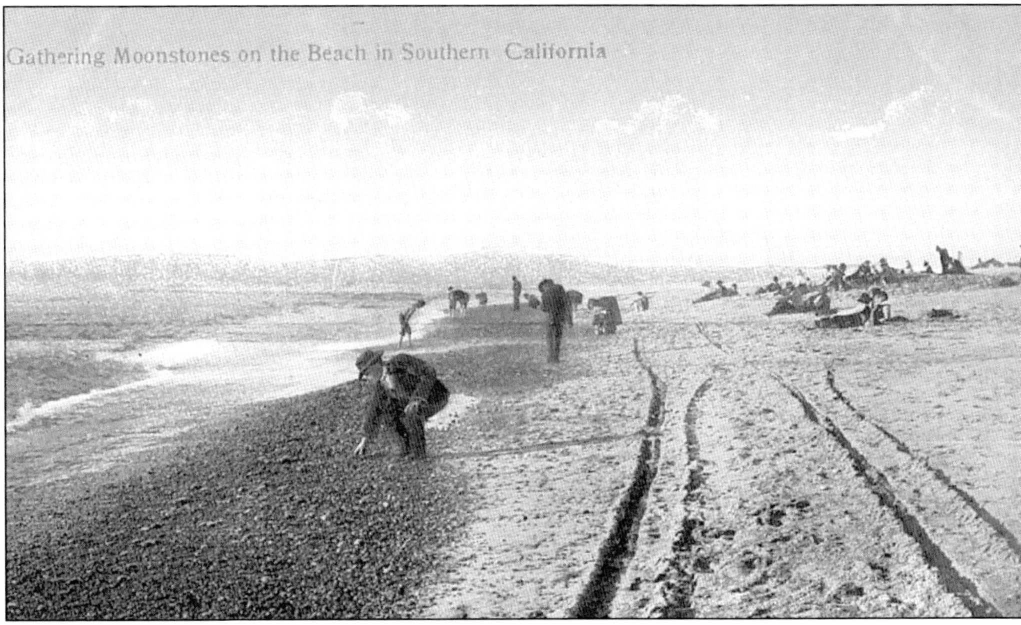

Gathering Moonstones on the Beach in Southern California. Who can resist picking up a stone or a shell while beachcombing? Today's participants in this activity are not as formally attired. (P/P: M. Rieder, Los Angeles, No. D 17.)

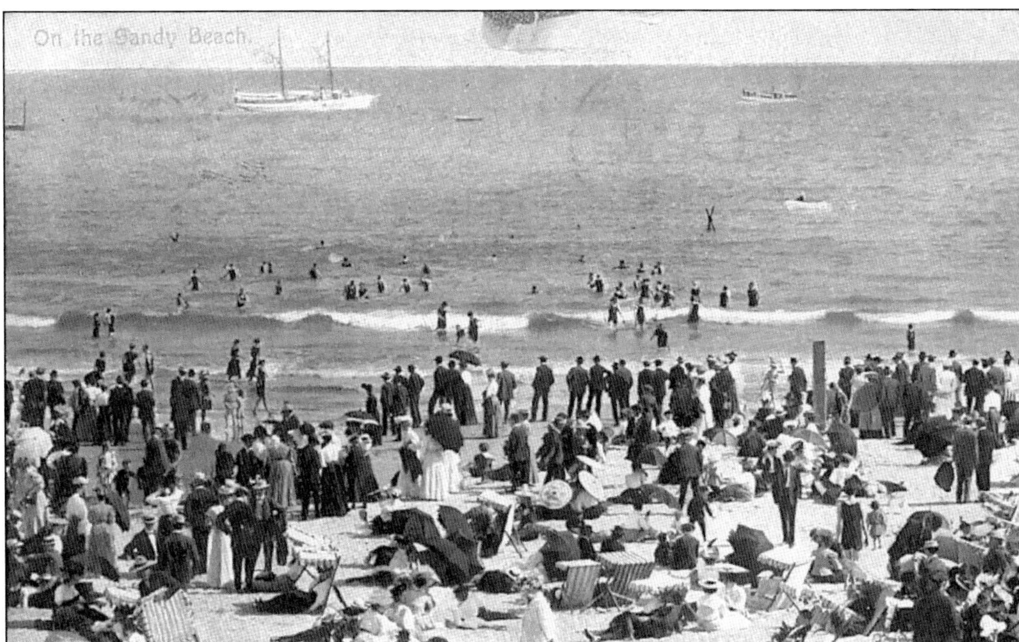

On the Sandy Beach. There is not too much danger of overexposure to the sun for most of those in this picture. (P/P: Newman Post Card Co., Los Angeles, No. D 12; made in Germany; postmark: September 1909.)

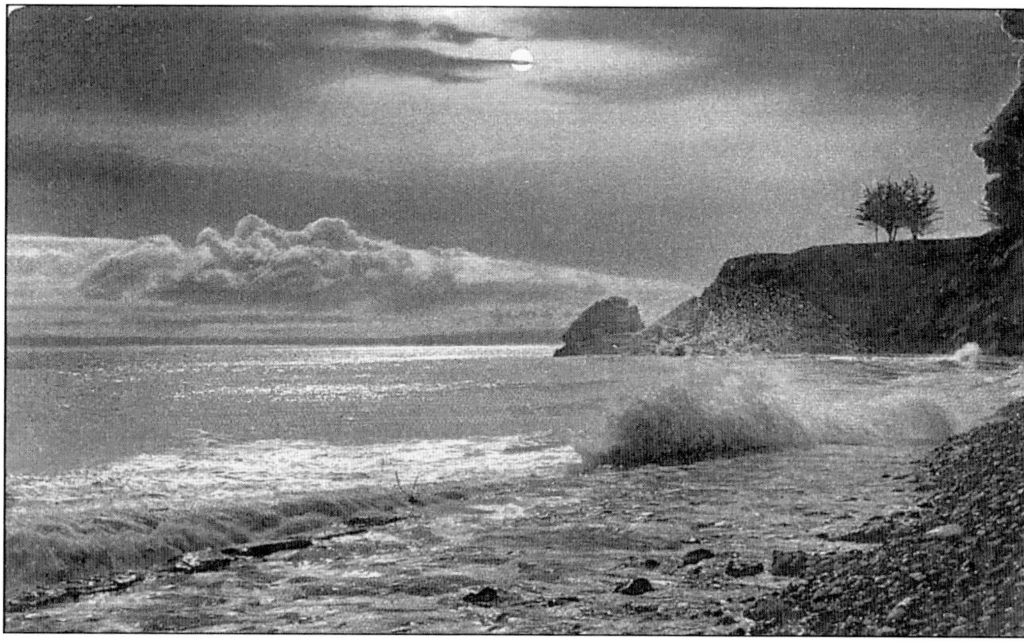

THE SURF BY MOONLIGHT, PACIFIC COAST. This postcard captures a moonlight view of another favorite California place, the Pacific Ocean. (P/P: M. Rieder, Los Angeles, No. 4495; made in Germany.)

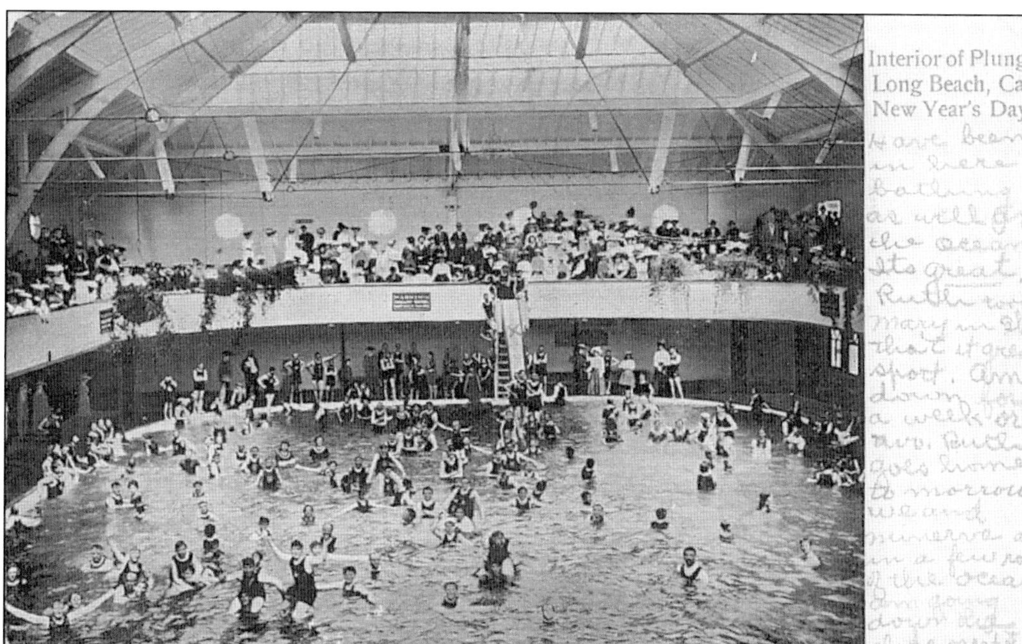

INTERIOR OF PLUNGE, LONG BEACH, NEW YEAR'S DAY. The sender wrote this message: "Have been in here bathing as well as the ocean. It's great." (P/P: M. Rieder, Los Angeles, No. 3326; made in Germany; postmark: June 1907.)

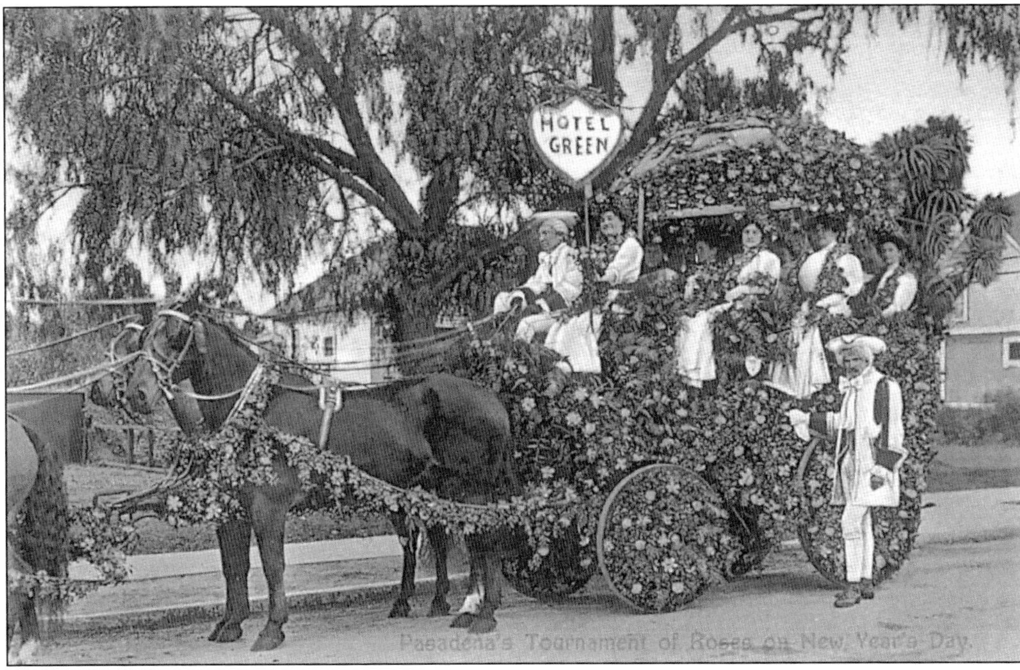

Pasadena's Tournament of Roses on New Year's Day. Before the days of television, this is how images of the Rose Parade were shared across the country. (P/P: Newman Post Card Co., Los Angeles, No. B 112; made in Germany.)

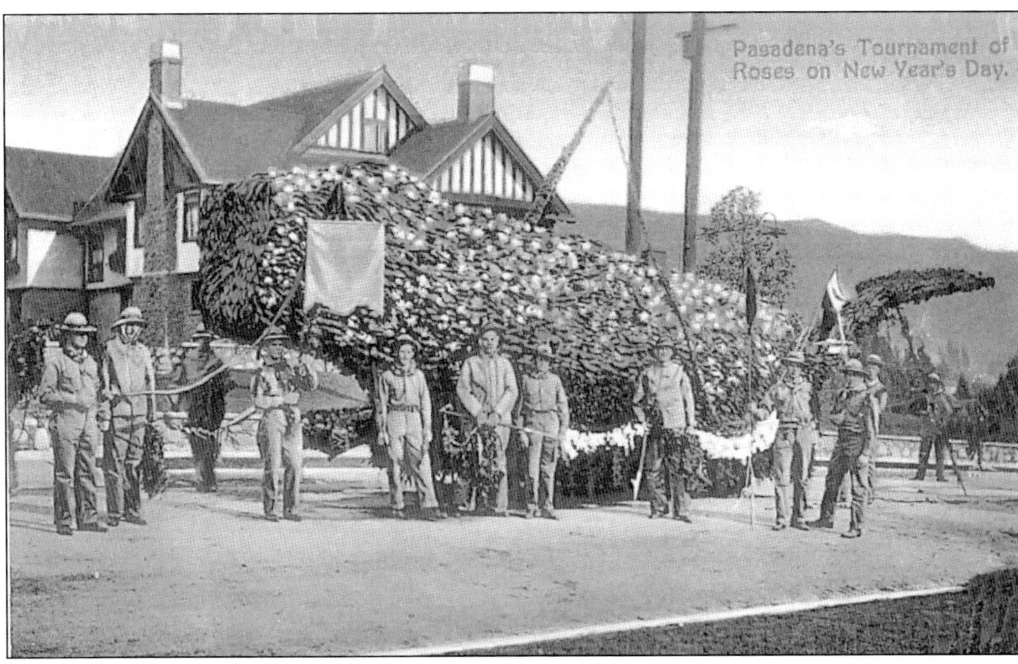

Another View of Pasadena's Tournament of Roses. The sender wrote, "This is to represent a whale, but does not show very plainly in the picture." (P/P: Newman Post Card Co., Los Angeles, No. B 117; made in Germany; postmark: April 6, 1909.)

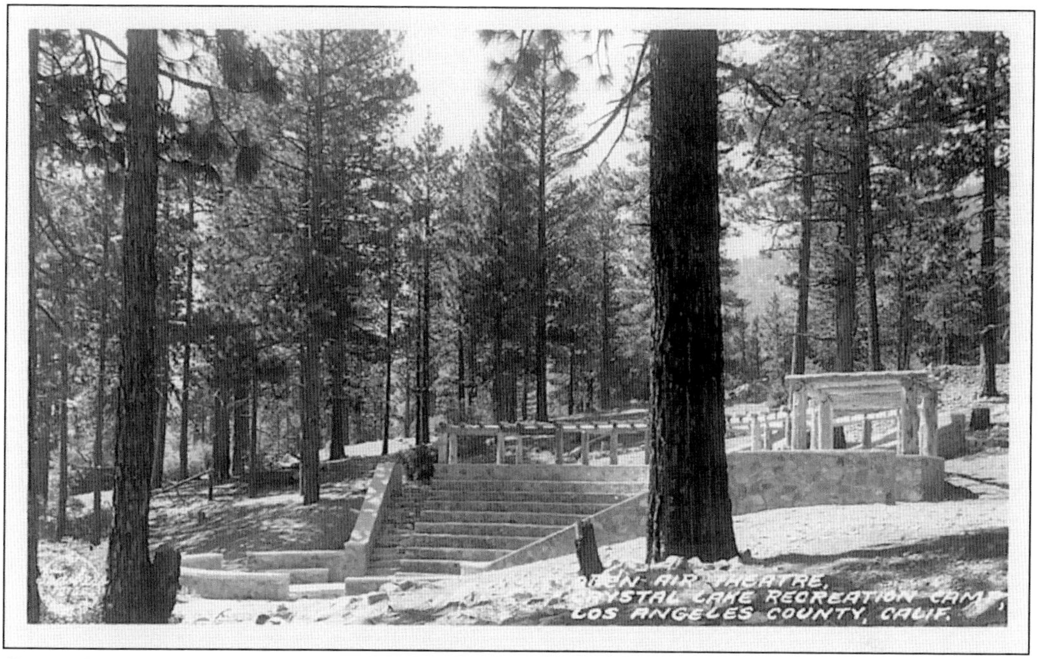

Open-Air Theatre, Crystal Lake Recreation Camp, Los Angeles County. The out of doors has always appealed to Californians. (P/P: Frashers, Pomona.)

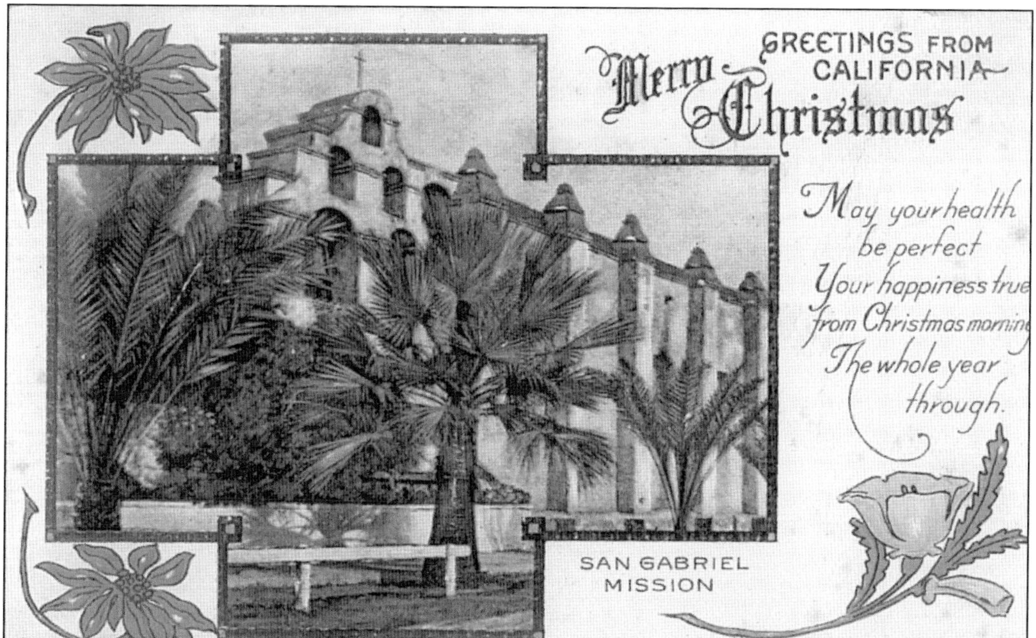

Greetings from California, San Gabriel Mission. San Gabriel Mission was the nearest to Lordsburg/La Verne of the 21 missions built by the Spanish padres throughout California in the 1700s. (P/P: M. Kashower Co., Los Angeles; made in the U.S.A.)

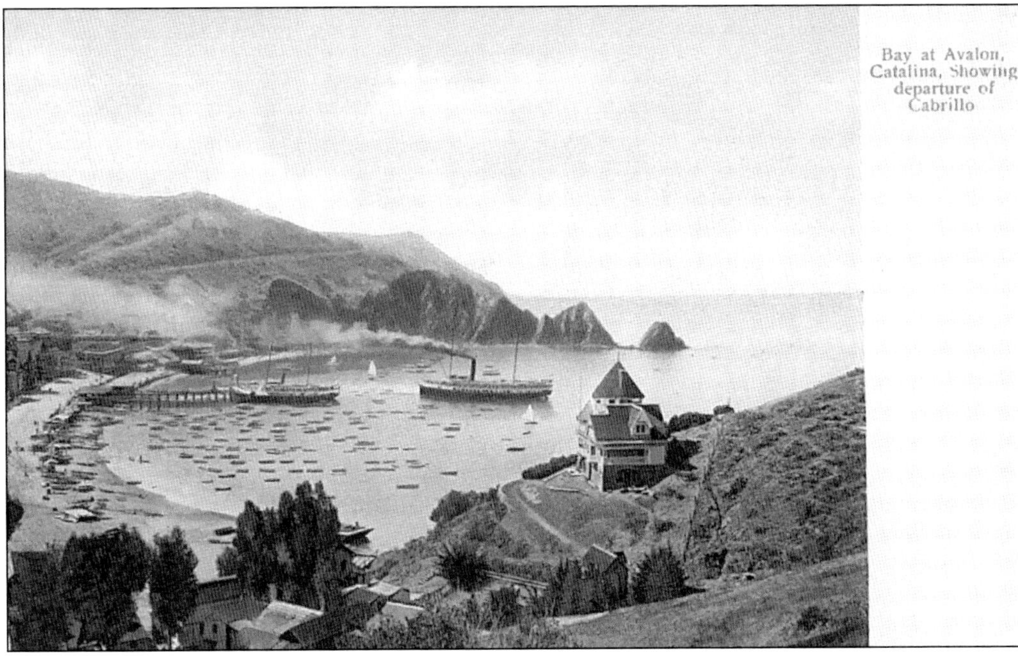

Bay at Avalon, Catalina. This card shows the departure of Cabrillo at California's popular off-shore resort area. (P/P: M. Rieder, Los Angeles & Leipzig, No. 3309; back side for address only; postally unused; card purchased in Weimar, Germany, June 1999.)

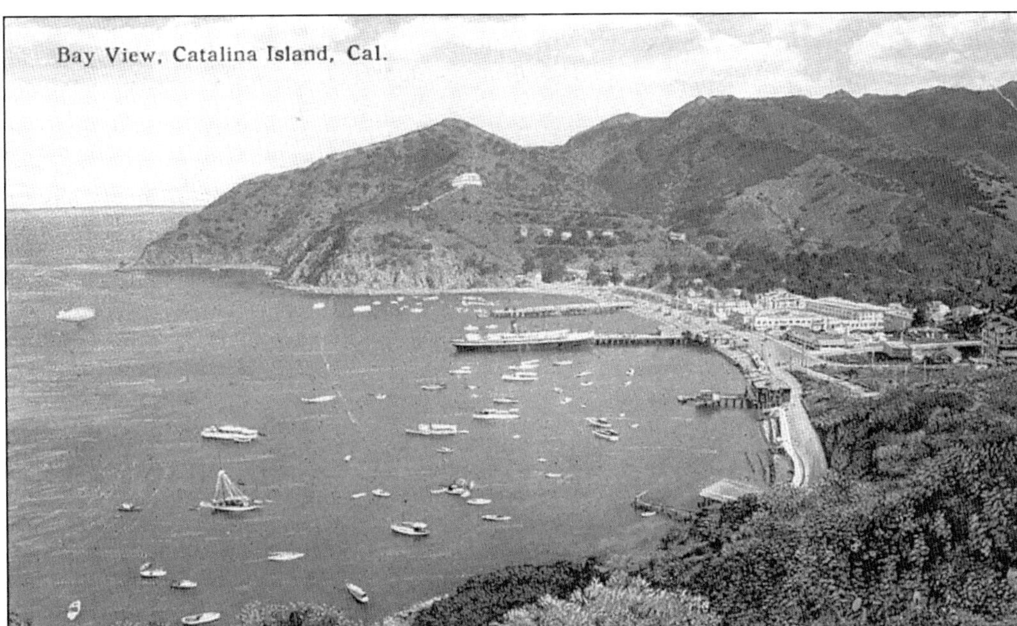

Bay View, Catalina Island. Formerly reached only by steamer, today's hydroplane boats are the means of travel for most people who go "out" to Catalina for a day or a longer stay. (P/P: Catalina Novelty Co., Catalina Island, No. A 87603; made in the U.S.A.; postmark: August 1922.)

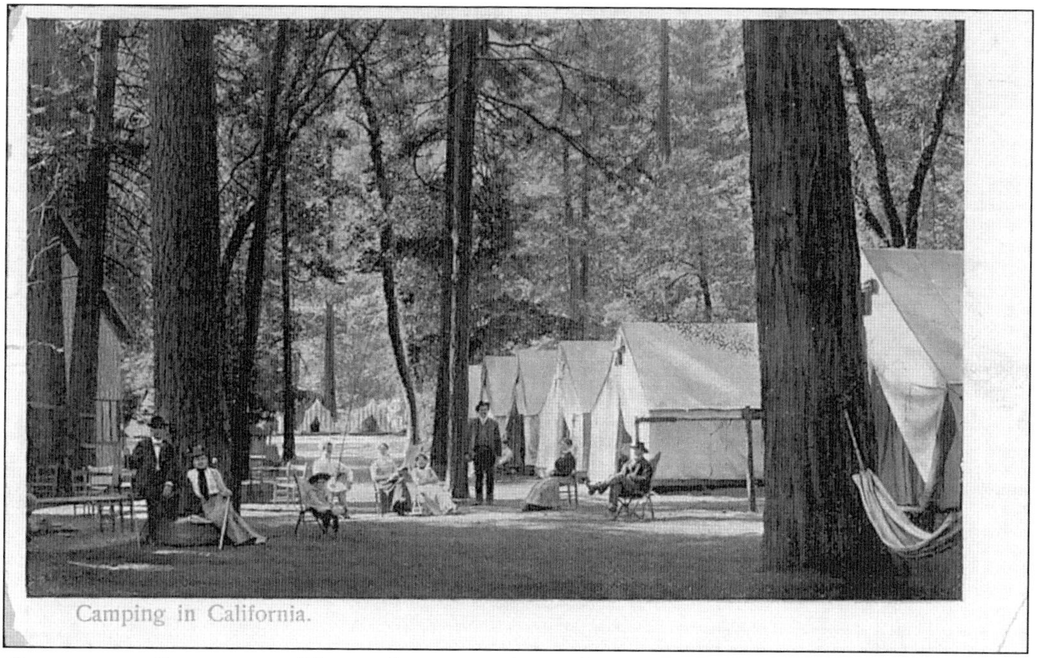

Camping in California. The sender wrote, ". . . this camping place is up in the mountains about 60 miles from here. It is called Yosemite. It is nice and cool here in the Summer." (P/P: M. Rieder, Los Angeles, No. 3852; made in Germany; postmark: October 1908.)

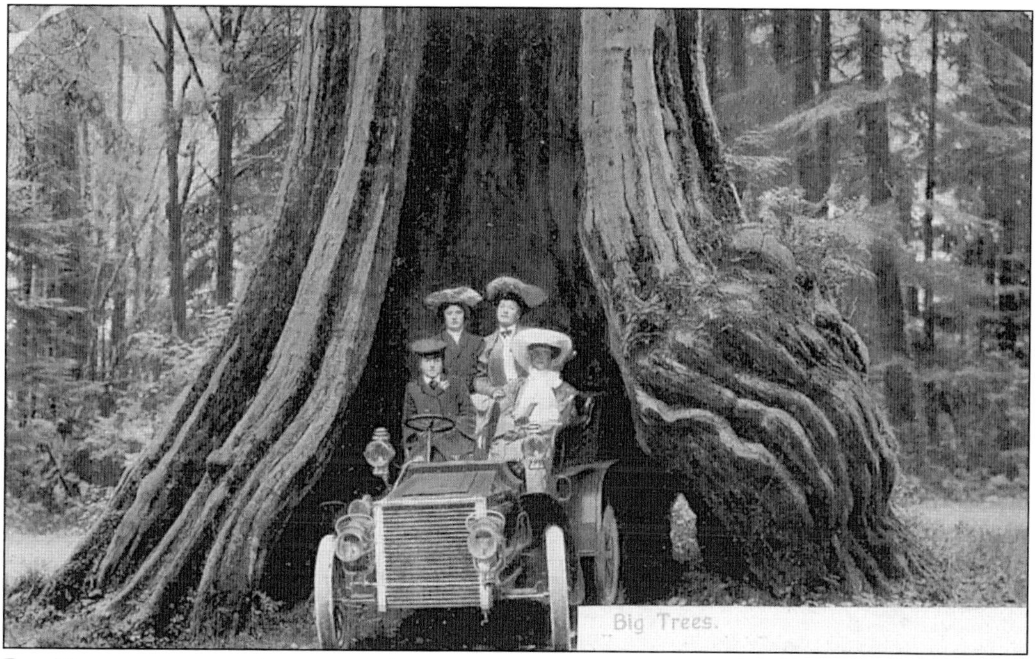

Big Trees. A very early automobile travels through the famous Sequoia tree in the Mariposa Grove in Yosemite National Park. An early Southern Pacific Railroad advertisement said of Yosemite, "No dust. Stage roads are sprinkled daily." (P/P: Newman Post Card Co., Los Angeles, No. A. B.1; made in Germany; postmark: June 1908.)

ACKNOWLEDGMENTS

Thank you to the following who shared information, donated postcards for inclusion, gave postcards to me, gave postcards to the University of La Verne Wilson Library, helped with identification of photos, gave encouragement, advice, etc.

Galen Beery, President, SOLVE/La Verne Historical Society; Betty Castellano, La Verne; Dolores Cole, Monrovia; Charles and Dorothy Doyen, La Verne; Ernestine Hoff Emerick, La Verne; Evelyn Hollinger, La Verne; Rex and Karen Huigens, La Verne; Nadine Johnson, La Verne; E. Louise Larick, La Verne; Verniel Lundquist, Evanston, IL; Jack McCaskill, Arcadia, CA; Roynon family members, La Verne; Adalyn S. Watts, Montclair, CA; Gary Williams, Claremont, CA; City of La Verne Planning Department; and University of La Verne, Wilson Library Archives.

Thanks also go to my wife, Shirley Heckman, and editors at Arcadia Publishing Anne Phipps and Allison Carpenter.

Index of Publishers/Photographers

This volume is dedicated to

ROBERT P. DYER

inveterate swap meet/yard sale explorer

who is always on the lookout for things to share with others

while keeping a keen eye out for his own collectibles.

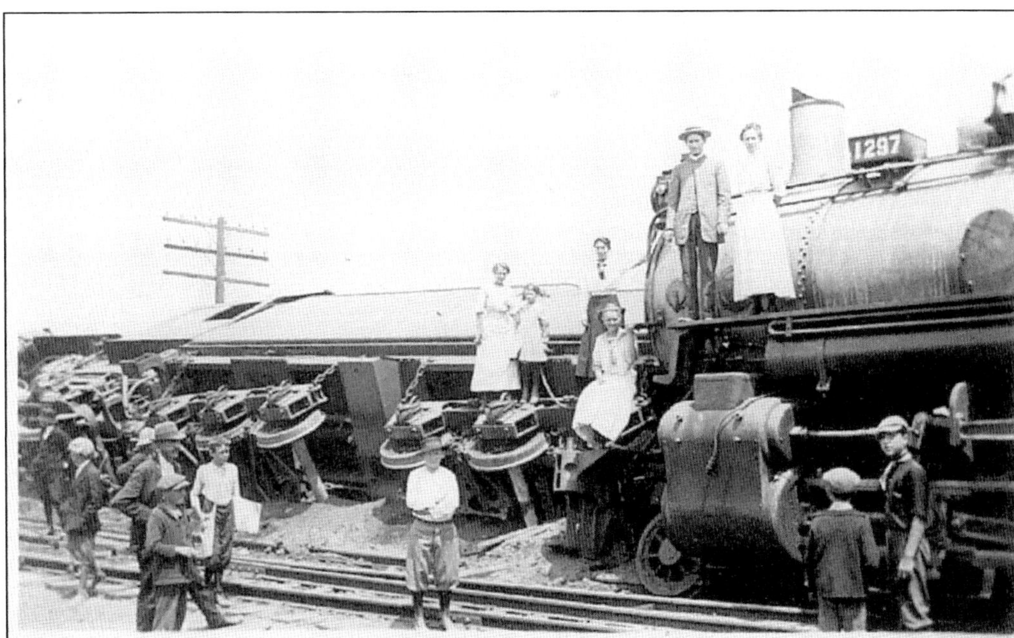

DECEMBER 24, 1899, TRAIN WRECK IN LORDSBURG. The *Lordsburg Sunbeam* for Saturday December 30, 1899, reported that on Christmas Eve, "the 6:47 local came down White Avenue and left the curve at Cypress, causing the worst smash-up that Southern California has ever experienced." There were 4 deaths and 30 injuries. (P/P: unknown; courtesy Ernestine Hoff Emerick.)